普通高等教育“十一五”国家级规划教材

U0795342

◉ 大学英语选修课／学科课程系列教材

跨文化交际视听说

A Multimedia Approach to Intercultural Communication

■《大学英语选修课／学科课程系列教材》项目组 编

高等教育出版社·北京

《大学英语选修课 / 学科课程系列教材》

总 主 编：王海啸　余渭深
总 策 划：周　龙　贾　巍

《跨文化交际视听说》
主　　编：樊葳葳
副 主 编：钟　华
编　　者：胡艳红　张迎丰　惠海峰　康　莉　范　蕾　徐　敏　Paul Wright

策　　划：徐艳梅
项目编辑：贾　巍　徐艳梅　邓中杰
责任编辑：徐艳梅
封面设计：王凌波
版式设计：刘　艳
责任校对：徐艳梅
责任印制：刁　毅

《大学英语选修课/学科课程系列教材》总前言

随着我国经济、文化、科技的不断发展，社会对大学生的英语水平提出了更高的要求，大学英语教学改革已成为社会关注的热点之一。为了推动大学英语教学改革，教育部在总结近年来教学改革经验的基础上，对2004年公布的《大学英语课程教学要求（试行）》进行了全面修订，并于2007年8月正式颁布了《大学英语课程教学要求》。与以往的《大学英语教学大纲》相比，新的《大学英语课程教学要求》从以下三个方面为大学英语教学带来了新的变化：1. 培养目标的变化。《大学英语课程教学要求》提出，大学英语要培养学生的英语综合应用能力，在坚持其通用基础学科定位的同时，提出了与专业学习相结合的专门用途英语，以及以人文、国际交流为核心的文化素质课程的定位；2. 教学思想的变化。提出了自主学习的思想，鼓励学生自主选择学习内容和学习方式；3. 教学模式的变化。鼓励在教和学的过程中使用以计算机为基础的教育技术，拓展英语学习的渠道，增加语言练习的机会，提高语言输入和输出的质量。

面对新的改革形势，我们明显感到，现行的以英语基础能力发展为核心的大学英语教材体系难以适应新形势的需要，广大师生也盼望着更多与国际文化知识、专业知识、学术交流相结合的新型英语教材，满足正在出现的大学英语的多重定位、学生自主选择学习内容和基于计算机技术的自主学习方式等变化的需要。为此，我们提出开发《大学英语选修课/学科课程系列教材》。

本系列教材为“普通高等教育‘十一五’国家级规划教材”，主要供完成《大学英语课程教学要求》中规定的“一般要求”后，继续学习“较高要求”和“更高要求”英语课程的学生使用，也可供研究生及广大专业技术人员学习专业英语、学术英语，提高英语综合应用能力使用。

本系列教材包括语言技能发展、跨文化交际能力发展和通用学术交流能力发展三个子系列。语言技能发展系列教程着重发展学生的通用英语技能。在该系列教材的开发中，我们将分期、分批建设若干门大学英语高级技能发展课程教材，其中包括：网络视听、翻译实践、网上阅读、高级阅读、口译技巧、应用写作等。跨文化交际能力发展系列教程着眼于扩展学生的国际文化视野，培养学生将英语作为国际交流语言使用的能力。在该系列教材的开发中，我们拟建设的教材有中西方文化概论、英语文化解读、英语演讲与辩论、跨文化交际、世界文明与文化导论、科技与人文、文学选读、经典作品欣赏、影视欣赏等。通用学术交流能力发展系列教程重在发展学生使用英语进行相关专业学术交流的能力。在该系列课程的开发中，我们将重点建设两大类别的专业学术英语课程，即A类教材和B类教材。其中，A类教材以学术研究和职业技能为基础，包括学术写作、学术会议、批判性思维等；B类教材以专业知识为基础，提供能供双语教学使用的专业通用基础教材，从而将专业学习与语言学习有机地结合起来。

本系列教材的开发是我们的一个新的尝试，新教材强调英语学习与文化学习、专业学习、学术交流和工作交流的结合，突出英语学习的实用性、学术性和人文性，充分反映国内外新式教学思想和理念，突出学生的参与和自主学习，强调信息技术的使用和教材的立体开发。我们相信，该系列教材的出版一定会给广大师生带来新的感受和新的教学体验，进而深化我国大学英语教学改革，创造出大学英语教学的新范式。

由于编者水平有限，加之时间仓促，疏漏和不妥之处在所难免，恳请读者不吝指正。

《大学英语选修课/学科课程系列教材》项目组

2008年1月

前 言

随着全球化进程的深入中国与国际接轨的步伐不断加快，中国与世界的跨文化交际不仅关系到国家的经济发展和文化交流，对国家形象的建立、国际关系的维护和国际地位的提升都起着举足轻重的作用，跨文化交际人才培养成为21世纪人才培养的一项至关重要的任务。为了迎接时代的挑战、满足社会对人才的渴求，跨文化交际能力的培养已被写入教育部最新制定的《高等学校英语专业教学大纲》；2007年教育部颁布的《大学英语课程教学要求》也第一次明确地将“跨文化交际”列为大学英语教学的主要内容之一。

语言是重要的交际工具，语言能力是成功的跨文化交际必不可少的。然而，语言能力并不等同于跨文化交际能力。跨文化交际能力除了语言交际能力之外，还包括对母语文化和异文化差异的敏感性、宽容性和处理文化差异的灵活性。为了更好地实现这一目标，20世纪90年代后期以来，越来越多的高校在语言课程之外增设了“跨文化交际”课程，各种跨文化交际教材也相继出版，这些都有力地促进了跨文化交际能力的培养。然而，迄今为止，国内尚无以影视片段等视听材料来辅助跨文化交际教学的视听说教材。

本教材的编写宗旨是以影视片段、相关文章和交际案例等视听素材为载体，通过视听、阅读，以及师生之间、生生之间的口语交互活动来促进跨文化理解、增强跨文化意识。全书共分为六个部分。第一部分介绍了文化、交际、跨文化交际等基本概念。第二部分介绍了最具影响力的几个文化价值观理论，只有对这些“隐蔽文化”深刻理解才能深入地洞察“外显文化”。第三、四部分分别阐释了跨文化语言交际和跨文化非语言交际。第五部分讨论了跨文化适应过程中的障碍和跨越障碍的桥梁。第六部分集中讲述了国内最常见的两大跨文化情境（教育情境和商务情境）中的种种跨文化实践。全书共十六章，每一章都由影视片段、阅读材料和案例分析三部分组成。影视片段通过真实的跨文化交际情境使学生对跨文化交际产生感性的认识。阅读材料是在参考国内外相关资料和研究成果的基础上、根据我们自己多年的教学经验编写而成的，语言简洁、精炼，深入浅出地讲解跨文化理论和知识，可以作为课堂上教师的讲稿，也可供学生课外自学之用。案例分析是在透彻理解的基础上运用相关理论和知识去解决跨文化交际的实际问题。每一部分都设计了相关练习。练习有两种类型：一类旨在促进对影视、阅读和案例的理解；另一类以帮助学生进行深入思考为目的。每一章的教学大约需要2个课时，整个教材大约需要32课时。

本书是集体智慧和劳动的结晶。樊葳葳教授主持召开了多次编写会议，教材的整体构思、章节的敲定、影片的选择、阅读材料的编写和全书体例等等都是在集体讨论中确定下来的。参加编写的作者们全都是奋战在跨文化交际教学第一线的老师。美国自由撰稿人 Paul Wright 先生对本书的编写提出了很多建设性意见，还在百忙之中抽出时间对全书的语言做了修改和润色。在此我们对他表示诚挚的感谢。

本书内涵丰富，集知识性和趣味性为一体，可作为大学生跨文化交际课程教材，也可供从事跨文化交际实践的人们自学之用。

本书是国内第一本跨文化交际视听说教材，教材的编写从内容到形式都有不少新的尝试。由于条件和水平有限，难免有疏漏和不当之处，恳请广大读者和同行批评指正。

编　者
2008年10月
于华中科技大学

Contents

Part I

Basic Concepts

Chapter 1

Culture

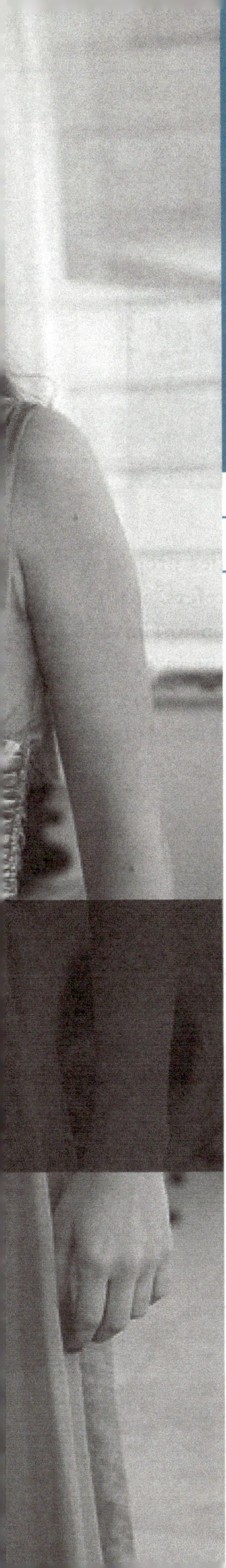

Section A Movie clip

Introduction to the Movie *Legally Blonde*

Elle Woods, majoring in fashion merchandising, is a blonde sorority girl who is about to graduate from CULA (City University of Los Angeles). She has what she thinks is a perfect life, and is fully expecting her boyfriend to propose marriage before he takes off for Harvard Law School. All of this changes the night her ambitious boyfriend breaks up with her telling her she's not good enough to be a future senator's wife. Elle decides that the only way to get him back is to go to Harvard Law School herself. After managing to get herself admitted, she has trouble initially fitting into the life of a typical law student at Harvard, but she works her way through the tough times. Eventually, she becomes a law firm intern working on a difficult murder case. By using her somewhat unconventional methods, she solves the case and gains respect from her peers. She proves that people can do anything they set their mind to.

Introduction to the Selected Scene

To apply for Harvard Law School, Elle Woods undergoes difficulties preparing for the LSAT entrance examination, foregoing the fun activities she prefers. With a score of 179 on her LSAT, she finally meets the requirement for admission to Harvard Law School. She also prepares a video essay in her application, in which she introduces herself and offers her qualifications. Watching her imaginative essay, the men on the admissions committee sit at a table piled high with applications, stunned. Finally one of them speaks.

Script of the Scene

Elle: Hi, my name is Elle Woods, and for my admissions essay, I'm gonna tell all of you at Harvard why I'm gonna make an amazing lawyer.

Elle: As president of my sorority, I'm skilled at commanding the attention of a room and discussing very important issues. It has come to my attention that the maintenance staff is switching our toilet paper from Charmin to generic. All those opposed to chafing please say "aye."

Girls: Aye.

Tutor: A, neither type of opera or neither type of rap is on sale. B, neither type of jazz and neither type of opera is on sale. C, neither type of opera and neither type of soul...

Boys: Party! Delta Nu, we love you!

Elle: I'm able to recall hundreds of important details at the drop of a hat.

Margot: Hey, Elle, do you know what happened in *Days of Our Lives* yesterday?

Elle: Why, yes, Margot, I do. Once again, we join Hope in the search for her identity. As you know, she's been brainwashed by the evil Stefano.

Serena: Get set and go!

Margot: One forty-three.

Elle: I feel comfortable using legal jargon in everyday life. I object!

Amy: It's here!

Elle: What?

Amy: It's here! The LSAT score! It's here!

Girls: Open the score! What's the score? This is so exciting. Tell us! What is it?

Elle: One seventy-nine! One seventy-nine!

Elle: And that's why you should vote for me, Elle Woods, future lawyer for the class of 2004.

Admissions Guy 1: She does have a 4.0 from CULA, and she got a one-seventy-nine on her LSATs.

Dean of Admissions: A fashion major?

Admissions Guy 2: Well, sir, we've never had one before, and aren't we always looking for diversity?

Admissions Guy 3: Her list of extracurricular activities is impressive.

Dean of Admissions: She was in a Ricky Martin video.

Admissions Guy 1: Clearly, she's interested in music.

Dean of Admissions: She also designed a line of faux fur panties for her sorority's charity project.

Admissions Guy 2: She's a friend to the animals as well as a philanthropist.

Dean of Admissions: Elle Woods… welcome to Harvard.

New Words

aye *adv.* yes 是的；不错

chafing *n.* soreness or irritation of the skin caused by friction 皮肤发炎

extracurricular *adj.* outside the regular academic curriculum 课外的

generic *adj.* common 普通的

philanthropist *n.* someone who makes charitable donations intended to increase human well-being 博爱主义者；慈善家

sorority *n.* a social club for female undergraduates 女生联合会

Phrases and Expressions

at the drop of a hat
quickly and easily; without needing to decide 一发出信号；马上

faux fur panties
man-made short underpants for women and children 人造皮毛的紧身短裤

Notes

Days of Our Lives

A soap opera that has aired nearly every weekday since 1965 on the NBC network in the United Stated.

Charmin

A well-known brand of toilet paper produced by Procter & Gamble American Company.

Essay

Also known as college application essay. A good essay serves to distinguish yourself from hundreds or even thousands of applicants with similar grades, activities, and SAT scores. To achieve this, your entrance essay must not only demonstrate your achievements, but also paint a vivid picture of your personality and character.

Delta Nu

The name of the sorority

4.0 from CULA

4.0 is the GPA (grade point average) Elle gets in her studies in CULA (City University of Los Angeles). GPA is important to admissions committees, not because it signifies a student's intelligence, but because it is a long-term indicator of a student's motivation and his/her ability to do consistently good or bad work. Generally, most master's programs require minimum GPAs of 3.0 or 3.3, and most Ph.D. programs require minimum GPAs of 3.3 or 3.5.

Hope

A character in *Days of Our Lives*.

LSAT

Law School Admissions Test. It is designed to measure skills that are considered essential for success in law school, including knowledge, logic and the ability to draw inferences etc. In this movie, Elle is told by her advisor that if she wants to enroll in Harvard Law School, she will need at least one seventy-five on her LSAT.

Ricky Martin

The most well-known pop singer in the world and winner of a Grammy Award and a Latin Grammy Award. He was chosen to sing the anthem of the 1998 FIFA World Cup—The Cup of Life.

Stefano

A character in *Days of Our Lives*.

Understanding and Speaking Interculturally

Exercise 1 The following is a list of abilities Elle presented to Harvard Admissions Committee. Fill in the blanks to make it complete.

GPA	________ from CULA

LSAT score	________
Major	________
________ **activities**	In a Ricky Martin video Designed a line of faux fur panties for her ________ Skilled at ________ the attention of the members of her sorority
Others	A friend to the animals and a ________
	Able to ________ hundreds of important details
	Feel comfortable using ________ jargon in everyday life

Exercise 2 In her application, what examples have been given to illustrate her points?

1. I'm able to recall hundreds of important details.

2. I feel comfortable using legal jargon in everyday life.

3. I'm skilled at commanding the attention of the members of my sorority.

4. I'm interested in music.

Exercise 3 Decide whether the following statements are True or False according to the movie clip you have just watched. Write "T" for true and "F" for false.

_____ 1. Elle's 4.0 GPA is not good enough for admission to Harvard Law School.

_____ 2. Her LSAT score is not good enough for admission to Harvard Law School.

_____ 3. According to the Dean of Admissions, a fashion major is not good enough for the admission to Harvard Law School.

_____ 4. The Harvard Law School Admissions Committee is always looking for diverse applicants.

Exercise 4 Roleplay the scene showing the discussion among members of the Harvard Law School Admissions Committee.

Exercise 5 Explore interculturally.

1. Why is Elle Woods considered diverse by Harvard Law School? And why is Elle Woods admitted by Harvard Law School? What can we learn from it about American culture?

2. Discuss in groups the strengths and weaknesses of the American and Chinese education systems. Present your ideas to the whole class after your discussion.

3. Why do Chinese and Americans develop different education systems? What are the cultural factors underlying the differences?

Section B Reading

Defining Culture

When you think of the word "culture", what enters your mind? Perhaps music, architecture, the arts. Many people associate these areas with culture. Others may think of philosophy, history, and literature. Still others may think of beliefs, customs, values, and worldview.

Perhaps the earliest formal definition of culture, put forward by E. B. Tylor in 1871, is also one of the best known. He conceived of culture as "that complex whole which includes knowledge, belief, art, morals, law, custom, and any other capabilities and habits acquired by man as a member of society." (Tylor, 1871) Since Tylor's definition, more than 500 different versions have emerged, but still no consensus has been reached up to the present. Defining culture is difficult mainly because scholars have different understandings of it. One definition, for example, treats culture as everything that is human-made. Another scholar, however, has proposed that "culture is communication and communication is culture." (Hall, 1976)

The authors of this book agree with most anthropologists' view that culture refers to the total way of living of particular groups of people. It includes everything that a group of people think, say, do, and make. Traditional Chinese medicine, Chinese Gongfu, Peking Opera and Chinese Cuisines are among the most frequently mentioned symbols of Chinese culture. Besides, examples of culture can also be found in every aspect of our life. These include the customs we observe for naming our children, the way we address our family members, our mode of entertaining our guests, the way we spend our money, how we take our vacation, the way we raise our children, as well as the table manners we expect, the clothes we wear, the vehicles we drive, the utensils we use for meals, and so on. In a word, culture is a whole collection of our living patterns and behaviors.

Metaphors of Culture

As a large and pervasive concept, culture is often compared to an iceberg, suggesting that only a small part of it is visible while most of it lies concealed. Our customs, habits and the artifacts made and used by humans lie atop the iceberg, easy to discover. The hidden dimension, however, is mainly composed of the underlying worldview, value systems, ways of thinking, national character and any other deep concepts of our mind that serve as the foundation of the visible part and that account for our customs, habits and artifacts. In China, for instance, we often greet each other by asking "Where are you going?" and give a general answer to it when greeted. The strong emphasis on social relationships and the heavy interdependence between Chinese people are some underlying reasons that account for this habit. To an American, this same sentence may be interpreted as an intrusion into one's privacy. The underlying individual-oriented relationship is the invisible part of the iceberg.

Culture is also compared to the "software of our mind" (Hofstede, 1991) and the grammar of our behavior. Levi Strauss once said, "All societies construct their own realities in accordance with mental or psychological principles... We thus invent the world we inhabit." (Hawkes,2003) The society around us is not an entirely objective reality, for every one of us helps to construct our world. Culture is this shared set of mental and psychological principles that exist in people's minds. This collective agreement then governs people's behavior and gives people guidelines about what things mean, what is important, and what should or should not be done. Chinese people are well known for their modesty. Confucian teachings, which originated in the group-oriented cultures, are the guidelines that help shape their behavior.

Another popular metaphor for culture is to compare it to the rules of the game everybody is playing in any particular society although we generally are not highly aware of the rules at any given moment. These shared rules of the game tell us how to communicate with others and how to interpret the behavior of those around us. Egyptians, for instance, tend to use more similes and metaphors in their compliments than Americans. "He is like a brother to me" is often heard in their conversation. Besides, "May God protect him" is often addressed to a pregnant woman or a child to protect the individual from bad luck. Americans, on the other hand, seem to compliment more frequently than Egyptians though their compliments are often shorter and include fewer metaphors and similes. Thus, culture is everything an individual needs to acquire in order to be well accepted into a society.

Characteristics of Culture

However, one does not become a member of a culture by birth. Culture is learned. We learn our culture from those people with whom we interact in our process of socialization: our parents, teachers, friends, and even strangers. A human infant will learn wolf culture if he lives with wolves since his birth. We also learn the expectations others may have for our behavior through our religious institutions and the mass media. Television, for example, not only provides us with views of reality but also teaches us many of the day-to-day norms of our culture.

Another characteristic of culture is that it is transmitted from one generation to another. Culture is passed down from parents or other adults to children, who in turn grow up and teach their own children the culture's customs and expectations. Parents often teach us the norms and rules of our culture by modeling how to behave and correcting us when we violate them. In the US, for example, most children are asked from a very early age to make their own decisions. In many other cultures, a parent seldom or never asks a child what he or she wants to do. Instead, they simply tell the child what to do. Culture can also emerge in groups, as is the case often with younger people, who form their culture apart from parents or other adults.

Culture is also a dynamic system that is changing constantly. The only thing that remains unchanged is the fact of "change" itself. There are lots of reasons to explain the changing nature of culture: for example, economic development, shifts in political systems, and technological innovations. Consider the example of China. Tremendous changes have taken place in China since the introduction of policies of reform and economic and social opening. Together with these changes are some traditional Chinese values. For example, the idea of saving and thrift was once considered a very important Confucian principle. Now it is a principle seldom observed among the younger generations of China, who are more concerned about enjoying life in the present.

Subculture and Coculture

It is not true to say that each country has only one culture. In the US, there is not only the so-called "White Anglo-Saxon Protestant" (WASP) culture, but also African-American culture, Arab-American culture, Asian-American culture, Hispanic-American culture, and many others, which are labeled as subcultures within the US. This term, however, has connotations that suggest subordination to the larger Euro-American culture. Thus, the term "coculture" is occasionally employed in an effort to avoid the hierarchical implication of subculture.

There are also other kinds of subcultures (cocultures). We can, for example, talk about a student subculture, a business subculture, a middle-class subculture, and a southern (or other regional) subculture. Each of these groups shares many common cultural ideas with a larger culture but observes some of its own that are unique.

For communication purposes, however, we usually focus on the dominant cultural patterns. For instance, when we say differences between Chinese and American cultures, we mean differences between the dominant Han culture and the dominant Anglo-Saxon American culture. This will probably change a lot, as minority groups together become the majority in the US. For example, much of American music, such as jazz, is influenced by African-American culture. In addition, we have to remember that individual differences always exist. Within a dominant cultural pattern there are always some people who deviate to varying degrees from the pattern.

Understanding and Speaking Interculturally

1 Class work: Brainstorm examples of culture. Then classify them into the visible and invisible part of the iceberg below.

2 Question: Why is culture compared to the software of people's mind and the grammar of people's behavior? Cite some examples to illustrate it.

3 Group work: Do you have some different values from your parents' generation? What are they?

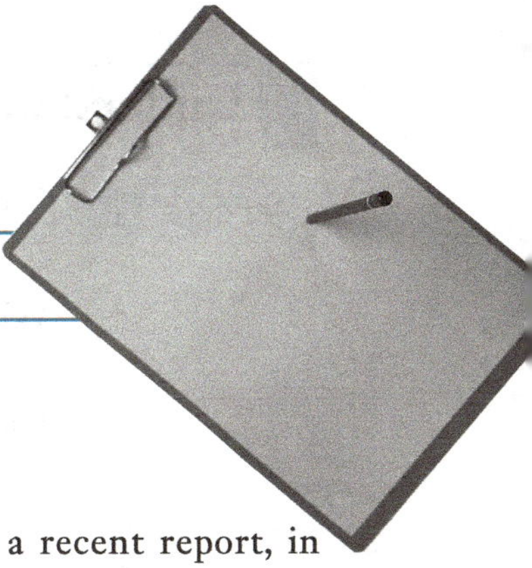

Section C Case

Introduction to the Case

According to a recent report, in 2006 there were more than 39 000 elderly Chinese living in New York State. Most of them went to America for the sake of their children, who had decided to settle in the United States after graduating from an American university.

The Scenario

An Elderly Chinese Farming in America

Zhao Xinggui, 62 years old, had been a farmer in Shaanxi. To relieve Zhao's loneliness after the death of his wife, his only son, who had settled in America for years, working as a librarian in an American university, asked his father to come to live with him. When his son went to work, Zhao spent most of his time sitting in front of the TV. He often dreamed of his friends and neighbors in China, who often talked, drank tea and played *mahjong* together during their leisure time. "America is a good place, but it's too dull," he said.

What Zhao did not expect was that his farming life could continue in America. Like many university towns established in agricultural areas, the surrounding land was a major source of income for the university. All the teachers and students, after paying a nominal rent, were able to enjoy the pleasure of farming. Different from most of the American families, who casually used their parcels of land to raise flowers, Chinese tenants grew vegetables. Zhao was one of those tenants and one of the most famous for his farming talents. Many elderly Chinese came to ask him for advice, and they often conversed while selling their spare vegetables. That summer was the happiest time for Zhao.

Understanding and Speaking Interculturally

Exercise 1 Listen for the first time and answer the following questions.

1. Why did Zhao go to America?

2. Did Zhao enjoy his American life?

Exercise 2 Listen for the second time and fill in the blanks.

1. To ______ Zhao's loneliness after the death of his wife, his only son, who had ______ in America for years, working as a ______ in an American university, asked his father to come to live with him.

2. He often ______ of his friends and neighbors in China, who often talked, drank tea and played ______ together during their leisure time. "America is a good place, but it's too ______," he said.

3. Like many university towns established in ______ areas, the ______ land was a major source of income for the university. All the teachers and students, after paying a nominal ______, were able to enjoy the pleasure of farming.

4. Different from most of the American families, who ______ used their parcels of land to raise flowers, Chinese ______ grew vegetables. Zhao was one of those tenants and one of the most famous for his farming ______.

Exercise 3 Explore interculturally.

1. Why did Zhao say "America is a good place, but it's too dull"? What can we learn about Chinese culture?

2. Why did most Chinese families decide to grow vegetables instead of flowers on their land? What can we learn about Chinese culture?

3. Culture is often compared to the "software" of people's minds. Cite the examples in this case to explain the sentence.

Communication

Section A Movie clip

Introduction to the Movie *Serendipity*

Jonathan Trager and Sara Thomas meet while shopping for gloves for their respective lovers. A night of Christmas shopping turn into romance. Jon wants to explore things further but Sara isn't sure whether their love is meant to be. They decide to test fate by splitting up and seeing if destiny could bring them back again. Many years later, having lost each other that night, both are engaged to be married. Still, neither can shake the need to give fate one last chance to reunite them. Many opportune moments bring the two close to meeting a number of times, but fate will have the final word on whether it is meant to be.

Introduction to the Selected Scene

After spending a beautiful night with Jonathan, Sara decides to write down her phone

number. All of a sudden, the wind wrenches the number from Jonathan's hand into a pile of blowing trash on the sidewalk. Sara takes it as a sign, thinking fate is telling them to back off. Seeing that Jonathan doesn't share this view, Sara decides to test fate, asking Jonathan to write his number on a $5 bill…

Script of the Scene

Jonathan: Legible, legible.
Sara: Yeah, yeah, yeah. I can't believe I'm doing this.
Jonathan: Please please let fate take its proper course.
Jonathan: Oh. That was an accident! Write that down again please?
Sara: I can't! That's a sign. Fate's telling us to back off.
Jonathan: If fate didn't want us to be together, then why did we meet tonight? Gotcha!
Sara: I don't know, but it's not an exact science. It's a feeling.
Jonathan: What if you're wrong? Huh? What if it's all in our hands and you just walk away? No names, no phone numbers, nothing. What do you think's gonna happen? Do you think good fate is gonna deliver my information right to your doorstep?
Sara: You know, that's the best idea you've had all night.
Jonathan: What's the best idea?
Sara: Here you go. Write your name and number down.
Jonathan: On this $5 bill?
Sara: Yeah, just do it.
Jonathan: You are a strange and interesting woman. Now what?
Sara: Wait there.

Jonathan: Hey! What the hell was that?

Sara: Well, if that $5 bill makes its way back into my hands, I'll be able to call you, and when you hear my voice on the other end, then you'll believe in fate, won't you?

Jonathan: Hey! What about me?

Sara: What do you mean?

Jonathan: Well, we have to send something out in the universe with your name on, shall we? I mean, that's the only fair thing.

Sara: That is the only fair thing. What have I got, even? Ooh, no, I have a really good idea.

Jonathan: That's a lot of tubas.

Sara: Okay, see this book?

Jonathan: Yeah!

Sara: Okay, so when I get home tonight, I'm gonna write my name and number inside this book. And then first thing tomorrow morning, I'll sell it to a used bookstore.

Jonathan: Which one? You're not gonna tell me, you're not gonna tell me? Why not?

Sara: Well, now, every time you pass an old book store, you're gonna have to go inside to see if it's there!

Jonathan: This is just wrong! You don't just have the most incredible night of your life with a perfect stranger and then leave it all to chance, do you? Do you?

Sara: Come with me a second.

Jonathan: What, we're gonna get a room? I'm kidding. But I wanna know you more. Come on. Where are we going?

Sara: Now you stay here.

Jonathan: Okay.

Sara: No. Stay there. Stay there. Don't make me come over there. Okay?

Jonathan: Okay.

Sara: Right. If we both randomly pick the same floor, we're meant to be together now.

Jonathan: You're insane.

Sara: Come on. Okay, get in. Take a breath, and then when the door closes, hit a button.

Jonathan: I don't understand this.

Sara: You don't have to understand. You just have to have faith.
Jonathan: Faith in what?
Sara: Destiny. Hey! It's Sara. My name's Sara.

New Words

destiny *n.* fate 命运

faith *n.* a strong belief in a supernatural power or powers that control human destiny 信任；信仰

incredible *adj.* beyond belief or understanding 难以置信的

insane *adj.* mad, crazy 疯狂的

legible *adj.* (of handwriting, print, etc.) able to be read 清晰的；易辨的

randomly *adv.* without any definite plan or aim 随意地；任意地

tuba *n.* a large brass wind instrument that produces the deepest sound 低音喇叭

Phrases and Expressions

back off
move backwards 后退；放弃

leave it to chance
let it decided by fortune and luck 凭运气

let fate take its proper course
let it follow the ordinary course of things 任其自然发展

Notes

Gonna

It is used in spoken English, meaning "going to."

Gotcha

It is used in spoken English, meaning "(I've) got you." 难倒你了；问倒你了

I'm kidding

It is used in spoken English, meaning "I'm joking."

Wanna

It is used in spoken English, meaning "want to."

Understanding and Speaking Interculturally

Exercise 1 Put the following sentences in the right order according to the movie clip you have just watched.

(   ) 1. Sara promises to write down her phone number inside a book and sell it to a used bookstore.

(   ) 2. Jonathan loses the paper with Sara's phone number written on it.

(   ) 3. Sara asks Jonathan to get into a hotel with her.

(   ) 4. Sara spends the $5 bill in a little grocery store.

(   ) 5. Sara writes down her phone number on a small piece of paper.

(   ) 6. Sara asks Jonathan to write down his phone number on a $5 bill.

(   ) 7. Sara tells her name to Jonathan.

( ) 8. Sara proposes that she and Jonathan pick the same floor in the lift randomly.

Exercise 2 Fill in the blanks according the movie clip you have just watched.

	What Jonathan thinks of it	What Sara thinks of it
Jonathan loses the paper with Sara's phone number.	Just an ________	A ________ of the fate to tell us to ________ off
Sara asks Jonathan to write his number on a $5 bill.	A ________ and interesting woman.	To see whether the bill could come back into my hands again.
Sara decides to write her number inside a book and sell it to a used bookstore.	This is just wrong. You can't leave it all to ________.	To see whether Jonathan could finally get this book.
Sara asks Jonathan to get into a hotel with her to see whether they could randomly pick the same floor in the lift.	You're ________.	You have to have ________ in destiny.

Exercise 3 Explore interculturally.

1. In the movie, Jonathan wants to get Sara's phone number, but their process of communication fails. What elements go wrong in this process?

2. In the movie, how many things does Sara do in order to test fate? And what are they? What do you think of these behaviors?

3. A famous anthropologist once said that "Culture is communication and communication is culture." Do you agree? Why or why not?

Section B Reading

Defining Communication

As social animals, humans employ communication in every aspect of daily life. It serves to facilitate human socialization, maintain social relationships, and develop personality. Although experts have not agreed upon precisely one definition, communication generally refers to the process in which participants create and share information with one another as they move toward reaching mutual understanding.

A Model of Communication

As our understanding of this subject has deepened, the models we use for communication have evolved from the linear to the circular. The following model indicates the transactional view of communication.

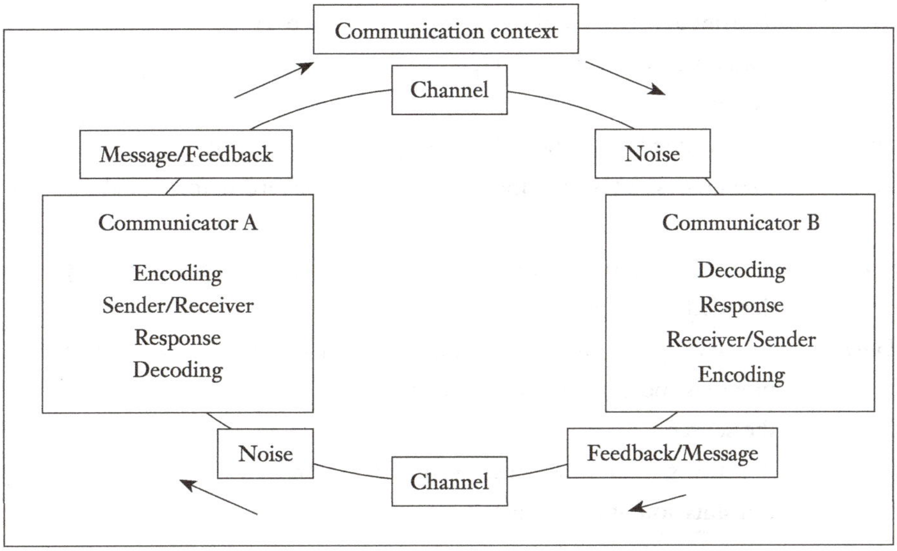

Figure 2.1 A Model of Communication

Elements of Communication

As is shown in the above model, there are ten major elements or aspects of communication. The following is a conversation between two colleagues who meet in an elevator on the way to their offices. It serves as a useful example to illustrate these ten elements. Table 2.1 presents explanations, along with illustrations, for each aspect.

Male: Hi, how've you been?
Female: Not bad. 'N you?
Male: Oh, can't complain. Busy.
Female: I know. Me, too.
Male: Oh well, gotta take off. See ya.
Female: Bye. Take care.

Elements	Explanations of the elements	Illustrations in this conversation
Context	A setting or situation in which communication occurs	An elevator on the way to the office
Sender	The individual who originates a message	The man
Encoding	The process by which an idea is converted into a message	Converting the idea of greeting into a verbal message
Message	The information being sent	A verbal greeting (How've you been?)
Channel	The means by which a message is transmitted from its origin to its destination	Face-to-face
Receiver	The intended destination of a message	The woman
Decoding	The process by which the message is converted into an idea	Converting the verbal message into the idea of greeting: He's greeting me.
Response	The reaction of the receiver to the decoded message	Positive response to the greeting
Feedback	A message about the effects of a previous message that is sent back to the source	A verbal message sent back: "Not bad. 'N you?"
Noise	Anything that interferes with the transmission of a message	None

Table 2.1 Elements of Communication

Please note that, while the above analysis focuses only on the first two lines of the conversation, we can follow the same approach for the rest of the exchange. Since most human communication is a mutual process rather than a one-way message flow, the participants frequently exchange roles as message originators and message receivers in the ongoing process of communication.

Another thing worthy of notice is that in this conversation the communication is going on smoothly without any "noise." There is no physical noise since there are no other people aboard the elevator and, thus, the two communicators can hear each other perfectly well. There is no mental noise either since neither of them is distracted mentally, and they both are attentive to the conversation. Neither is there any cultural noise because both speakers are from the same culture and share the same cultural background.

However, human communication is never as perfectly effective as this example suggests. The receiver does not always decode a message into exactly the same meaning that the source had in mind when encoding the message. Misunderstandings or even conflicts are especially likely to occur when the source and the receiver lack a common value-base, culture or perspective. According to a recent survey, for example, non-native English speakers are found to have difficulty performing the speedy greeting in which time is very limited as illustrated in the above example of the elevator talk. Some are unable to shorten their greetings sufficiently. Others may keep silent, unable to continue the conversation after answering the initiator's greeting. Still others may only smile at the speaker, or nod the head, instead of offering a verbal response. To native speakers, these behaviors may seem either inappropriate or not quite polite.

Classifications of Communication

There are different ways of classifying communication. Depending on the message, communication may be verbal or nonverbal, for example. Depending on the degree of feedback, communication may be one-way or interactive. Depending on the channel used, communication may be direct or indirect. Depending on level and context, communication may be interpersonal, interorganizational and mass media-based. Depending on the cultural background of the sender and receiver, communication may be intracultural and intercultural. In addition, communication may be intrapersonal (communicating with oneself) and interpersonal (communicating with others), intentional and unintentional (indicating whether the source is encoding and sending the message intentionally or unintentionally), successful and unsuccessful communication, effective and ineffective communication, or appropriate and inappropriate communication. Ideally, successful communication should be both effective and appropriate.

Understanding and Speaking Interculturally

1. The passage only analyzes the ten ingredients of the first two lines of the talk in the elevator. Please continue the analysis process until the last line.

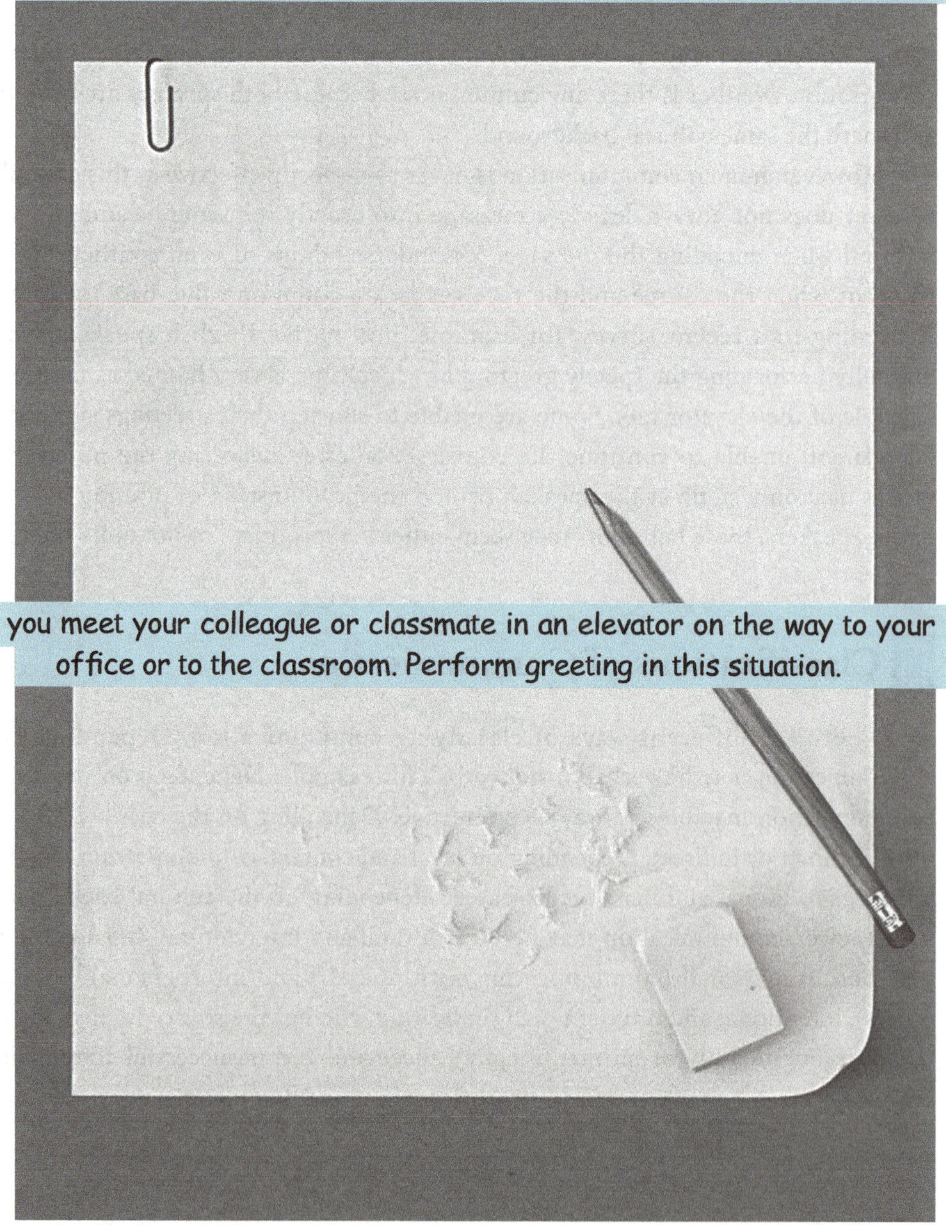

2. Suppose you meet your colleague or classmate in an elevator on the way to your office or to the classroom. Perform greeting in this situation.

Section C Case

Introduction to the Case

Human beings are social animals. Communication occurs every moment in every corner of the world. While people adopt different approaches to communication for various reasons, culture is one of the most important factors. Culture drives the way in which people communicate. People in different cultures usually favor different styles and patterns of communication.

The Scenario

An Intercultural Classroom

It was a hot day. Since it was still too early to use the air-conditioner, according to the regulations of the university, every class kept its door open to make the classroom cooler. While I was lecturing on Chinese grammar in Class 4, waves of laughter came from the neighboring Class 5.

A German student named Stephen raised his hand and stood up. "The laughter from Class 5 is bothering us. I think we should go to their class to protest," he said.

His deskmate, a student from Japan, shook his head. "Is it necessary to protest over such a minor issue? I can tolerate this noise. And there are some Japanese friends of mine in Class 5. I don't want to make my friends unhappy just because of their laughter."

Another Japanese girl stood up, "Let me close our door. Although that will make it hotter, it will be quieter."

She was stopped by a French student. "Why should we close our door and suffer from the heat? Class 5 should close their door in order not to bother other classes."

A few students from Africa suggested, "Why not strike our desks like drums to protest?"

A girl from Russia agreed, "Our class could also laugh together to let them know what the noise sounds like."

Two Korean students whispered to each other, "Western students really have a hot temper. They just don't know how to stay calm. How could we get along well with other classes if we can't control ourselves?"

A Hungarian girl happened to overhear their comments. She disagreed, "I don't understand you Asians. You won't protest even when your rights have been violated."

More laughter came from Class 5. Stephen stood up, "No matter what you think about it, I'm going to protest." He went to Class 5 and asked, "How happy you must be today! May we share in your happiness?" Laughter stopped. After a while, Class 5 closed their door.

Stephen came back satisfied and told his Japanese classmates, "Now you Asians can enjoy the peace won by us Westerners." After the class was over, a few European students from Class 5 came to apologize to me. They weren't aware that their happy laughter might have bothered Class 4. The Japanese students from Class 5, however, adopted a Chinese nickname for Stephen "*Jin jin ji jiao*" (people who haggle over every ounce).

Understanding and Speaking Interculturally

Exercise 1 Listen for the first time and answer the following questions.

1. What bothered Class 4 on a hot day?

2. How many different solutions did Class 4 propose?

Exercise 2 Listen for the second time and fill in the blanks.

Who	Nationality	Proposal
Stephen	German	
Stephen's classmate		
A girl student		Let me close our door.
	French	
		Why not strike our desks as the drum to protest?
A girl student	Russia	
	Korean	
	Hungarian	

Exercise 3 Explore interculturally.

1. What is the mode of communication favored by Asians? What cultural values underlie it?

2. What is the mode of communication favored by Westerners? What cultural values underlie it?

3. Hall, an anthropologist, once said, "Communication is culture. Culture is communication." Do you agree? Why or why not?

Chapter 3

Intercultural Communication

Section A Movie clip

Introduction to the Movie *The Guasha Treatment*

Based on a real story of a Chinese family living in the United States, the movie describes cultural misunderstanding and intercultural adaptation. Working as a designer of video games, Xu Datong receives many awards and regards himself as a successful Chinese immigrant who has realized his American dream. When Datong's father visits from China, he performs Guasha, a traditional Chinese medical practice, to treat his young grandson, Dennis. Though painless, the treatment leaves bright red marks on the skin. Soon the Child Welfare Agency accuses the family of child abuse and takes the boy away from them. In order to get their only son back, the family undergoes much hardship, only to find it's too difficult to overcome the cultural barriers.

Introduction to the Selected Scene

Suspecting that young Dennis has been subject of neglect and abuse, the Child Welfare Agency accuses the family of child abuse. A judge presides over a special hearing to see

whether there is sufficient evidence to hold a trial in the matter. Xu Datong invites his best friend, John Quinlan, to defend him. Shocked by the red scar visible on the boy's back, John gets too angry to defend Datong. Xu Datong has to defend himself by proving that Guasha is a traditional Chinese medical treatment.

Script of the Scene

Quinlan: No problem, your honor. John Quinlan, attorney for the defendant.

Judge: Why is that I've never seen you around before, Mr. Quinlan?

Quinlan: I've never had the honor, your honor. I deal mostly in intellectual property right cases.

Judge: Apples and oranges, Mr. Quinlan. The two areas of law have virtually nothing to do with each other.

Quinlan: Yes, of course. So I told my client, but he insists on my representing him. Also I'd like to have the record show that my client only had two days' notice of this hearing, so for me I only had twenty-four hours' preparation time.

Judge: I think you are putting the cart before the horse, counselor. This hearing is for the purpose of determining whether there is sufficient evidence to run court proceedings. So take off your lawyer caps. And before we get to the court in these formalities, let's just talk about the matter. Would the Child Welfare Agency care to start?

Davis: Yes, your honor. We're preparing the proceeding anyway you see fit it. Three days ago we received a telephone call from the social worker on duty in St. Matthew Hospital, informing us of a possible case of child abuse discovered as a result of medical examination by Doctor Michael Longman. Upon administering treatment in the ER to Dennis Xu, Doctor Longman had reason to suspect that Dennis has been the subject of physical abuse.

Judge: I've read the report, Miss Avery, very thorough as usual.

Davis: As you can see, the medical report indisputably proves that Dennis Xu has been the subject of deliberate, long-term neglect and abuse.

Quinlan: Objections, no foundation, just conjecture and speculation.

Judge: This is a hearing, not a trial, Mr. Quinlan. But you made a fine point.

Davis: In order to supplement the medical report, you note that we provided additional evidence.

Quinlan: Your honor, we haven't received any copies, or any evidence or reports related to this case.

Margaret: I, I thought you provided them copies.

Davis: Sorry, your honor. No recite.

Margaret: I, I don't know how this could have happened.

Davis: Your honor, the CWA is currently carrying out a full investigation of this case, and has located a considerable number of witnesses, all of whom are prepared to testify regarding Mr. Datong Xu's violent nature, and the neglect and abuse he has inflicted on his young son Dennis.

Quinlan: And I can produce a hundred witnesses to testify he's a good husband and father who'd rather die than see his family harmed. I count myself chief among those witnesses.

Margaret: As my colleague just stated we're in the midst of full investigation, but we'll not be calling any witnesses. We feel there's no need.

Xu: She knows she doesn't have any witnesses.

Quinlan: Or I think she doesn't need any.

Margaret: Your honor, I have incontrovertible evidence that I feel quickly settle this matter in the court's mind.

Quinlan: Your honor, perhaps I don't understand family law, but I do understand Datong Xu. These accusations are ludicrous, laughable.

Margaret: Perhaps you don't understand your friend as well as you think you do. According to the doctor's report, the condition and coloration of the bruises went within two days prior to the Dennis' head injury. We believe that these photographs are sufficient evidence to demonstrate that Dennis Xu lives in a dangerous home environment and should remain under the protection of the State.

Judge: Please return to your seats.

Quinlan: How can you do this to your son? Is there something that you forgot to inform me of? Did you think nobody would notice your son's back was like a piece of roast beef?

Xu: That is *Guasha*, a traditional Chinese medical treatment. Dennis had a stomachache that day, and Guasha is simply a cure. A home remedy, we call it. I had this on me endless time when I was a kid.

Quinlan: If this is what you call some kind of treatment, I hate to see what you consider to be child abuse.

Judge: If you two would chitchat, we can all go home. Does the defendant have something more to add?

Quinlan: No.

Xu: Yes, I do. I think you don't understand. *Guasha* is a traditional Chinese medical treatment, used for nearly all kinds of illnesses. For thousands of years, Chinese medicine has recognized that there're seven *Jin* and eight *Mai*. An example, it's like a small stream that runs into rivers, and in turn falls into the sea. A person's body has an invisible but very complex system of vital network, just like the computer network. And also the human *Qi* from *Dantian* finally goes through *Dantian*. It's the same principle.

Judge: Your client, what did he say?

Xu: It's a kind of...

Judge: It doesn't mind whether we could understand what you say. Perhaps I should provide another way. What does it say on every Missouri license plate?

Xu: Show Me State.

Judge: Precisely. Can you get an authoritative medical expert to back your testimony in plain English that an old country judge can understand?

Xu: Yes, I can try.

Judge: Did you do this *Guasha* to your son yourself? Mr. Xu?

Xu: Yes, I did it myself.

Jian: No, it was't him.

...

Judge: I warn you. This hearing must be conducted in a language we all can understand. Do you have something else to the discussion?

Jian: No, your honor.

Judge: Let me ask you one more time for sake of clarity. Did you do this *Guasha* to your son?

Xu: Yes, I did.

Judge: Until I was shown otherwise, I have no choice but to conclude that Dennis Xu lives in an unsafe home environment, and should be kept under the supervision of the Child Welfare Agency, pending a full trial on the charges.

New Words

abuse *n.* mistreatment 虐待

attorney *n.* lawyer 律师

bruise *n.* an injury that shows up as a discoloration on the skin 瘀伤；擦伤

chitchat *n.* light informal conversation 闲谈；聊天

conjecture *n.* a hypothesis that has little hard evidence 推测；臆测

hearing *n.* a legal proceeding where evidence is taken for the purpose of determining an issue of fact and reaching a decision based on that evidence 听证会

incontrovertible *adj.* impossible to deny or disprove 无争论余地的

indisputably *adv.* cannot be disputed 无争论余地地

inflict *v.* impose something unpleasant 施以；加害

ludicrous *adj.* inviting laughter 荒谬的；可笑的

neglect *n.* lack of attention and due care 疏忽；怠慢

pending *adj.* waiting to be decided or settled 待决的

speculation *n.* a guess based on incomplete evidence 推测；臆测

testimony *n.* something that serves as evidence 证词

Phrases and Expressions

put the cart before the horse
to have things in the wrong order 本末倒置

Notes

CWA

Child Welfare Agency, a government organization intended to protect the rights of children

Guasha treatment (scraping therapy)

A traditional Chinese medical treatment in which a wooden board repeatedly slides across the patient's acupuncture points. It works on the basis of principles similar to those of acupuncture and massage. Thus, ailments that can be treated by acupuncture and massage can be helped with Guasha as well. It can help reestablish the human body's natural biological circulation.

ER

emergency room

Show Me State

A nickname for Missouri, a Midwestern state in the central United States. This term appears on automobile license plates for Missouri.

Understanding and Speaking Interculturally

Exercise 1 Match the words on the left with their speakers on the right.

1. "Perhaps you don't understand your friend as well as you think you do."

2. "No, it wasn't him."
3. "Yes, I can try."
4. "How can you do this to your son?"
5. "I think you are putting the cart before the horse."
6. "Dennis Xu has been the subject of deliberate, long-term neglect and abuse."

a. Xu Datong
b. Judge
c. John Quinlan
d. Margaret Avery
e. Davis
f. Jian Ning

Exercise 2 Fill in the blanks according to the movie clip you have just watched.

1. **Judge:** Why is that I've never seen you around before, Mr. Quinlan?
   Quinlan: I've never had the honor, your honor. I deal mostly in ______ ______ cases.
   Judge: Apples and oranges, Mr. Quinlan. The two areas of law have virtually nothing to do with each other.
   Quinlan: Yes, of course. So I told my client, but he insisted on my representing him.
2. **Judge:** This hearing is for the purpose of ______ whether there is sufficient ______ to run court proceedings. So take off your ______ caps. And before we get to the court in these formalities, let's just talk about the matter.
3. **Davis:** ... Three days ago we received a telephone call from the social worker on ______ in St. Matthew Hospital, ______ us of a possible case of child ______ discovered as a result of ______ examination by Doctor Michael Longman.
4. **Davis:** As you can see, the medical report indisputably proves that Dennis Xu has been the ______ of ______, long-term ______ and abuse.
5. **Davis:** ... The CWA is currently carrying out a full ______ of this case, and has located a ______ number of ______, all of whom are prepared to testify regarding Mr. Datong Xu's ______ nature, and the neglect and ______ he has inflicted on his young son Dennis.

6. **Judge:** Until I was shown ________, I have no choice but to conclude that Dennis Xu lives in an ________ home environment, and should be kept under the ________ ________ of the Child Welfare Agency, pending a full ________ ________ on the charges.

Exercise 3 Decide whether the following statements are True or False according to the movie clip you have just watched. Write "T" for true and "F" for false.

_____ 1. John Quinlan is a lawyer of intellectual property rights.

_____ 2. Family law and the law of intellectual property rights are closely related to each other.

_____ 3. The judge believes Dennis Xu has been the subject of deliberate, long-term neglect and abuse.

_____ 4. Xu Datong performed Guasha on Dennis.

_____ 5. John Quinlan believes Xu Datong.

Exercise 4 Explore interculturally.

1. In the hearing, why does Xu Datong invite John to be his lawyer although John is not familiar with family law? What can you learn from it about Chinese culture?

2. Why doesn't John defend Xu Datong in the hearing? What can you learn from this?

3. Why does Xu Datong tell the judge he performed *Guasha* on Dennis? What can we learn from this about Chinese culture?

4. Debate: Divide the class into two groups and debate on the topic: "Who shall we ask for help when we get into legal troubles, our relatives and friends, or a lawyer." One group argues for relatives and friends, and the other group argues for the lawyer.

Section B Reading

A Case of Intercultural Communication

John, an American student, has a classmate named Mohammed, who comes from Egypt. The following is a conversation between them on a day when Mohammed bought a new cassette tape.

John: Nice cassette tape.

Mohammed: This is nothing. Please take it.

John: (surprised)

What surprised John and made him lose his words? One reason is that he didn't expect Mohammed to say "This is nothing" because his American classmates won't belittle the object being complimented. The second is that John didn't expect Mohammed to offer the tape to him in response to his compliment. This never occurs in American culture. Besides, if the object is "nothing", why do you send it as a gift to your friend? In Mohammed's culture, however, this practice is quite common.

As mentioned in the previous chapter, there are ten main elements of communication. Among the ingredients, encoding and decoding are of special significance to intercultural communication, which generally refers to the communication between culturally diverse people. Misunderstanding or breakdown of communication may occur as a result of the different cultural context in which the encoding and decoding take place. Another classic example is that the encoded message of "Have you eaten?" serves as a greeting according to Chinese cultural norms, but is decoded as an invitation to a meal in Western culture.

A Practical Discipline

As a human activity, intercultural communication is not a new concept and has existed in human history for thousands of years. However, it was not until the end of World War II that government officials and scholars became seriously interested in the understanding of intercultural interactions.

One of the major reasons for this shift was the ineffectiveness of many international development projects, and the failure to conduct the American government programs designed to offer economic and scientific expertise to aid developing countries in the 1950s. Much misunderstanding occurred as a result of ignorance about the vital role culture plays in the process of communication.

During the 1960s, anthropologists' insights into intercultural communication were applied not only to the training that diplomats were required to undergo, but also to training programs offered to business people, immigrants, missionaries, international students and Peace Corps volunteers. These programs helped to develop multicultural understandings for dealing with the frictions common in intercultural encounters, to smooth the adjustment to new cultural environments, and to inspire in participants a greater global awareness. Cultural illiteracy came to be viewed as an important problem to address.

Ever since then, rapid development has taken place in the understanding of culture and communication from a variety of perspectives, including psychology, sociology, anthropology, communication, and linguistics. As a result, skill in intercultural communication has acquired significant and practical value for the growing numbers of people who choose to work, study, travel, or live abroad.

Increasing Waves of Intercultural Contact in China

As we all know, "global village" is a term used to describe the shrinking world brought about by the rapid development of telecommunication technology and transportation networks. With China's great leaps in economic development and globalization, especially China's entry into the World Trade Organization, increasing waves of intercultural contact have occurred between Chinese people and the world at large, in business, education, the arts and in personal lives.

Since 1978, the total number of Chinese people who have gone overseas to further their education has reached one million. In 2005 alone, approximately 118000 Chinese people traveled overseas. This number is expected to grow about 30% in 2008. Meanwhile, more than 22 million foreigners visited China in 2006 for business and pleasure. In addition, the number of foreign students who come to Chinese universities to study has been increasing by an average of 15.3% annually.

The 29th Olympic Games were held in Beijing in August 2008. This was the first time that China, a country with 5000 years of civilization, hosted such a large international event. To attend, millions of people visited this ancient country, providing an invaluable opportunity for China to show itself to the world and for the world to get to know the real China. The Olympics afforded every citizen of China the privileged opportunity to introduce China to the world.

Elements of Intercultural Communication

One major goal of intercultural communication study is to discover the specific variables affecting the quality of intercultural communication. Although it is impossible to list all these variables, the major cultural elements fall into four general groups: perception, verbal processes, nonverbal processes and contextual elements (Samovar, Porter & Stefani, 2000).

The perception variables that influence intercultural communication include beliefs, attitudes, values, and worldviews. These cultural value systems serve as message filters that determine, to a certain extent, the meaning each person assigns to messages he encounters and thus, how to perceive the events these messages describe. In group-oriented cultures, for example, people's styles of communication tend to be indirect and tentative with a heavy emphasis on the context of communication, since maintaining harmony within the group is accorded priority. In individual-oriented cultures, however, people are more direct and less dependent on the context surrounding their conversation because their worldview tends to radiate outward from themselves. Thus, understanding different cultural ways of thinking allows us to perceive and predict the ways in which individuals from a given culture will respond to specific intercultural interactions.

Language is a major means of communication, heavily influenced by the culture in which it is developed. In other words, an individual's culture shapes the meaning of a verbal message. In American English, to be "embarrassed" is to feel mildly uncomfortable, but to Spanish-speakers, to be "embarassada" connotes "to be pregnant". That's why the Spanish translation of the English advertisement of the bottled ink produced by Parker Pen Company "To avoid embarrassment, use Parker SuperQuink" was decoded into "To avoid pregnancy, use Parker SuperQuink."

Communication also involves signs and symbols. The meaning of these nonverbal codes such as body language, time, and space etc., are also culturally determined. In most cultures, nodding the head means "yes" and shaking the head means "no." In Bulgaria, Iran and some places of Greece, however, they mean the opposite. In some cultures, people often schedule their activities and take time commitments seriously. In other cultures, however, schedules are very flexible and plans often change. Personal space also varies from culture to culture. In high-contact cultures, people feel comfortable standing close to each other and making physical contact. In low-contact cultures, the comfortable distance between people is larger and tolerance for touching much lower.

As mentioned in the previous chapter, communication takes place in a certain context. The contexts where intercultural encounters most likely occur are business, education and health care. In business, not only does a company's advertising content vary, but also the style of negotiation and the method of decision making differ according to the culture that most influences the company. A conventional function of the education system is to teach people the norms and the desired behavior of the local culture. In recent years, the classroom has become increasingly multicultural, with teachers and students coming from diverse cultural backgrounds. Cultural influences are also found in health care settings in which doctors and patients from different cultures have different explanations of illness and prefer different practices to treat illness as well as different ways of defining the patient-doctor relationship.

It is very important to keep in mind that the categories of variables described here are not separate elements independent of each other. Rather, they are interactive and work together to influence the process of intercultural communication. These elements will be explored in greater detail in the next chapters of this textbook.

Understanding and Speaking Interculturally

1 Group work: As mentioned in the passage, intercultural communication has existed in human history for thousands of years. Work in groups of three or four to name some intercultural encounters in Chinese history and in Western history.

2 A contest on English expressions of Chinese culture:

Step1: Divide the class into two groups.

Step2: In five minutes, each group prepares ten words or expressions in Chinese language that represent Chinese culture. (eg. *Qipao*, *Duanwu Jie* etc.)

Step3: Each group hands in the ten words or expressions to the teacher. (Once the order is fixed, it can never be changed.)

Step4: Start the contest. Group A expresses in English the words and expressions written by Group B. Group B expresses in English the words and expressions written by Group A. The group wins one point when they express one word correctly. Take turns doing this.

Step5: The group that gets more points wins the game.

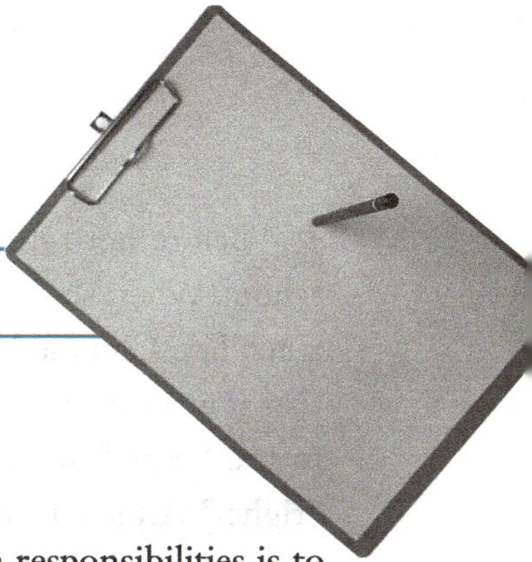

Section C Case

Introduction to the Case

For most elderly Chinese living in the United States, one of their main responsibilities is to help take care of their grandchildren. Since most of their grandchildren were born and grew up in America, it's not an easy job for them.

The Scenario

Grandparents and Grandchildren

When Mr. Xin arrived in America, he was very happy to meet Mike, his ten-year-old grandson, who had been born in America. His son, who was educated according to the traditional "beating" principle of China, warned Mr. Xin that according to the local law, physical punishment of children was forbidden. Mr. Xin always remembered this caution until one day. During the lunchtime, Mr. Xin couldn't control himself when Mike, who hated vegetables, picked out all the vegetables from his plate and threw them aside. Spanked by his grandfather for the first time, Mike didn't cry. He went to pick up the telephone and called the police. Mr. Xin thought Mike was calling his mother, and was shocked when a police car arrived at the door fifteen minutes later.

Before her retirement, Xue Suling used to be a teacher of Chinese language in a primary school. When she was invited by her daughter to help take care of her grandson, she decided to teach him Chinese language and made a detailed plan on how to do it. What she didn't expect is that it was very difficult to carry out her plan, even though she was an experienced teacher. Born in the United States, the six-year-old grandson already knew how to protect his time and his "rights". After returning home from school each day, he refused to spend half an hour sitting in front of the desk to practice reading and writing Chinese. He kept asking his grandmother why the other children didn't have to learn it. Things went better when Xue decided to learn English from her grandson. Every time she learned an English word, she taught him the equivalent Chinese word. In this way, both of them learned from each other.

Understanding and Speaking Interculturally

Exercise 1 Listen for the first time and answer the following questions.

1. According to Mr. Xin's son, what is not allowed in the United States?
2. What did Mike do after being spanked by his grandfather?
3. What did Xue Suling do before her retirement?
4. Did she find it easy to carry out her plan?

Exercise 2 Listen for the second time and fill in the blanks.

1. When Mr. Xin arrived in America, he was very happy to meet Mike, his ten-year-old grandson, who had been born in America. His son, who was educated according to the traditional "______" principle of China, ______ Mr. Xin that according to the local law physical

punishment of children was forbidden. Mr. Xin always remembered this caution until one day. During the ______, Mr. Xin couldn't control himself when Mike, who ______ vegetables, picked out all the vegetables from his plate and threw them aside. ______ by his grandfather for the first time, Mike didn't cry. He went to pick up the telephone and called the ______. Mr. Xin thought Mike was calling his mother, and was shocked when a police car arrived at the door fifteen minutes later.

2. Before her ______, Xue Suling used to be a teacher of Chinese language in a ______ school. When she was invited by her daughter to help take care of her grandson, she decided to teach him Chinese language and made a ______ plan on how to do it. What she didn't ______ is that it was very difficult to carry out her plan, even though she was an experienced teacher. Born in the United States, the six-year-old grandson already knew how to ______ his time and his "rights." After returning home from school each day, he ______ to spend half an hour sitting in front of the desk to practice reading and writing Chinese. He kept asking his grandmother why the other children didn't have to learn it. ______ went better when Xue decided to learn English from her grandson. Every time she learned an English word, she taught him the equivalent Chinese word. In this way, both of them learned from each other.

Exercise 3 Explore interculturally.

1. Could you understand why Mike called the police? What can we learn about American culture and Chinese culture?

2. Why couldn't Xue Suling carry out her original plan of Chinese language teaching? What can we learn about American culture and Chinese culture?

Part

II

Cultural Value Orientations

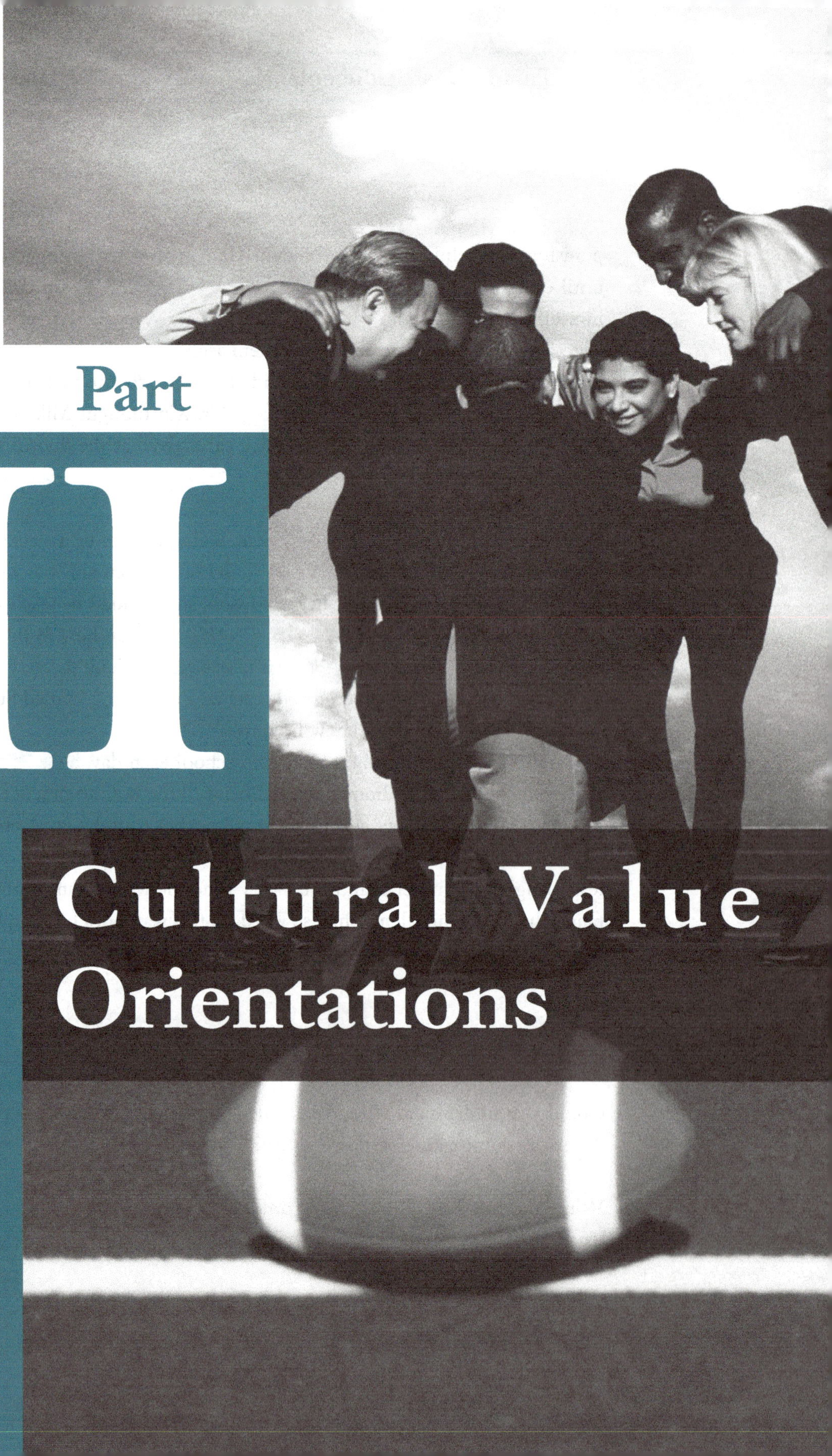

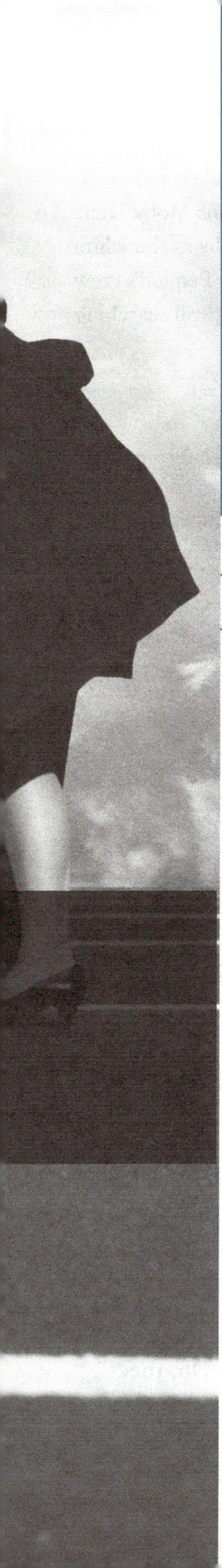

Chapter 4

Kluckhohn and Strodtbeck's Model

Section A Movie clip

Introduction to the Movie *Moby Dick*

In New Bedford, Connecticut, in the 1800s, the crew of the whaling ship Pequod, under Captain Ahab, know their mission is to hunt whales. However, what they don't realize is that Ahab once lost a leg to the magnificent white whale known as Moby Dick, and that he'll risk anything to avenge himself on the animal that cost him a leg... including himself and every member of his crew.

Shortly after meeting the Rachel, another whaling ship, the crew spots Moby Dick. For three consecutive days, Ahab sends out small boats to capture the whale. On the first day, Moby Dick crushes Ahab's boat between his jaws. The entire crew of the small boat escape unharmed. On the second day, Moby Dick once again destroys Ahab's boat, this time killing one of the sailors. On the third and final day, Moby Dick ignores the pursuing Ahab and rams the Pequod itself. The awesome power of the whale is too much for the ship, which sinks. As the ship goes down, Captain Ahab finally harpoons Moby Dick. The harpoon line catches Ahab around the neck and pulls him into the depths as the white whale dives beneath the surface, never to be seen again. Every member of the Pequod's crew is killed, except for Ishmael, who was thrown clear of the wreck. The Rachel, still searching for its missing crew, discovers Ishmael and rescues him.

Introduction to the Selected Scene

Captain Ahab finally has the chance to fight Moby Dick, to gain his revenge. However, as the harpoon line loops around Ahab's neck, he is pulled into the sea as the white whale dives beneath the surface, never to be seen again.

Script of the Scene

Ahab: ... Show us your crooked jaw... Show us your wrinkled brow! Rise! Birds, the birds!

The Crew: He rises! Him...Hold him!...

Ahab: Let the thing go. Hold him, closer! He'll not escape. Thunder! What the hell is wrong with him! Oh, the whale, the damned whale!

The Crew: Ahab! Ahab!

Ahab: From hell's heart I stab at thee; for hate's sake I spit my last breath at thee. Thou damned whale!

...

Starbuck: No more this, no more this!

New Words

crooked *adj.* not straight or level; twisted, bent or curved 歪的；扭曲的；弯曲的

jaw *n.* either of the bone structures containing the teeth 颌

spit *v.* send saliva from the mouth; do this as a sign of contempt or anger 吐口水，吐唾沫，吐痰；啐唾沫（以示鄙夷或愤怒）

stab *v.* pierce (sth) or wound (sb) with a pointed tool or weapon; push (a knife, etc) into sb/sth 戳（某物），刺伤（某人），用（刀等）捅

wrinkled *adj.* having or showing wrinkles 有皱纹的；显出皱纹的

Notes

Captain Ahab

Ahab has become a part of America's popular mythology. Having lost a leg in an earlier encounter with Moby Dick, the great whale, it was this encounter that provoked his desire for revenge. He wears a false leg carved, appropriately, from the jaw bone of a sperm whale.

Moby Dick

The great white whale Moby Dick, a creature of legendary size, ferociousness, and appearance, has become a subject of great scholarly speculation.

Understanding and Speaking Interculturally

Exercise 1 Answer the following questions according to the movie clip you have just watched.

1. What are all the sailors looking for as the clip starts?
2. How does Ahab alert the sailors that Moby Dick is coming?
3. What are the physical characteristics of Moby Dick?
4. What kind of personality has Ahab displayed during his fight with the whale?

Exercise 2 Decide whether the following statements are True or False according to the movie clip you have just watched. Write "T" for true and "F" for false.

_____ 1. The birds' arrival heralds the coming of the whale.

_____ 2. Ahab is pursuing Moby Dick for money.

_____ 3. Ahab successfully kills the big whale.

_____ 4. Ahab dies in his fighting with the whale.

Exercise 3 Discuss the image of the whale as a symbol of nature, and Captain Ahab's attitude towards it.

Section B Reading

What is Value?

We have already discussed various ways of defining culture. However, visible objects and customs, such as paintings, clothing and food are only the tip of the cultural iceberg. In order to get under the water line for a larger view of the "iceberg", we need to examine its core—value.

Consider the definition of "value" offered by the *American Heritage Dictionary*:

Value: "A principle, standard, or quality considered worthwhile or desirable."

Thus, value represents a kind of principle or standard. That means it can serve as a kind of guide. It is applied in every aspect of our life, not just limited to a specific field or to a certain category of things. Value is normative: it sets norms. (Dou, 2007) In other words, values deal with what is required or forbidden, what is considered by the majority in society to be good or bad. Values lie at the core of every culture. The chief goal of culture is concerned with what ought to be, not what is. (Martin & Nakayama, 2007) For example, we all share the ancient belief that all men are created equal, but still we are quite clear that differences of gender, class and ethnicity do exist.

Kluckhohn and Strodtbeck's Model

Intercultural communication studies take different approaches. Among the most influential and pioneering research has been the work carried out by Harvard professors Kluckholn and Strodtbeck during the mid-twentieth century. They selected 5 communities in the Southwest and conducted a study of their differing values. The results of the study appeared in their book *Variations in Value Orientations* (1961). They suggested that members of all cultural groups must answer, consciously or unconsciously, the following important questions:

1. What is human nature?
2. What is the relationship between humans and nature?
3. What is the relationship between humans?
4. What is the preferred personality?
5. What is the orientation toward time?

According to Kluckholn and Strodtbeck, there are three possible responses to each question as they relate to shared values. (See Table 4.1)

Range of Values			
Human nature	Basically good	Mixture of good and evil	Basically evil
Relationship between humans and nature	Humans dominate	Harmony	Nature dominates
Relationship between humans	Individual	Group oriented	Collateral
Preferred personality	Doing	Growing	Being
Time orientation	Future oriented	Present oriented	Past oriented

Table 4.1 (Adapted from Martin & Nakayama, 2007)

The Nature of Human Beings

As the above table shows, there are three possible responses to this question. In European countries and the US, where many people are Christians, especially before the mid-nineteenth century, the dominant view toward human nature was that man is born with original sin. As a result of the biblical Adam's fall, men have to labor to get food, and women have to endure pain to bear children. They thought that man had to receive constant instruction and exhortation to ensure him to fight against his evil nature and to receive God's favor. Many held that all men were sinners before God. That partly explains why during the eighteenth century there appeared so many conduct books in Europe. Many writers, when satirizing man's folly and corruption, trace the associate evil with man's fall. This is a deep-rooted view. It was particularly the case with Calvinists, who held a much more pessimistic view of man's depravity. Later, with the rise of humanism, people began to adopt a more optimistic worldview. The Age of Enlightenment, with its important notions about reason and science, convinced people of a bright future and thus changed their fundamental view of human nature. The most significant shift happened in the twentieth century. Many people no longer regarded man as basically evil. They began to adopt a mixed attitude.

Social views of human nature have a deep impact on people's lives in many respects. We can often see their manifestations in legal systems. The wide adoption of the principle of "presumption of innocence," (in which the accused is presumed to be innocent until declared guilty by a jury or court) is a notable example. The burden of proof is thus on the prosecution (representing the State), which must convince the court of the accused's guilt. Moreover, a society's view of human nature affects not only the judicial process, but also applies to convicts. As Martin and Nakayama (2007) have pointed out, "Societies that hold this belief [men are basically evil] would be less interested in rehabilitation of criminals than in punishment." Thus it becomes more understandable that in some countries even a minor offense may result in the cutting of one's hand. The same thing happened in Britain during the sixteenth and seventeenth century. Aristocrats regarded the poor to be potential vagabonds or mob, and punished them cruelly for the tiniest offense.

In China and in some other Asian countries, people traditionally held that men are born innocent, but corruptible. For thousands of years, Chinese people have been disciplined more by moral than legal standards, one of the most important reasons explaining the comprehensive development of the moral-based system in Chinese society. But we should keep it in mind that when we discuss value systems, we refer to the dominant standards or principles in a society, where many different or even contradictory opinions may be held simultaneously.

The Relationship Between Man and Nature

As noted earlier, in addition to the question of human nature, man's relation with Nature is also a significant cultural drive. A society's approach to this issue will guide its conduct and attitude when dealing with nature, a fact that has far-reaching impact on its culture. The traditional Western view of this relation also stems from the Bible, a reflection of Judeo-Christian beliefs. According to biblical tradition, God created the earth and all the living things in it for man. He gives Adam the right to name every living thing and to have dominion over the earth. This view has long influenced the West's use and conquest of Nature. In the Industrial Age, due to break-through technological innovations, man's productivity increased drastically. At the same time man's unrestrained exploitation of natural resources also surged. As a result, environmental degradation occurred and Nature, as Engels pointed out, was seen to take her revenge. With the rise of ecology as a branch of study and a growing interest in environmental protection, people began to embrace a harmonious relationship with nature. In many countries, there has been a call for sustainable development.

In China, the notion of the unity of man and Nature is nearly as ancient as our civilization. The Taoists especially advocate a harmonious relation ship with Nature, enabling man to reach a higher state. The theories underlying traditional Chinese medicine are the best-known manifestation of the Chinese people's harmonious view of human society and Nature. The 24 solar terms, for example, which serve as a practical guide for framework, also reflect this view. Elsewhere, geomancy, or the practice of *fengshui*, builds on this view for its theoretical basis, as well, although the scientific nature of geomancy is still under heated discussion. It is ironic that, with the development of China's economy, some Chinese people are blinded by short-term profit and exploit nature excessively, causing great damage to the environment. Fortunately, the importance of environmental protection has been realized by the central government, which propagates awareness of this through the slogan of "building a harmonious society."

A very different attitude, man's subjugation to nature, usually exists in primitive societies and cultures, where man's power with respect to Nature is viewed as comparatively weak. In these societies, people are quite fatalistic and tend to believe that everything in their lives is predestined, and human beings have no choice at all.

The Relationship Between Humans

Man, according to Socrates, is a social animal. The fundamental relationship within a society is that between individuals, or groups of individuals. This relationship regulates our behavior toward others in every aspect. According to different approaches to this question, we can roughly distinguish two types of society. Individualism, often regarded as the fundamental value held by Westerners, places more importance on personal competence and responsibility. People in Western societies tend to take actions on their own and shoulder the responsibility for themselves. They are more assertive; tend to make decision for themselves instead of consulting their colleagues or others around them. Asking for advice and help from their supervisors is usually regarded as evidence of lack of competence. Thus, their working environment is usually more competitive. Employers are more attentive to employees' personal performance and usually track their achievements in order to decide whom to reward or promote. In contrast, those from more collectivistic societies, such as Asia, and many Arab societies where tribal or clan considerations may predominate, place more emphasis on cooperation, teamwork, group loyalty, and collective decision. They usually seek suggestions from their friends, family members and colleagues. In case of difficult situations in business, some will often ask their supervisors to decide for them. That is strongly avoided in a society where individualism is valued. But for those living in group-based societies, they tend to regard such tasks as pertaining to the whole group instead of to themselves alone. Thus, their view is that they are doing, not to shift responsibility, but for the benefit of the whole group.

Nowadays, with the rise of globalization, these two values begin to merge. The emphasis on cooperation and teamwork in many US-based companies is already commonplace, while many Chinese companies begin to focus more on individual competence and achievements. The synergistic power of these two values is becoming clear.

Activity Orientation

With the quickening pace of modern life, people now are more and more adopting a "doing" orientation. Those who are quick to catch opportunities and take action are favored. People pay more attention to personal achievements. International companies are especially famous for their preference for quick and incisive action.

"Being" orientation has a longer history. In the days of feudal society, social status and position counted more than personal merit. The landed aristocracy thus became averse to productive behavior. After many generations, they could not longer be compared to their glorious ancestors. After all, they didn't have to do anything to hold their social positions. Their ancestry guaranteed that they would be respected and allowed them to live on inherited wealth, without endeavoring to do anything productive, quite contrary to the lives their landed tenants generally led. "Being" societies are usually more static.

"Growing" orientation is somewhere in between being and doing.

Sense of Time

Some countries enjoy a long history. People in these countries tend to pay heavy attention to tradition. History can always serve as guide. In times of crisis, history can often offer precedents in which the wisdom of the ancestors is worth following. Apart from this, in such a country, the force of tradition and customs is usually strong, and sometimes it becomes rather an obstacle to fundamental changes or reforms.

Some cultures are more present-oriented. They put more emphasis on the present. They work, they earn, in order to enjoy the present life. Mexicans are famous for their energy and enjoyment in their daily life. The following report is good evidence.

> *I had a wonderful experience in Mexico. I like the energy—there was ALWAYS so much going on in the streets, and in the zocalo, all hours of the day and night. And when I returned to the US, the streets seemed so dead—everyone individually alone in their own little houses here. I felt suddenly so sensory-deprived!!!* (Martin & Nakayama, 2007)

Some societies are more future-oriented. The custom of mortgage is a good indicator. People consider how much they may earn in the future and decide their expenditure. With the mortgage and the credit card, it is easy and enjoyable. The famous joke about two old women, one from China, who deposits money in the bank for so many years to buy a house, the other from the US, who before her death has paid up her mortgage, is well-known. But its moral is still powerful.

Understanding and Speaking Interculturally

1 Pair discussion: Do you think human nature is basically good or evil? Do you have any reason supporting your belief? Or is it just a generalization instilled to you by your parents?

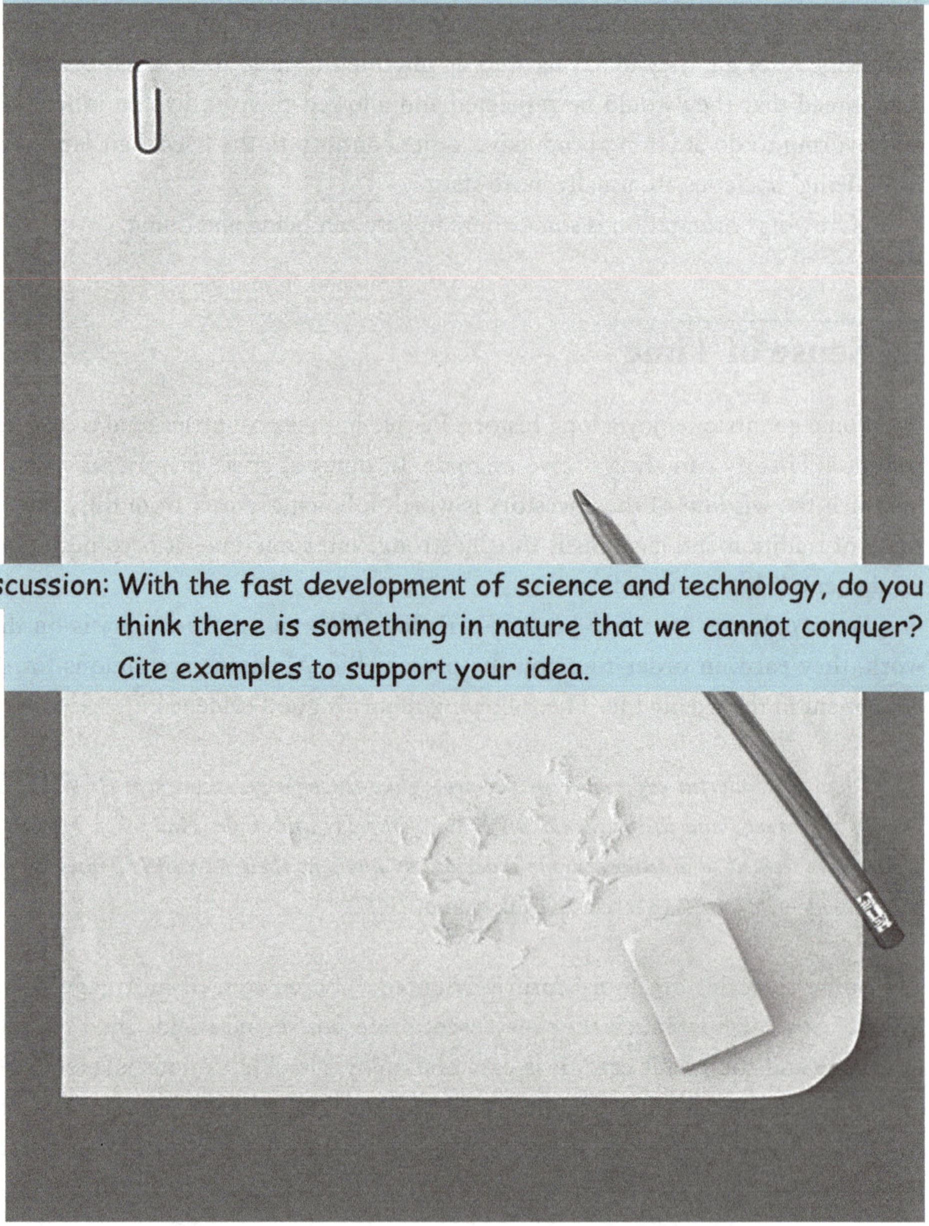

2 Group discussion: With the fast development of science and technology, do you think there is something in nature that we cannot conquer? Cite examples to support your idea.

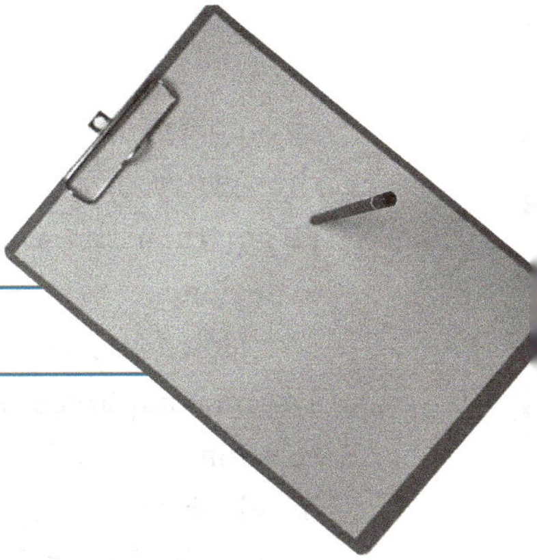

Section C Case

Introduction to the Case

The following is a case about an American company's management in one of its Mexican branches. In this case, the issue of interpersonal relationship plays a crucial role in management. Listen to the case and try to discover the problem.

The Scenario

Managing Your Company Culturally

In order to further expand its activities, USAHP, an American multinational company, purchased a plant in Axcala, Mexico, from a Mexican group called PAMEX. At the moment this plant has over 500 employees and produces a million cases of products per month. The plant has state of the art technology with almost completely automatic production lines. The two companies have very different ways of conducting business.

For the managers and engineers remaining from the previous company, the culture change accompanying USAHP's acquisition of the Axcala plant was enormous. Most of the employees felt, accurately, that their jobs were at risk because of the remarkable differences in philosophy between the two companies. PAMEX promoted, rewarded, and retained employees based on their loyalty to the firm and to their immediate supervisors, and on interpersonal (usually family) connections. In contrast, USAHP's policy is to hire technical experts to start as supervisors and then grow within the company, advancing to managerial positions. Similar differences were apparent in the reward systems of the two companies. Under PAMEX, managers' salaries were based on their friendships with the owner or the Board of Directors of the company. As a result, their salaries were far larger than the USAHP salary structure allowed, given their training, performance and experience.

However, one of USAHP's first steps raised questions about the fairness of the company's reward system. Employees in all cultures view fairness as an important aspect of worker-organization relationships and react negatively to actions that they perceive are unfair. However, the way in which "fairness" is defined varies across cultures, focusing on in-group relationships in Mexico and on "objective" assessments of credentials and performance in the US. In sum, in the new plant rewards, promotions, and retention were based on objective measures of individual performance. Each of these changes was appropriate given the strategic model on the basis of which USAHP operated. But, for the PAMEX employees, they created uncertainty and ambiguity and directly threatened their job security. To make matters worse, they were imposed by outsiders, who in many ways had carelessly exaggerated their alien status.

In many ways, the Axcalan acquisition provides a textbook case of the kinds of problems that can occur when business operations cross cultural boundaries. In this case, the American firm attempts to introduce change to its newly-acquired Mexican operations, which inevitably engenders resistance.

Understanding and Speaking Interculturally

Exercise 1 Listen for the first time and answer the following questions.

1. Why did many staff remaining from the previous company have fears?
2. How had they been rewarded previously?
3. How were they rewarded after USAHP bought the company?

Exercise 2 Listen for the second time and fill in the blanks.

1. Most of the employees felt, accurately, that their jobs were ________ ________ because of the remarkable differences in ________ between the two companies. PAMEX promoted, rewarded, and retained employees based on their ________ to the firm and to their immediate supervisors, and on ________ (usually family) connections.

2. In contrast, USAHP's policy is to hire ________ to start as ________ and then grow within the company, advancing to ________ ________.

3. In sum, in the new plant ________ were based on objective measures of ________. Each of these changes was appropriate given the strategic model on the basis of which USAHP operated. But, for the PAMEX employees, they created ________ and directly threatened their ________.

Exercise 3 Explore interculturally.

1. What can you learn about Mexican culture from the reward system of PAMEX?

2. What can you learn about American culture from the reward system of USAHP?

3. How do you explain the phenomenon in this case, applying the theory of the relationship between humans? What cultural differences caused the resistance of the local staff in PAMEX after the acquisition?

4. If you were one of the managers from USAHP, concerning the local culture, what measures will you take to promote the motivation of the original staff in PAMEX?

Chapter 5

Hofstede's Cultural Dimensions

Section A Movie clip

Introduction to the Movie *Anna and the King*

This film depicts a true story of a woman who challenged the heart of a king and inspired the destiny of a nation. When an English schoolteacher, Anna Leonowens, arrives in the exotic land of Siam to educate the fifty-eight children of King Mongkut, her Western sensibilities clash with the ruler's Eastern ways. If she has preconceived notions about the East, the King has similar notions about the West. The tension builds as Mongkut learns that outside forces are conspiring against his regime. With the political intrigue set to explode, Anna and the King must become allies in a daring fight to save Siam from dangerous enemies bent on destruction. Amid the danger of growing political unrest, their

respect for each other slowly turns into something more. This film is a masterpiece filled with passion and adventure.

Introduction to the Selected Scene

The selected scene reflects the different attitudes that Westerners and those in the East have about power distance, individualism, collectivism, as well as the masculinity and femininity, as proposed by Hofstede. Regarding the question of where Anna would live, the king has promised Anna to provide her with a dwelling outside of the palace, but he seems to have no intention of making good on his promise. Anna reminds the king of his promise, but the king replies that it is his pleasure to have Anna living in the palace. When Anna insisted that it was not her pleasure, the king shouts at her: "You should obey." All the women present kneel down on the ground in fright, while Anna refuses to submit to his authority, claiming that she was the guest rather than the servant.

When the prince of Thailand boasts about his father's power and influences, he concludes his speech by saying "And (my father's) power reaches everywhere." Anna's son, who has little understanding of this kind of power, replies, "But in my house they don't." This statement immediately fills the prince with anger, as he has been deeply influenced by the ideology of authority and power.

Script of the Scene

Servant 1: It appears sir must wait to meet His Majesty another day.

Anna: No. I do not think so. Come along.

Servant 1: Mem Leonowens. Mem Leonowens. Mem Leonowens! Mem, wait!

Anna: Please! Your Majesty... I am Anna Leonowens. I'm a school—

King: Stop!

Louis: Aah!

King: Who? Who?

Servant 1: You Majesty, Mem Anna Leonowens and son Louis.

Anna: Your Majesty... we have been kept waiting for nearly 3 weeks. And although I appreciate that you have issues of...

great importance. I would imagine that your son's education would be far more—

King: Silence! Has she no understanding of protocol?

Servant 1: She has been advised.

King: You... are teacher?

Anna: Yes, Your Majesty, I am.

King: You do not look sufficient of age for scientific teaching. How many years have you?

Anna: Enough to know that age and wisdom do not necessarily go hand in hand, Your Majesty.

King: I doubt you would say same for being bold and English.

Anna: They are rather inseparable, I'm afraid.

Servant 1: His Majesty has not dismissed you. Follow him!

Anna: Come along, Louis. Up, up, up. Quickly. Uh, pardon me.

King: You articulate logical answer under pressure, Mem Leonowens.

Anna: That is very kind of you, Your Majesty.

King: But irritating superior attitude, King find most unbeautiful. However, it will serve you well, given decision I now make.

Anna: First impression can often be very misleading.

King: Along with my eldest son... you shall now teach all my children. Come. The royal family. 23 wives... 42 concubines... 58 offspring, and 10 more on the way. Each one unique, each one my hope for the future. I understand your surprise. Not as many as emperor of China, but he did not spend half of life in monastery. King making up for lost time.

Louis: Mother, what's a concubine?

Anna: Shh.

King: Attention, my most blessed and royal family, we have company. Two who have sailed from far, far way. Presenting original pupil and heir apparent Prince Chulalongkorn. This, my son, is your new teacher.

Anna: It is a great honor, Your Highness.

Prince: Have I done something to offend you?

King: Of course not.

Prince: Then why do you punish me with Imperialist schoolteacher?

Louis: He doesn't look too happy about it.

King: Dearest family, I desire you all, when of a appropriate age, to be educated in English language, science and literature. This is a necessary and practical gift I give to you, and you must never forget to honor your renowned teacher Mem Anna Leonowens.

Anna: Ahem! Uh... Hello, Your Highnesses, I am pleased to meet you. This is my son, Louis.

King: Oh. Must not forget head wife the Lady Thiang.

Anna: It is my pleasure.

King: That you help make her fine scholar also.

Lady: Welcome, Mem teacher.

King: Prince... Thongkon Yai. Prince Suk Sawat. Princess Kannika Kaeo. And Princess Fa-ying.

Fa-ying: I'm not princess. I'm monkey.

King: Ha ha! My deepest apologies. I study her in English myself.

Anna: Well, Your Majesty, I am most flattered by your welcome, and I find the opportunity to be in school an exciting one. Such devotion to progress is to be commenced.

King: Reform is vital for my country's survival. As tiny feet change, so, too, will Siam.

Anna: But being in a country with so many unique customs, if I am to raise my son to be like his father, which I very much hope he will be, then I must feel free to follow our own traditions.

King: As a father, I understand.

Anna: Good. Then His Majesty will appreciate why having a home outside the palace walls is of such great importance to us. A home which... had been promised, but so far has not been provided.

King: It is my pleasure that you live in the palace.

Anna: But it is not mine, Your Majesty.

King: You do not set conditions of your employment. And you shall obey!

Anna: May I respectfully remind His Majesty that I am not his servant, but his guest!

King: A guest who's paid. Education begins tomorrow.

Woman: He sounds absolutely dreadful, if you ask me.

Anna: Did unnerve me, I must say.

Louis: Moonshee, why does the king have so many wives?

Man: That is an excellent question… for your mother.

Louis: Mother…

Anna: I heard you, Louis. Well, uh… Siam is a monarchy, just like England, and one way that a royal family maintains its control in the face of war and disease is to have as many children as possible.

Louis: So he needs s lot of wives to take care of them.

Anna: A keen observation, darling. Time for bed. Come give us a kiss.

Louis: Does he love all of them?

Anna: In a way.

Louis: Like you loved father?

Anna: Things are very different here, Louis. Even love. Go on. Off to bed.

Louis: Mother, why doesn't Queen Victoria have a lot of husbands?

Together: Good night, Louis.

Man: I'll never forget you, never. My heart is yours, Tuptim. I will always love you, always, Tuptim. I will never forget you, remember.

Lady: Presenting royal school, sir. Is anything wrong, sir?

Anna: No. No, no. Nothing at all, Lady Thiang. Louis, that'll be your desk. Yes. Well, I suppose class is now in session. Sit down.

Prince: Greetings, Mem Leonowens. My father wish to give sir this to put on path of good teaching.

Anna: Well, I shall… certainly bear that in mind, Your Highness. Uh, may I complement you on your English.

Prince: Siam… population 6 million, spreading across 49 bountiful provinces, from Burma in west to Cambodia in east. Presided over by King Maha Mongkut, lord of life, whose strength and power reach everywhere.

Louis: Not in my house, they don't.

Prince: Son of teacher is forgetting I am son of King. Son of teacher couldn't care less. You will sit somewhere else.

Louis: I will not.

Anna: Louis, remember what I told you.

Louis: I'm sorry, Mother, but he started it.

Prince: In my country, man never tell woman he is sorry about anything. Ever. If you had father, you would know that.

Louis: You don't have a father! You have a map!

Anna: Louis.

Prince: Is forbidden to touch royalty!

Louis: I didn't touch you! I shoved you! Why don't you get one of your slaves to shove me back?!

Anna: Let me through. Stop. Stop. That's enough. That's enough.

New Words

articulate *v.* pronounce distinctly and carefully; enunciate 说话；明白表示；清楚地表达

concubine *n.* in certain societies, a woman contracted to a man as a secondary wife, often having few legal rights and low social status 妾；情妇

flatter *v.* compliment excessively and often insincerely, especially in order to win favor 过分夸赞；奉承

inseparable *adj.* impossible to separate or part 分不开的或不可分离的

irritate *v.* rouse to impatience or anger; annoy 激怒激起不耐烦或愤怒

monarchy *n.* government by a monarch; A state ruled or headed by a monarch 君主国；由君主统治或领导的国家

monastery *n.* a community of persons, especially monks, bound by vows to a religious life and often living in partial or complete seclusion 全体修道院修士；立誓皈依某一宗教的人的组织

protocol *n.* the forms of ceremony and etiquette observed by diplomats and heads of state; a code of correct conduct 外交礼节；礼仪正确的行为方式

unnerve *v.* to deprive of fortitude, strength, or firmness of purpose; to make nervous or upset 使…失去意志，使…失去坚韧；使…紧张或慌张

Phrases and Expressions

go hand in hand
关系密切地；手拉着手地

in session
在开会，在开庭，在上课

Notes

Siam

Thailand's official name was Siam until 23 June 1939, when it was changed to Thailand; it was renamed Siam between 1945 and 11 May 1949, after which the name Thailand was once again adopted. Also spelled *Siem*, *Syâm* or *Syâma*, it has been identified with the *Sanskrit Śyâma*, dark or brown. But the names Shan and A-hom seem to be variants of the same word and Śyâma is possibly not its origin but a learned and artificial distortion.

Buddhist monastery

Thailand is one of the most strongly Buddhist countries in the world. The national religion is Theravada Buddhism which is practiced by more than 95% of all Thais. Buddhism is so intensely interwoven with the life of a nation from the king to the lowest subject, and where the talapoins or bonzes play such an important role in the national life, so that every male subject, the king and the crown prince not excepted, has to live in a Buddhist monastery and join the ranks of the talapoins for a short period.

King Maha Mongkut

also known as Rama IV, ruled Siam (now Thailand) from 1851 to 1868, during which time he successfully negotiated with Western powers, modernized his nation and served as the inspiration for the story *Anna and the King of Siam*. Mongkut ascended the throne upon the death of his half-brother, Jetta (Rama III), after spending 27 years as a Buddhist monk. Educated and multi-lingual, Mongkut negotiated with the United States and European powers to open Siam to international trade. He also brought in missionaries to teach his concubines and children about modern science and culture. Among the missionaries was Mrs. Anna Leonowens, who left Siam after Mongkut died of malaria (1868) and then gained fame for her book *The English Governess at the Siamese Court*. Her story was turned into the popular book *Anna and the King of Siam* (1944) by Margaret Landon, and later became the subject of movies and a Broadway musical (*The King and I*).

Understanding and Speaking Interculturally

Exercise 1 Answer the following questions according to the movie clip you have just watched.

1. After watching the selected scenes, could you describe the status of women in Siam?

2. Why did Anna refuse to live in the palace?

3. Could you explain what different viewpoints the prince and Louis hold?

Exercise 2 Fill in the blanks according to the movie clip you have just watched.

1. But being in a country with so many ______ customs, if I am to raise my son to be like his father, which I very much hope he will be, then I must feel free to ______ our own traditions.

2. Good. Then His Majesty will ______ why having a home outside the palace walls is of such great importance to us. A home which… had been ______, but so far has not been provided.

3. But it is not mine, Your Majesty. ... May I ______ remind His Majesty that I am not his servant, but his guest!

Exercise 3 Divide the class into several groups and perform the scene with the help of the script.

Organize into small groups with 4 or 5 students each. Assign the roles of Anna, the King, the prince and Louis. After rehearsing, students will perform their roles, and vote for the best actor and the best actress.

Section B Reading

Based on his survey of over 88 000 employees of IBM, a large multinational business organization with branches in 66 countries, Dutch scientist Geert Hofstede identified four dimensions that drive cultural differences: individualism-collectivism, power distance, uncertainty avoidance, and masculinity-femininity. More recently abundant research has shown that Hofstede's dimensional model applies not only to work-related values but also to cultural values, in general.

Individualism vs. Collectivism

Generally speaking, the values, norms and beliefs associated with Individualism emphasize that every individual is unique. Accordingly, popular comments about individuals tend to be mainly based on their personal achievements, status and other features. By contrast, societies organized along collectivist lines prefer to characterize an individual according to his family, social class, and group. Individualism indicates that a society is a loosely knit social framework while Collectivism indicates a tight social network. The following table is a comparison of the major characteristics of individualists and collectivists.

Attitudes and Behaviors	Individualists	Collectivists
Self	Each person is separate from others; children learn to think in terms of "I"	Each person is part of a group; children learn to think in terms of "we"

Identity	Identity is based on the individual	Identity is based on the social network
Communication	Low context	High context
Social values	Speak your mind and tell the truth	Maintain harmony and avoid confrontation
Decision-making	Personal freedom is more important than equality	Equality is more important than personal freedom
Group membership	Follow universal rules; the decision-making process is important	Fulfill obligation to in-group members; relationships are important
Conformity	The individual belongs to many groups but his attachment to them is relatively weak	The individual belongs to few groups but feels strongly attached to them
Behavior toward in-group and out-group members	Group has relatively little influence on the behavior of group members	Group greatly influences the behavior of members
Relationships with group members	Relatively little difference in behavior toward in-group and out-group members	Big difference between in-group and out-group behaviors
Competition	Less intimate with in-groups and less hostile to out-groups	More intimate with in-groups and more hostile to out-groups
Cooperation	Occurs within groups as well as between groups	Cooperation with members of in-groups but not with members of out-groups
Strangers	Value meeting new people; meet them easily	Formal and distant with strangers
Self-reliance	It is a pleasure to do as much by yourself as possible	People depend on each other but should not burden in-group members unnecessarily
Typical relationship pattern	Short-term, voluntary, less intensive relationships	Long-term, involuntary, more intensive relationships

Table 5.1 Contrasts Between Individualism and Collectivism

Country or region	Ranking	Country or region	Ranking
USA	1	Venezuela	40
Australia	2	Colombia	39
Great Britain	3	Pakistan	38
Canada	4	Peru	37
Netherlands	5	Taiwan	36

Table 5.2 Ranking of the First and Last Five Countries or Regions on Individualism-collectivism Dimension

Table 5.2 is a display of the most individualistic cultures and the most collectivistic cultures based on the ratings of 40 countries included on Hofstede's individualism-collectivism dimension. It is very interesting to find that most of the highly individualistic cultures happen to be native-English speaking countries. According to linguists, English is the only language that capitalizes the pronoun "I" in writing. Is it just a coincidence? Or is there some kind of relationship between the language and the culture it invented?

Power Distance

The "power distance" dimension reflects the degree to which the culture accepts the unequal distribution of power. Cultures with a high power distance index are said to accept inequality as the cultural norm. Such a culture is vertical and hierarchical. Some people hold higher status while others have lower status. Authoritarian-style communication is common. Persons in authority enjoy more privilege and most people tend to depend on them for decision-making. However, cultures with a low power distance index are more horizontal. People have formed the habit of fighting for equal treatment and questioning authority.

In Mexico, for example, employees tend to respect authority. Individuals in authority tend to maintain certain social distance from their subordinates, and show reluctance to empower employees. Conversely, in North America, where society values fair competition and independence, those in authority are expected to earn the people's respect. Subordinates think of superiors as being the same kind of people as themselves, and vice versa. In addition, children raised in high power-distance cultures are expected to obey their parents and comply with the requests of their teachers. In low power-distance cultures, however, children are taught to challenge their parents and teachers. Asking questions is highly encouraged instead of being regarded as a threat to authority.

Country or region	Ranking	Country or region	Ranking
Philippines	1	Austria	40
Mexico	2	Israel	39
Venezuela	3	Denmark	38
India	4	New Zealand	37
Former Yugoslavia	5	Ireland	36

Table 5.3 Ranking of the First and Last Five Countries or Regions on "Power Distance" Dimension

Table 5.3 displays the ten cultures at the two extremes of the "power distance" dimension, with the Philippines ranking at the high end and Austria at the low end. As suggested by Hofstede, population size is one of the important predictors of power distance. Generally speaking, the larger the population, the greater the power distance is likely to be. In order to cope with the increased complexities that arise from their large population, these cultures tend to adopt a political hierarchy that enables them to function effectively and efficiently. In addition, climate and distribution of wealth may also account for the different preferences of power distance.

Uncertainty Avoidance

Uncertainty avoidance indicates norms, values and beliefs related to the toleration of ambiguity. Cultures with a high uncertainty avoidance index ranking, Japan and Korea for example, seeks to establish social systems that prize rules and social expectations. Risk seems to cause them anxiety, tension and stress. Laws are of great importance to them. People in these cultures choose to avoid conflicts and have difficulty tolerating deviant or abnormal people and views. Members of these societies tend to defer to experts and individuals in authority. Uniformity is preferred. In cultures with a low or weak uncertainty avoidance index ranking, people enjoy less stress from ambiguity. They welcome new ideas, try new things and are more tolerant of people and views considered deviant. Singapore, Denmark, USA, India, and Great Britain are good examples. Table 5.4 displays the five high-uncertainty-avoidance cultures and five low-uncertainty-avoidance cultures.

Differences in this area also manifest themselves in the business context. In high-uncertainty-avoidance cultures, for example, employers tend to hire those people who are faithful and committed to them and their organizations. Those who have unusual longevity in the organization would be promoted. Since employees would think that being faithful to the organization is a kind of virtue, they try to avoid conflicts and competition. In low-uncertainty-avoidance cultures, however, employers appreciate flexibility and prize employee initiative. Such organizations tend to have fewer rules, enabling employees to enjoy more freedom.

Country or Region	Ranking	Country or Region	Ranking
Greece	1	Singapore	40
Portugal	2	Denmark	39
Belgium	3	Sweden	38
Japan	4	Hong Kong	37
Former Yugoslavia	5	Ireland	36

Table 5.4 Ranking of the First and Last Five Countries or Regions on Uncertain Avoidance Dimension

Masculinity vs. Femininity

In all cultures, men and women adopt distinct norms of socialization and tend to play differentiated roles in society. However, different cultural expectations of male and female occur across cultures. Masculine cultures prefer rigid gender roles, and esteem achievement, success and money, as well as self-reliance. Feminine cultures tend to accept fluid gender roles, and appreciate traits such as affection, compassion, and interpersonal relationships, placing an emphasis on responsibility and nurture. In masculine cultures, men dominate in the culture and assume decision-making roles. Societies with lower masculinity scores tend to enjoy more flexible sex roles and equality between sexes. Quality of life is valued over money.

Japan, Austria, Venezuela, Italy, Switzerland, Mexico, Ireland, Germany, Great Britain, and Philippines are cultures with the highest masculinity-index scores. The countries with the highest feminine scores are Sweden, Norway, Netherlands, Denmark, Yugoslavia [Note: The former Yugoslavia. This is no longer a country], Finland, Chile, Portugal, Thailand. China traditionally used to be a typical masculine society. With its great social and economic transformation, its profile is changing. For example, Hong Kong ranked 17 while Taiwan ranked 27 in the survey.

Please note that many scholars today do not agree with the exact ranking of the forty cultures placed along these four dimensions, which was set about two decades ago. However, Hofstede's cultural dimensions are still very enlightening and illuminating.

Understanding and Speaking Interculturally

1 How does Individualism differ from Collectivism in terms of attitudes toward "self" and "identity"? Please cite some examples in daily life to illustrate it.

2 What are the differences between masculine and feminine cultures? It is said that "China traditionally used to be a typical masculine society. With its great social and economic transformation, its profile is changing." Do you agree or disagree with it? Could you use some TV commercials to illustrate your opinion?

Section C Case

Introduction to the Case

The following cases illustrate the cultural differences presented by Hofstede. The first case talks about the "uncertainty avoidance" dimension. The second case shows the "individualism-collectivism" dimension, in which a Chinese professor tends to seek help from people in her own culture and expects them to look after her.

The Scenario

Case 1 Certain or Not Certain

In China, the staff who are working at the Foreign Affairs Office often get international calls from foreign teachers. Before foreign teachers come to China, they frequently ask the staff for information. The staff often tell them that they will discover everything they need to know once they arrive in China. Some foreign teachers are doubtful of that, and continue to call. The staff repeat again and again that the Foreign Affairs Office and the teaching departments will arrange everything for them. Besides, every foreign teacher has a contact person to help with problems about teaching and daily life when they are in China.

Case 2 Permission to Use the Library

One day, Professor Wang wanted to get access to some particular books for her research work. She discovered that the books were available in the library of another university. She was unsure whether she could get the books she wanted since she didn't have library privileges at that university. Fortunately, when she went there, she happened to meet a former classmate, who was working as the librarian. With the help of her classmate, she had no trouble getting the books she needed.

Some years later, Professor Wang went to America as a visiting scholar. When she ran into the same problem, her instant thought was to turn to her network of connections to ask for help. Instead of getting help, she was told that she could call to find out if there were any special procedures for using the library in another university. She realized that she would receive the same service in America whether or not she had friends working there.

Understanding and Speaking Interculturally

Exercise 1 Listen for the first time and answer the following questions.

1. What do foreign teachers do before they arrive in China?
2. What did Professor Wang do in China to solve her problem? What did she do in America to solve the same problem? What was she expected to do in America?

Exercise 2 Listen for the second time and decide whether the following statements are true or false.

( ) 1. Before foreign teachers arrive in China, they frequently ask the same question.

( ) 2. Chinese officials assign people to aid foreign teachers when they are in China.

( ) 3. When Professor Wang was in China, she had her in-group to help her.

( ) 4. When Professor Wang was in U.S., she found out that her friends would not help her in the same way.

Exercise 3 Explore interculturally.

1. What can we learn from the first case? Use Hofstede's "uncertainty avoidance" dimension to explain your answer.
2. If you are in America, what will you do to get a book you need? What can we learn from this case? Use Hofstede's "individualism-collectivism" dimension to explain your answer.
3. Please discuss the following topics with your partners: What does "friend" mean to Chinese? What does "friend" mean to Americans? Are there any different implications?

Chapter 6

Hall's Culture Context Model

Section A Video clip

Introduction to the TV Program

First launched on June, 1999 on CCTV, *Outlook English Magazine* is a brand-new English teaching and learning program. This program has made a breakthrough in style, departing from the traditional mode of lecturing, and adopting a magazine-like format with different "articles" and topics of interest to the viewers. The magazine's topics have new information about the world, including fashion, language, news, movies, music and culture, in simple English, to stimulate the viewers' language learning. Zhao Yinqi and Zhu Hua are the host and hostess of the thirty-minute program respectively. The program's slogan is "Making your outlook brighter." The *Star of Outlook English Talent Competition* has been held annually since 2000, and has attracted thousands of English learners, who have made use of this opportunity to show their excellence in English.

Introduction to the Selected Scene

Let's Talk, with Elyn and Rebecca as co-hostesses, was once a feature of *Outlook English Magazine*. The topics included everyday conversation and cultural discrepancies between East and West. Viewers developed a new understanding of the difficulties they confronted in English learning in a lively and light atmosphere.

Script of the Scene

Rebecca: Offering a compliment is just a way to make you feel good and it's very common in English.

Elyn: I think in Asian societies, it's possible that people would think if he says, "I like your sweater." He means "I don't like your sweater." Or maybe it might mean "I want your sweater." Or maybe it might mean "your sweater is nice." It's not clear what the meaning of "I like your sweater." is. But in the West it's almost always just "How are you?" "Your sweater is nice." And there is no other possible meaning, so don't think that your foreign friends want your sweater when they say "I like your sweater."

Rebecca: It's very clear. It's just a way of making conversation, and it is a simple common way of giving your compliment.

Elyn: When I first came to China, I went to an artist friend's house and I looked at all the paintings on her wall and I said, "Oh! I like this painting!" In English that just meant you've painted many paintings, this one is very nice. But my friend was thinking differently because she is Chinese. And so when I went home she handed me a package. When I got home and opened it up I found the painting. I was so shocked and I was so surprised. I almost fainted because that was never my thinking and I thought "Oh dear, there is a difference in our culture, and there is a difference in our language."

New Words

compliment *n.* a remark that expresses admiration of someone or something 恭维语

package *n.* a box or bag for containing or shipping objects 包；邮包

Understanding and Speaking Interculturally

Exercise 1 Fill in the blanks according to the program you have just watched.

When I first came to China, I went to an ________ friend's house and I looked at all the ________ on her wall and I said, "Oh! I like this painting!" In English that just meant you've painted many paintings, this one is very nice. But my friend was thinking differently because she is Chinese. And so when I went home she handed me a ________. When I got home and opened it up I found the painting. I was so shocked and I was so surprised. I almost ________ because that was never my thinking and I thought "Oh dear, there is a difference in our culture, and there is a difference in our language."

Exercise 2 Answer the following questions according to the program you have just watched.

1. What is a very common way of making conversation in English according to the program?

2. What happened to Elyn one day when she visited a Chinese friend's house?

Exercise 3 Fill in the blanks according to the program you have just watched.

	In Asian societies	In the West
I like your sweater.		

Exercise 4 Explore interculturally.

1. Why is the meaning of "I like your sweater" very clear in the West?

2. Why is the meaning of "I like your sweater" not clear in Asian Societies?

3. Elyn said, "...there is a difference in our culture, and there is a difference in our language." What are the differences between Chinese and Western culture? What are the differences between Chinese and Western language? Cite some examples in your daily life to illustrate the sentence.

Section B Reading

In 1976, the well-known anthropologist Edward Hall, the father of intercultural communication, originated the concepts of high-context culture and low-context culture. Hall based his concepts on the degree to which meaning comes from the context or from the words being exchanged. In high-context culture, much information is implied in the context. Context includes the situation or surrounding circumstances, relationships of the communicators, their family background, title, age, sex, education, status, and social networks. Relatively, little is provided in the verbal message itself. In low-context cultures, however, the majority of the information is contained in the verbal code, and the message is stated clearly and explicitly without depending on the context of the communication. According to Hall, most cultures contain both high-context characteristics and low-context characteristics, but usually there is a clear tendency toward one end of the continuum or the other. (Hall, 1976)

Communication Styles

Background information

Collectivistic cultures are usually high-context cultures. In these cultures, such as Japanese, Arab, African-American, and Latino cultures, people are very homogeneous and share much background information. Therefore, it is not necessary to articulate every detail of the information explicitly. Consequently, people find it easy to understand the most subtle information provided through gestures, the use of space, and even silence. A simple example of high-context communication can be found in the interactions that take place between two people with a long-term relationship. They are often able to interpret even the slightest gesture or the briefest comment.

In the low-context cultures, such as American and British cultures, people are usually from diverse background and do not share much common information. This lack of a large pool of common experiences means that each time they interact with others everything needs to be stated directly and overtly. Therefore, conversations in a low-context culture tend to be clear, to the point and more explicit, with low dependence on the use of nonverbal codes.

Let's take a daily example to illustrate it. When you talk about an activity, like driving and parking a car, with someone who is also very familiar with these activities, you don't have to specify every aspect of your ideas because those you are speaking with know what you mean easily. However, when you talk to someone who knows little about the subject, you will have to explain more, add more specific details and provide more background information to help your listeners understand.

Another example is found in the well-known movie *Lust, Caution*. Some conversations take place among Wang Jiazhi, Mr. Yi and Mrs. Yi when they are playing *mahjong* together with some friends. Although the talks are generally short and brief, a subtle facial expression, turning of the eyes, and a little gesture or movement of the hands contain abundant information. Unfortunately, most of the information is very hard for Western audiences to understand, who, as a result, may find the situation of *mahjong* playing quite ambiguous and boring. Just as what the *Globe and Mail* movie reviewer said, "We can feel it, but we cannot figure it out."

Face concerns

Another reason for the indirect and subtle nature of the high-context communication is people's great concern over "face." In high-context cultures, an important purpose in communicating is to promote and sustain harmony among the participants in these cultures. Therefore, people are extremely polite, trying to avoid threatening the "face" of their conversational partner. Even if a conflict occurs, it should be dealt with subtly. Therefore, what is not said may be more important than what is said, and reactions are likely to be reserved and constrained as well.

An interesting case is found in Rogers and Steinfatt's book about how to decline a potential spouse in an arranged marriage in South India, a high-context culture (Rogers & Steinfatt, 1999). The boy's family has visited the girl's home in order to look over the potential bride and decide upon the marriage. After the visit, they send an emissary who conveys this message: "We really enjoyed meeting all of your family members. Usha is a fine cook and is a very nice young woman. But we wish that tea had been served with the mangos instead of coffee." The real meaning of this message is that "We do not want our son to marry your daughter." Hurting the other party's feelings is avoided at all costs with great emphasis on saving face.

In low-context cultures, however, people are more individualistic and more concerned about their own face rather than that of others. Therefore, they are not afraid of confrontations and conflicts. They mean what they say. Being frank and explicit characterize their interpersonal communication. The same can be said of people's reactions, which are readily observable. When confronted with people from high-context cultures, they will often feel uncomfortable with the vagueness and ambiguity of the message, and become puzzled, frustrated, impatient or even irritated. They may find it difficult to grasp the point from a spiral of widely scattered details. In a business discussion involving most people from high-context cultures, for example, businessmen from low-context cultures could not even be sure as to who disagreed with whom.

In China, the words "We will consider it" are often heard as a reply to a request or an application. While Chinese usually take this sentence as a tentative decline or a half-decline at least, Western students who just arrive in China might miss the implied message and experience disappointment when hearing the same answer again and again on later inquiries.

Many other examples can be found in daily life. For instance, the communication in literary works tends to be high-context, whereas in scientific reports it tends to be low-context. Conversations between females tend to be high-context whereas talks between males tend to be low-context.

Nonverbal codes

Silence is often regarded as a very important nonverbal code highly valued by people in high-context cultures. Just as a proverb says, "Empty cans clatter the loudest", high-context people may perceive talkative low-context people as less credible. However, in the eyes of people in low-context cultures, who hate ambiguity and value clarity, silence is usually associated with negative meanings such as indifference, anger, hostility, disagreement, shyness, embarrassment, ignorance, boredom or coldness.

In films produced in low-context cultures, the verbal statement of "I love you" is often heard. In high-context cultures, statements of affection are rare. Sparkling eyes, blushing face, intimate space and a gentle touch all connote passionate love. However, in the recent movies produced in China, a high-context culture, explicit verbal expressions of emotion are increasingly valued, indicating a shift toward low-context communication, especially in the younger generations.

In-groups and Out-groups

In addition to differences in communication styles, there are other manifestations of high-context and low-context cultures.

In high-context cultures, the commitment between people is very strong and deep, and loyalties to families and friends are long-lasting and unchanging. Long-term relationships, in turn, strengthen the high-context communication between in-groups. In addition, people make a clear distinction between in-group members (intimate friends generally) and out-group members (casual acquaintances generally). Therefore, it is very easy to determine the in-groups, who usually share a lot of unspoken rules in communication and act according to these norms. And it is also easy to detect who is not a member of the group, for he is often deviating away from these norms.

In low-context cultures, the bonds between people are, by comparison, quite fragile. Group membership changes rapidly. The extent of involvement and commitment is low. Therefore, the distinction between in-groups and out-groups is not clear-cut. To be explicit and articulate is always emphasized as an important skill in communication.

Orientation to Time

The final characteristic of high-context and low-context culture is their differing orientation to time. In the former, time is viewed as more open, less structured. People are more responsive to the immediate needs of the others, and less subject to time constraints. In the latter, time is highly organized and carefully scheduled. In the former, people are often 5 to 10 minutes late for work in the morning, and no one in the office seems to notice or to care. When an explanation has to be given, reference to unexpected situations such as a traffic jam, is often made. In low-context cultures, people are expected to be punctual on business, and often social occasions. When offering an explanation for a late coming, people usually start with "I'm sorry I'm late", followed by an explanation of why.

Understanding and Speaking Interculturally

1 The following table summarizes the most important attributes of high-context cultures and low-context cultures. Please complete the table.

High-context cultures	Low-context cultures
Indirect, implicit mode of communication	
	Overt, explicit and plainly coded messages
Heavy dependence on nonverbal codes	
	Unconstrained reactions
Distinct in-groups and out-groups	

	Fragile people bonds
High commitment between people	
	Highly organized time

2 **Pair work:** With a partner, compare the characteristics of the following cultures and try to arrange them along the high-context and low-context dimension:
American, English, Chinese, Japanese, French, German, Korean, Arab

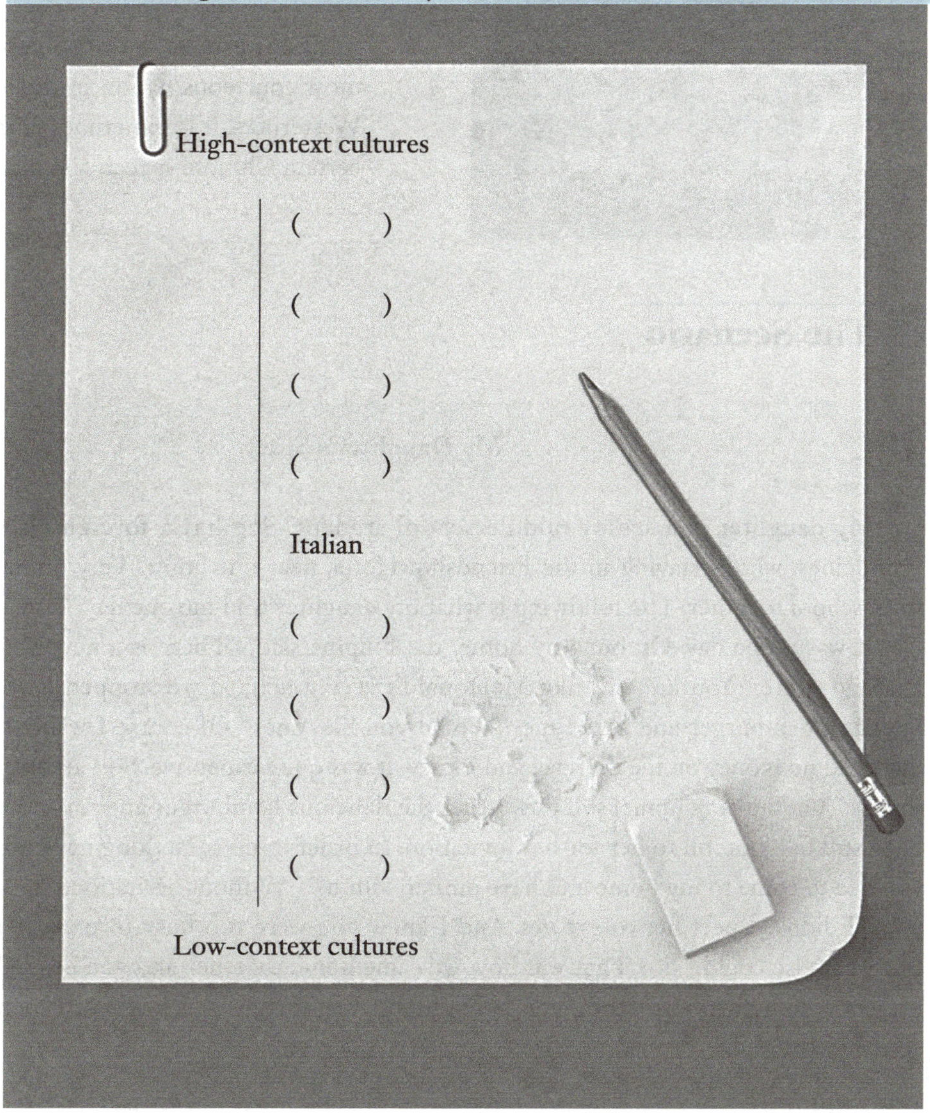

Section C Case

Introduction to the Case

Chinese have long been known as the most courteous nation in the world. For many Westerners, it is sometimes difficult to interpret certain Chinese speech and behaviors.

The Scenario

My Daughter's Story

My daughter is a senior middle school student. She has a foreign classmate from the Philippines, who is staying in the Friendship Hotel, near our home. Very often they come back from school together. The following is what my daughter told me one day:

It was a fine day. On our way home, the Filipina said, "There is a new McDonald's nearby. Let's go there." You know, I like McDonald's very much, so we stopped in. She immediately bought a hamburger and asked me, "Would you like one?" Of course I wanted one very much, but I had no money on me that day and I knew it was quite expensive. So I automatically said, "No, thanks." On our way home, she was eating the delicious hamburger and my mouth was watering, but I still felt grateful to her for her invitation. In order to do something in return, I said, "Would you like to come to my home and have dinner with us?" Without hesitation, she said, "Sure, thank you." I didn't expect her to say yes. And I knew you were too busy to prepare a formal dinner. But what else could I do? That was how we came home together and you blamed me for inviting someone home without letting you know first. I was sorry that I made you spend so much time cooking that night.

Understanding and Speaking Interculturally

Exercise 1 Listen for the first time and answer the following questions.

1. Why didn't the daughter buy a hamburger for herself?
2. Did she really want to invite her classmate to have dinner with her family?

Exercise 2 Listen for the second time and fill in the blanks.

1. On our way home, the ________ said, "There is a new ________ nearby. Let's go there."
2. On our way home, she was eating the delicious hamburger and my mouth was ________, but I still felt ________ to her for her invitation.
3. Without ________, she said, "Sure, thank you." I didn't ________ her to say yes.

Exercise 3 Explore interculturally.

1. Did my daughter really mean it when she refused her Filipino classmate's offer? What can we learn about her culture? Use Hall's culture context model to illustrate it.
2. What makes the Philippine girl consider the invitation as genuine? What can we learn about her culture? Use Hall's culture context model to illustrate it.

Part III

Verbal Communication

Cultural Connotation in Language

Section A Movie clip

Introduction to the Movie *My Fair Lady*

Henry Higgins, an arrogant professor of phonetics, wagers with a new acquaintance, Colonel Pickering, that he can teach any woman to speak so "properly" that he could pass her off as a duchess. The person whom he is shown thus teaching is one Eliza Doolittle, a young woman with a strong Cockney accent who is selling flowers on the street. Eliza goes through many forms of speech training. At first, she makes no progress but just as she, Higgins, and Pickering are exhausted and about

to give up, Higgins softens his attitude and gives an eloquent speech about the beauty and history behind the English language. Eliza begins to speak with an impeccable upper class accent. Higgins takes her on her first public appearance to the Ascot Racecourse, where she makes a good impression with her stilted, but genteel manners, only to shock everyone by a sudden and vulgar lapse into Cockney usage.

Introduction to the Selected Scene

The wager is won when Eliza successfully poses as a mysterious lady of patently noble rank at an embassy ball, despite the unexpected presence of a Hungarian phonetics expert trained by Higgins himself. Higgins's callous treatment of Eliza afterwards, especially his indifference to her future prospects, leads her to walk out on him, leaving him mystified by her ingratitude. Finally the inevitable confrontation occurs: Eliza has surpassed the teacher's expectations, but the teacher still considers her a common flower girl. How does one move forward in such a situation?

Script of the Scene

Pickering: Absolutely fantastic!
Higgins: A lot of tomfoolery.
Pickering: It was an immense achievement.
Mrs. Pearce: Well, Mr. Higgins?
Pickering: A triumph, Mrs. Pearce. A total triumph. Higgins, you were superb, absolutely superb. Tell us the truth now, weren't you a little bit nervous once or twice?

Pickering: Not during the whole evening?

Higgins: Not when I saw we were going to win. I felt like a bear in a cage hanging about.

Pickering: It was an immense achievement.

Higgins: If I hadn't backed myself to do it, I'd have given it up two months ago.

Pickering: Absolutely fantastic.

Higgins: Yes, a lot of tomfoolery.

Pickering: Higgins, I salute you.

Higgins: The silly people don't know their own silly business.

Pickering: Tonight, old man, you did it.
You did it, you did it!
You said that you would do it.
And indeed you did!
I thought that you would rue it.
I doubted you'd do it.
But now I must admit it.
That succeed you did.
You should get a medal, or be even made a knight.

Higgins: Oh, it was nothing, really nothing.

Pickering: All alone you hurdled every obstacle in sight.

Higgins: Now wait, now wait. Give credit where it's due. A lot of the glory goes to you.

Pickering: But you're the one who did it, who did it, who did it.
As sturdy as Gibraltar.
Not a second did you falter.
There's no doubt about it.
You did it.
I must have aged a year tonight.
At times I thought I'd die of fright.
Never was there a momentary lull.

Higgins: Shortly after we came in, I saw at once we'd easily win.
And after that I found it deadly dull.

Pickering: You should have heard the "oohs" and "aahs." Everyone wondering who she was.

Higgins: You'd think they'd never seen a lady before.

Pickering: And when the Prince of Transylvania asked to meet her

and give his arm to lead her to the floor, I said to him: You did it.
You did it.
You did it
They thought she was ecstatic and so damned aristocratic.
And they never knew that you did it.

Higgins: Thank goodness for Zoltan Karpathy. If it hadn't been for him, I would have died of boredom.

Mrs. Pearce: Karpathy? That dreadful Hungarian? Was he there?

Higgins: Yes, he was there all night and up to his old tricks.
That blackguard who uses the science of speech.
More to blackmail and swindle than teach.
He made it the devilish business of his
To find out who this Miss Doolittle is.
Every time we looked around
There he was that hairy hound from Budapest.
Never leaving us alone
Never have I ever known a ruder pest.
Finally I decided it was foolish not to
Let him have his chance with her
So I stepped aside and him dance with her.
Oozing charm from every pore
He oiled his way around the floor.
Every trick that he could play
He used to strip her mask away.
When at last the dance was done
He glowed as if he knew he'd won.
And with a voice too eager
And a smile too broad
He announced to the hostess that she was: a fraud!

Mrs. Pearce: No!

Higgins: Her English is too good, he said,
That clearly indicates she is foreign
Whereas others are instructed in their
Native language, English people aren't.
And although she may have studied with an
Expert dialecticians and grammarian,

I can tell that she was born: Hungarian!
Not only Hungarian, but of royal blood.
She is a princess
Her blood, he says, is bluer than the Danube is or ever was.
Royalty is absolutely written on her face.
She thought that I was taken in, but actually I never was.
How could she deceive another member of her race?
I know each language on the map, said he
And she's Hungarian as the first Hungarian rhapsody.

All: Congratulations, Professor Higgins
For your glorious victory
Congratulations, Professor Higgins
You'll be mentioned in history.

Maids/manservant: Congratulations, Professor Higgins
This evening sir you did it, You did it, you did it.
For your glorious victory.
You said that you would do it, And indeed you did.
Congratulations, Professor Higgins
This evening sir you did it, You did it, you did it.
We know that we have said it that you did it.
And the credit for it all belongs to you.

Higgins: Well, thank God, that's over. Now I can go to bed without dreading tomorrow.

Mrs. Pearce: Good night, Mr. Higgins.

Higgins: Good night, Mrs. Pearce.

Pickering: I think I'll turn in, too. Good night, Higgins. It's been a great occasion.

Higgins: Good night, Pickering. Oh, Mrs. Pearce? Damn, I meant to ask her to give me coffee in the morning instead of tea. Leave a little note for her will you, Eliza. And put out the lights.

Higgins: Must be downstairs. Oh, darn it. I'll leave my head behind one of these days. What the devil have I done with my slippers?

Eliza: Here are your slippers! There! And there! Take your slippers and may you never have a day's luck with them!

Higgins: What on earth? What's the matter? Is there anything wrong?

Eliza: No, nothing wrong with you. I won your bet for you, haven't I? That's enough for you. I don't matter, I suppose.

Higgins: You won my bet? You presumptuous insect! I won it! Why did you throw those slippers at me for?

Eliza: Because I wanted to smash your face. I could kill you, you selfish brute! Why didn't you leave me where you picked me up, the gutter? You thank God it's all over. Now you think you can throw me back again, do you?

Higgins: Oh, so the creature's nervous after all?

Higgins: Claws in, you cat! How dare you show your temper to me? Sit down and be quiet!

Eliza: Oh, what's to become of me? What's to become of me?

Higgins: How the devil do I know what's to become of you? What does it matter?

Eliza: You don't care. I know you don't care. You don't care if I was dead. I'm nothing to you. Not as much as them slippers.

Higgins: Those slippers?

Eliza: Those slippers! I didn't think it meant any difference now.

Higgins: Why have you suddenly begun going on like this? May I ask if you complain of your treatment here? Has anybody behaved badly? Colonel Pickering, Mrs. Pearce?

Eliza: No.

Higgins: Well you don't pretend that I have treated you badly?

Eliza: No.

Higgins: Well, I'm glad to hear that. Maybe you're tired after the strain of the day. Would you have a chocolate?

Eliza: No! Thank you.

Higgins: Well, it's only natural that you should be anxious, but it's all over now. Nothing more to worry about.

Eliza: No, nothing more for you to worry about. Oh, God, I wish I was dead.

Higgins: Why? In heaven's name, why? Now listen to me, Eliza. All this irritation is purely subjective.

Eliza: I don't understand. I'm too ignorant.

Higgins: It's just imagination. Nothing's wrong. Nobody's hurting you. Go to bed and sleep it off. Have a little cry and...

New Words

aristocratic *adj.* typical of nobleman or noblewoman 贵族的，贵族气派的

falter *v.* move or act hesitantly, usually because of weakness, fear or indecision 退缩，畏缩

lull *n.* interval of quiet or inactivity 稍息；稍止；间歇

presumptuous *adj.* excessively bold or self-confident 冒昧的，放肆的，不客气的

sturdy *adj.* strong and solid （性格等）坚强的，刚毅的，健全的

tomfoolery *n.* foolish behavior or act 愚蠢的举动；蠢事

Phrases and Expressions

darn it:
(inflammatory euphemism, used to express annoyance, impatience etc) 倒霉，该死

hang about:
be standing about (a place), doing nothing definite 闲逛，徘徊

Oozing charm:
beauty coming or flowing slowly and naturally 自然散发的魅力

once or twice:
a few times 一两次

Notes

Budapest

the capital city of Hungary. As the largest city of Hungary, it serves as the country's principal political, cultural, commercial, industrial, and transportation center and is considered an important hub in Central Europe.

Danube

the longest river in the European Union and Europe's second longest river after the Volga.

Gibraltar

a British overseas territory located near the southernmost tip of the Iberian Peninsula overlooking the Strait of Gibraltar. Today, Gibraltar is known colloquially as Gib or The Rock.

Hungarian Rhapsody

a set of 19 piano pieces based on Hungarian folk themes, composed by Franz Liszt during 1846-1853, and later in 1882 and 1885. The first fifteen were published in the year 1853, with the last four being added in 1882 and 1885.

Understanding and Speaking Interculturally

Exercise 1 Match the words on the left with their speakers on the right.

Well, it's only natural that you should be anxious, but it's all over now.	Mrs. Pearce
All alone you hurdled every obstacle in sight	Maids/manservant
I'm nothing to you. Not as much as them slippers.	Higgins
Karpathy? That dreadful Hungarian?	Pickering
You'll be mentioned in history.	Eliza

Exercise 2 Fill in the blanks according to the movie clip you have just watched.

1. **Higgins:** Not when I saw we were going to win. I felt like a bear in a ______ hanging about.
   Pickering: It was an immense ______.
   Higgins: If I hadn't ______ myself to do it, I'd have given it up two months ago.
   Pickering: Absolutely ______.

2. **Maids/manservant:** Congratulations, Professor Higgins
   This evening sir you did it, You did it, you did it
   For your ______
   Congratulations, Professor Higgins
   You'll be mentioned in ______.
   ...
   Higgins: Well, thank God, that's over. Now I can go to bed without ______ tomorrow.

3. **Higgins:** Why? In heaven's name, why? Now listen to me, Eliza. All this irritation is purely ______.
   Eliza: I don't understand. I'm too ignorant.
   Higgins: It's just ______. Nothing's wrong. Nobody' s hurting you. Go to bed and sleep it off.

Exercise 3 Decide whether the following statements are True or False according to the movie clip you have just watched. Write "T" for true and "F" for false.

_____ 1. Everybody is satisfied with Eliza's performance at the party.

_____ 2. Higgins is completely sure of his achievements in changing Eliza into a fair lady.

_____ 3. Zoltan Karpathy plays every trick to strip the mask of Eliza but failed.

_____ 4. Eliza is happy with her fake identity.

Exercise 4 Discuss in groups why Eliza was so sad in spite of her successful performance at the party. After the discussion, each group should present their ideas to the class.

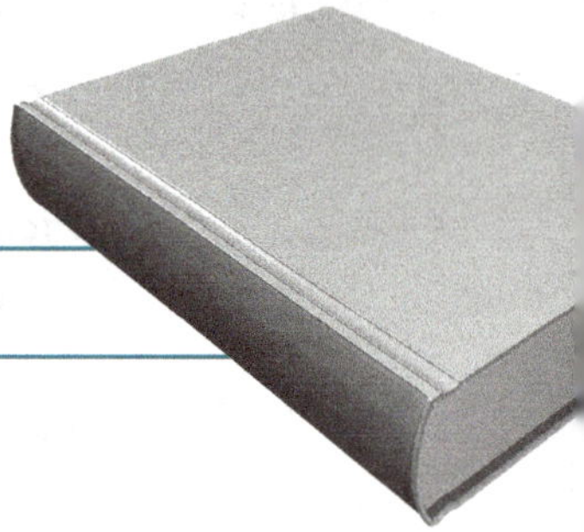

Section B Reading

Language

What is language? This sounds like an easy question. We speak and write with language every day, but, we seldom think about the thing we are most familiar with. Language, to put it most simply, is a set of codes and symbols, along with the rules for combining them together. Different groups of people speak and write different languages, that is, they have different codes, symbols and rules to facilitate their communication. For example, we use "*hua*" to name flowers, while French people use "*fleur*" to serve the purpose. We would enquire "*zhe shi shen me*?" when we refer to an object. British people would utter "*What's this?*", and French people would say "*Qu'est ce que c'est*?"

Language is the unique possession of human beings. No other animals enjoy the privilege. Dogs can bark, birds can sing, cows can moo. Some intelligent animals can learn to respond to simple verbal or non-verbal signals like "sit" and "jump." But none of them can use a systematic way to express complicated thoughts and feelings. With language, we human beings can communicate on different topics and on different levels.

Language and Culture

The world was said, once upon a time, to speak a single language and use the same words. In an action of overweening pride, men began to build the Tower of Babel, with its top in the clouds. The Lord was afraid, and thus confused men's speech by giving them different languages. That's why, today, we are scattered in different parts of the world, having our own systems of communication, and different ways of living.

The language we use and the culture in which we live are closely related. Some compare language and culture to a living organism: language is flesh, and culture is blood. Without culture, language would be dead; without language, culture would have no shape. In other words, they cannot be separated and exist alone. Some linguists have gone further and propose that the world we live in is based on the language we speak. Even the way of our thinking, they suggest, is "shaped" and "programmed" by our language. So, since no two languages are ever precisely alike, it follows that neither can any two social realities represented by language be considered the same. This is the well-known "Sapir-Whorf Hypothesis" proposed by two American linguists in the early years of last century.

Whatever the theory, we perceive culture through language, and any change in culture is likely to lead, in turn, to a change in language.

Cultural Connotations

As we know, words have meanings. When we use words, sometimes we use their literal meanings, that is, the basic meaning of the words. Yet, sometimes, we use the implied or figural meaning of words. For example, when we say *lang xin gou fei*, we don't mean, literally, that the person has the heart of a wolf and the lungs of a dog, rather, we refer to people who are cruel and fierce to their friends like wolves and dogs when these animals are attacking their enemy. This kind of implied meaning is also known as the "connotation" of a word. Connotations are in general closely related to the culture they are rooted in. When we learn about another culture or communicate with people from another culture, the "culturally loaded" aspect of the words they use require our special attention.

Categories of Cultural Connotations

When we study the cultural connotations of words, we can roughly divide words into three categories based on their similarities and differences. The following comparison is carried out between Chinese and English:

(Here, we use "c" to represent "connotation", "C" and "E" for "Chinese" and "English.")

1) cC = cE

In this category, the Chinese and English words have the same or similar connotations. For example, "*fox*" in both eastern and western cultures has the connotation of being cunning; and "*pig*" has the similar cultural image of being lazy and dirty. When using these types of words, many similar echoes certainly pass back and forth between people from these two linguistic cultures.

2) cC ≠ cE

Many words in two languages appear to have the same meaning. But actually their connotations are totally different.

The words used to describe different colors offer typical examples. For instance, "*red*" is a very lucky and festive color in Chinese culture. It is associated with important celebrations to commemorate weddings, success and popularity. In western eyes, however, "*red*" often connotes blood, revolution, and violence. Few good associations can be found. The novel "The Scarlet

Letter" can be used as an example here. However, "*white*" is generally preferred for weddings, and big celebrations. The color arouses sweet associations of peace and purity. This is, certainly contradictory to Chinese custom: white is usually used at funerals. "*Yellow*" is another color that bears different cultural connotations. In China, when people mention pornographic books or magazines, they would say "*huang se shu kan*." However, in the west, especially in the U.S., yellow journalism has nothing to do with pornography. It refers to the publications that exaggerate the news to create sensations and attract readers. This usage came from the use of yellow ink in printing "Yellow Kid", a cartoon strip in the *New York World*, a newspaper noted for sensationalism.

Some animal names also fall into this category. Besides the one we are most familiar with, "*dog*", which appears in many sayings and set phrases, "*dragon*", "*phoenix*", "*owl*" and "*peacock*" are also good illustrations of this type.

3) $cC = 0, cE \neq 0$ or $cC \neq 0, cE = 0$

In the last category, connotations of words in one culture seem to lack equivalents in the other. In other words, these words are common and plain in connotation to people from one culture, but have special meanings for people in the other. These words are key to understanding the unique characteristics of one culture.

For example, *mei, lan, zhu, ju,* are plants loved by Chinese people. The three flowers grow and fight against the hostile environment to put out fragrant blossoms, and thus are often used to describe qualities like integrity and nobility. While *zhu* grows straight upward and is hollow in its stem and branches, it is always associated with honesty, uprightness, and modesty. But for Westerners, they are simply plum blossom, orchid, bamboo, and chrysanthemum in their biological sense. Other words such as "pine, cypress, crane, and peach" are also favored by Chinese people, because their cultural image links them to longevity.

Often, numbers have special meanings to specific groups of people, as well. Eight and nine are numbers particularly loved by Chinese people when they are choosing a date for a celebration, choosing their car's license place number or cell phone number. Eight, in its Chinese pronunciation, is similar to "*fa*", which means prosperity. Nine shares the same sound with "*jiu*", which means "lasting forever." In English, it is widely known that thirteen is an unlucky number, originated from the religious story about Jesus.

Heroes in famous literary works are frequently used by the people in one culture to represent a certain type of person. It is unlikely, however, that people from an outside culture would have any idea about their meaning. For example, "*Li Kui*" in Chinese culture and "*Scarlett*" in the U.S.

It is impossible for us to master the connotation of every word when we communicate with people from a different culture. However, we should at least be aware that the words we choose to use may lead to misunderstandings and misinterpretations. To achieve successful intercultural communication, we should certainly NOT overlook cultural connotation.

Understanding and Speaking Interculturally

1 Group discussion: What do you think of the "Sapir-Whorf Hypothesis"? Do you agree that our way of thinking is determined by the language we speak? If so, can you give concrete examples to illustrate your idea?

2 Class work: Work individually first. Try to find more examples of similar and different cultural connotations between Chinese and English in each of the categories discussed above. Then exchange your list with other students in your class.

3 Group work: Translate the following excerpt from "*Hong Lou Meng*" (*The Story of the Stone / The Dream of Red Mansion*) into English.

（贾琏道）“你不用怕他！等我性子上来，把这‘醋坛子’打个稀烂，他才认的我呢！…”

Compare your version with those of your group members. Pick out the best one that might cause the least confusion and misunderstanding to your foreign friends.

Section C Case

Introduction to the Case

The dragon is a legendary creature of which certain interpretation or depiction appears in almost every culture worldwide. However, like most mythological creatures, dragons are perceived in different ways by different cultures.

The Scenario

Dragons and Branding

Has the dragon come to the end of its 7000-year reign as the symbol of the Chinese people? Earlier this year it was left off the list of the five Beijing Olympic mascots, which were selected with their international associations in mind—violent animals like the dragon were passed over.

And now a proposal has been put forward to retire the dragon altogether in favor of a more harmonious national symbol. Some commentators made the observation that the Chinese dragon could be given a new name to distinguish it from western dragons—"loong", for example.

Wu Youfu, a professor at Shanghai International Studies University, was interviewed last week on December 6, 2006 by Guangming Daily on the subject of image. In the course of the interview, Wu brought up the example of the dragon as an element of traditional culture that is misunderstood abroad when used as a national symbol. The western association of the dragon as a fearsome, threatening animal contrasts with its symbolism for honesty, good fortune, and happiness in the minds of Wu Youfu and Chinese people.

Naturally, the idea of a group of officials rejecting a national symbol merely to please some foreigners had upset many people. In a later report, Wu claimed that he had been misquoted and added that he only wished to change the dragon image into something more harmonious.

A view most closely associated with the modern poet Wen Yiduo says that the mythical dragon started out as some sort of snake before becoming the totem of a unified China by including elements of the totems of separate nations that made up the empire. This theory had obvious applications throughout much of the 20th century.

However, according to a scholar who has written a new, dragon-themed novel, Wen's explanation is utterly mistaken. Dragons were used as totems, says Yan Tie, author of "Traces of the Dragon" because, like other totem animals, they actually existed.

Yan's novel uses the framework of a thriller to lay out his theories—a group of adventurers set off in pursuit of a dragon-related artifact from the Xia Dynasty that vanished when its discoverer was being pursued by Japanese spies.

"Traces of the Dragon" is being promoted as a Chinese "Da Vinci Code", for similarities in plot. It's also being pushed as an answer to "Wolf Totem", the bestseller that identified the wolf as the soul of the Chinese people. Nonsense, says Yan—the dragon has always been the most important Chinese totem.

Understanding and Speaking Interculturally

Exercise 1 Listen for the first time and answer the following questions.

1. Was the dragon selected as one of the five Beijing Olympic mascots?

2. What is the difference between Western and Chinese associations with respect to the dragon?

3. According to the author of "Traces of the Dragon", why is the dragon used as a totem?

Exercise 2 Listen for the second time and fill in the blanks.

1. And now a proposal has been put forward to 1) ________ the dragon altogether in favor of a more 2) ________ national symbol. Some commentators made the 3) ________ that the Chinese dragon could be given a new name to distinguish it from western dragons—"loong", for example.

2. A 4) ________ most closely associated with the modern poet Wen Yiduo says that the mythical dragon started out as some sort of 5) ________ before becoming the totem of a 6) ________ China by including elements of the totems of separate nations that made up the 7) ________. This theory had obvious applications throughout much of the 20th century.

3. Yan's novel uses the 8) ________ of a thriller to lay out his theories—a group of adventurers set off in pursuit of a dragon-related 9) ________ from the Xia Dynasty that 10) ________ when its discoverer was being pursued by Japanese 11) ________

4. "Traces of the Dragon" is being 12) ________ as a Chinese "Da Vinci Code", for similarities in 13) ________. It's also being pushed as an answer to "Wolf Totem", the 14) ________ that identified the wolf as the 15) ________ of the Chinese people.

Exercise 3 Exploring Interculturally.

1. Do you think it is necessary to rename the dragon as Chinese symbol? Why?

2. Do other animals inspire different associations in China and Western countries? Discuss the question with your partner.

Chapter 8

Norms of Social Interaction

Section A Movie clip

Introduction to the Movie *Notting Hill*

Anna Scott is the world's most famous movie star. Her picture has been plastered on the cover of every magazine, and every time she makes a move, the entire world knows about it. William Thacker owns a travel bookstore and his business is stagnant. He has the roommate from hell and since his divorce, his love life is completely non-existent. For both, something or someone seems to be missing. And when Anna and William's paths unexpectedly cross in the eclectic neighborhood of Notting Hill, romance is the last thing on their minds. The couples come to face the ultimate question: Can two people fall in love with the whole world watching? Notting Hill, a charming romantic comedy, proves that love can

spring from even the most unlikely of circumstances.

Introduction to the Selected Scene

William, owner of an independent bookstore in Notting Hill, invites world-famous Hollywood actress Anna Scott to his sister Honey's birthday party. There, at Max and Bella's house, Anna feels at home with William's circle of friends. At the dinner party William, Anna, and his friends tell their sad tales in an attempt to win the last dessert brownie. From the game, William and his friends come to see Anna Scott not simply as a desirable woman, but as a complicated one, whose life doesn't make it easy for her to be happy. And the first "date" allows Anna to enjoy what is arguably the first normal evening she's had in years.

Script of the Scene

William: You-You'll be my date...to my little sister's birthday party?

Anna: If it's all right.

William: Well, yeah, I'm sure it's all right. My friend Max is cooking and he is generally acknowledged to be the worst cook in the world, but, um, you know, you could hide the food in your handbag or something.

Anna: Okay.

William: Okay.

Max: He's bringing a girl.

Bella: Miracles do happen.

Max: Does the girl have a name?

Bella: Don't know. Wouldn't say.

Max: Oh, Christ! What's going on in there?

[Doorbell Rings]

Max: Oh, God!

Max: Hi, Come on in. Vague food crisis.

Bella: Hiya! Sorry. The guinea-fowl is proving more complicated than expected.

William: He's cooking guinea-fowl?

Bella: Don't even ask!

Anna: Hi!

Bella: Hi! Good lord! You're the spitting image of...

William: Bella, this Anna. Right.

Max: Okay, crisis over.

William: Max, this is Anna.

Anna: Hi!

Max: Hello, Anna...Scott. Have some wine!

Anna: Thank you!

[Doorbell Rings]

Max: I'll get it.

William: Red or white?

Max: Oh. Hey.

Honey: Hi.

Max: Oh, yes, happy birthday!

Honey: Thank you.

Max: Look, your brother's brought this girl.

Honey: Hi, guys. Oh, holy fuck!

William: Hon, this is Anna. Anna, this is Honey. She's my baby sister.

Anna: Oh, Hi!

Honey: Oh, God. This is one of those key moments in life...when it's possible you can be really genuinely cool...and I... I'm going to fail just a hundred percent. I... I absolutely, totally and utterly adore you. And I just think... you are the most beautiful woman in the world. And more importantly, I genuinely believe, and I've believed for some time now, that we could be best friends. So what do you think?

Anna: Uh, haha. Lucky me!Well, happy birthday!

Honey: Oh, you gave me a present. We're best friends already, then. Marry Will. He's a really nice guy. Then we can be sisters.

Anna: Well, I'll think about it. [Chuckle]

[Doorbell Rings]

Max: That'll be Bernie. Hi,

Bernie: Hi, sorry I'm late. Bollocksed up at work again, I fear. Millions down the drain.

Max: Well done.

Max: Bernie, this is Anna.

Bernie: Hello, Anna. Delighted to meet you. And you, Honey bunny. Happy birthday to you!

Bernie: Hi, Bella.

Bella: Hi!

Bernie: It's a hat. You don't have to wear it or anything.

Bernie: Hi, Will.

William: Hi.

Bernie: Hi.

William: Hi.

Bernie: What?

Max: Wine, Bernie?

Bernie: Mm.

Max: You haven't slept with her, have you?

William: That is a cheap question, and the answer is, of course, no comment.

Max: No comment means "yes."

William: No, it doesn't.

Max: Do you ever masturbate?

William: Definitely no comment.

Max: You see, it means "yes."

Honey: Oh, my God!

Bernie: So, uh, tell me, um, Anna, what do you do?

Anna: I'm an actress.

Bernie: Oh, splendid.

Anna: What do you do?

Bernie: I'm actually in the stock market myself, so uh, not really similar fields. Though, um...um... I have done the odd bit of amateur stuff. Uh...uh, P. G. Wodehouse. Farce, all that, you know. "Careful there, vicar." Always imagined it's a pretty tough job, though, acting. I mean, the wages are a scandal, aren't they?

Anna: They can be.

Bernie: I see friends from university...clever chaps, been in the business longer than you. They're scraping by on seven, eight thousand a year. You know, it's no life. What sort of acting do you do?

Anna: Films, mainly.

Bernie: Oh, splendid. Oh, well done. How's the pay in movies? Well, I mean, last film you did.

Anna: Fifteen million dollars.

Bernie: Right. So, that's, fairly good.

Max: Well, I think we're ready.

Anna: Bella can you tell me where I can find...

Bella: Oh, sorry. Yeah, yeah. It's down the corridor on the right.

Honey: I'll show you. I'll show you.

Bella: [Whispering] Quickly, quickly, quickly. Talk very, very quickly. What are you doing here with Anna Scott?

Bernie: Anna Scott?

Bella/Max: Yes. Shut up!

Bernie: What, the film star?

Bella/Max: Shh!

Bernie: Oh, God!

William: What?

Bernie: Oh, God. Oh, goddy God.

William: What did you say to her?

Honey: I don't believe it. I actually walked into the loo with her. I was still chatting when she started unbuttoning her jeans. She had to ask me to leave.

Bernie: Oh, God!

William: So you knew who she was?

Honey: Of course I did, but he didn't.

Bernie: Well, not instantly, but I... I... I got away with it.

Bella: What do you think of the guinea-fowl?

Anna: I'm a vegetarian.

Bella: Oh, God.

Max: So, how's the guinea-fowl?

Anna: Best guinea-fowl I've ever tasted.

[song]

Max: Having you here, Anna, firmly establishes what I've long suspected...that we really are the most desperate lot of underachievers.

Bernie: Shame.

Max: I'm not saying it's a bad thing. In fact, I think it's something we should take pride in. I'm gonna give the last brownie as a prize...to the saddest act here.

William: Oh, Bern.

Bernie: Yeah, all right. Well, obviously, it's me, isn't it? I mean, I work in the city in a job I don't understand, and everyone keeps getting promoted above me. I haven't had a girlfriend since.... well, since puberty. And...nobody fancies me. And if these cheeks get any chubbier, they never will.

Honey: Nonsense. I fancy you.

Bernie: Really?

Honey: Yeah. Or I did before you got so fat.

Max: You see. And unless I'm much mistaken, your job still pays you a rather lot of money, whilst Honey here earns 20 pence a week... flogging her guts out in London's worst record store.

Honey: Yes! And I haven't got hair. I've got feather. And I've got funny goggly eyes. And I'm attracted to cruel men. And actually no one will marry me because, um, my boobsies have actually started shrinking.

Max: You see, it's incredibly sad.

Bella: Yeah. But on the other hand her best friend is Anna Scott.

Honey: True. I can't deny it. She needs me. What can I say?

Bella: And most of her limbs work, whereas I'm stuck in this thing day and night in a house full of ramps. And to add insult to serious injury, I've totally given up smoking, my favorite thing. And, um, well, the truth is, we can't have a baby.

William: Oh, Belle.

Bella: C'est la vie. C'est la vie. Still, um, we're lucky in lots of ways. But surely that's worth a brownie. [Chuckling]

Max: Well, I don't know. Look at William. Very unsuccessful professionally. That's true. Divorced. Used to be handsome, now kind of squidgy round the edges. And absolutely certain never to hear from Anna again...once she's heard that his nickname at school was Bernie: Floppy.

William: You did. I can't believe it, you did. Thanks very much. Thank you. Well, at least I get the last brownie.

Max: I think so, yes.

Anna: Well, wait. What about me?

Max: I'm sorry? You think you deserve the brownie?

Anna: Well, a shot at it at least, huh?

William: You'll have to prove it. This is a very, very good brownie, and I'm gonna fight for it.

Anna: I've been on a diet every day since I was 19, which basically means I've been hungry for a decade. I've had s series of not-nice boyfriends, one of whom hit me. Uh, and every time I get my heart broken, the newspapers splash it about as though it's entertainment. And... it's taken two rather painful, um, operations...to get me looking like this.

Honey: Really?

Anna: Really. And one day not long from now, my looks will go, they'll discover I can't act, and I'll become a sad, middle-aged woman who... looks a bit like someone who was famous for a while.

Max: No, nice try, gorgeous, but you don't fool anyone.

Anna: No.

William: Pathetic effort to hog the brownie.

Anna: Thank you for such a terrific time.

Max: I'm delighted.

Anna: That's a great tie.

Max: Now you're lying.

Anna: Okay, it's true. I told you I was bad at acting. It was lovely to meet you.

Bella: Yeah, and you. And you. I'll wait until you've gone before I tell him you're a vegetarian.

Anna: Good night.

Honey: Anna, I'm so sorry about the loo thing. I meant to leave. I just ... [Chuckles] Ring me if you want someone to go shopping with. I know lots of nice, cheap places, not that money is necessary... It was just so nice to meet you.

Anna: Happy birthday. You're my style guru.
Honey: Thank you.
Honey: Sorry, Can I just...
Anna: Oh.
Honey: Thanks.
William: Leave her.
Anna: Good night, everyone.
Bella/Max: Bye.
William: Max, Belle, we'll see you in a couple of days.
Bella/Max: Thank you, everybody.
William: Call us. Call us.
Anna: Bye, guys.
Bernie: Bye, Anna. Love your work.

New Words

brownie *n.* small rich cake made with chocolate and nuts 核仁巧克力饼

guru *n.* Hindu spiritual leader; (fig infml) respected and influential teacher or authority 古鲁（印度的宗教领袖）;（受尊敬、有影响力的）教师或权威

puberty *n.* stage at which a person is physically mature and becomes capable of having children 青春期，妙龄

pathetic *adj.* causing one to feel pity or sadness 可怜的；悲伤的

squidgy *adj.* soft and moist 湿软的

scandal *n.* a highly public situation that results in disgrace and public outrage 丑事；丑闻；耻辱

Phrases and Expressions

be stuck in
not able to move or continue doing something. 不能动；陷入困境

guinea-fowl
bird of pheasant family, with dark gray feathers spotted with white, often used as food 珠鸡（常供食用）

scrape by
barely manage to live (esp. to survive a difficult period on very little money, grain, etc.) 勉强生活（尤指依靠极少的钱、粮等勉强渡过困难时期）

the spitting image of
look exactly like someone or something 酷似，酷肖

Notes

Farce

A comedy written for the stage or film which aims to entertain the audience. Farce is, in fact, not merely a genre but a highly flexible dramatic mode that often occurs in combination with other forms, including romantic comedy. It is widely employed in TV sitcoms, in silent film comedy, and in screwball comedy.

loo

(Brit infml euph)lavatory

Notting Hill

An area in West London, England close to the north-western corner of Hyde Park, and lying within the Royal Borough of Kensington and Chelsea. It is a cosmopolitan district known as the location for the annual Notting Hill Carnival, the setting for the 1999 film Notting Hill starring Julia Roberts and Hugh Grant. Notting Hill has a contemporary reputation as an affluent and fashionable area; known for attractive terraces of large Victorian townhouses, and high-class shopping and restaurants.

P. G. Wodehouse

Sir Pelham Grenville Wodehouse was an English comic novelist, who enjoyed enormous popular success during a career of more than 70 years and continues to be widely read. Wodehouse was also a playwright and lyricist who was part author and writer of 15 plays and of 250 lyrics for some 30 musical comedies.

Understanding and Speaking Interculturally

Exercise 1 Answer the following questions according to the movie clip you have just watched.

1. In the movie, whose birthday are they celebrating?

2. What does Max suggest doing during the meal?

3. What kind of pain does Bella suffer?

Exercise 2 Fill in the blanks according to the movie clip you have just watched.

1. **William:** Hon, this is Anna. Anna, this is Honey. She's my ______________.
   Anna: Oh, Hi!
   Honey: Oh, God. This is one of those ______________ in life...when it's possible you can be really genuinely cool...and I... I'm going to fail just a hundred percent. I... I absolutely, totally and utterly ______________. And I just think...you are the most beautiful woman in the world. And more importantly, I genuinely believe, and I've believed for some time now, that we could be best friends. So what do you think?
   Anna: Uh, haha. ______________! Well, happy birthday!
2. **Bernie:** So, uh, tell me, um, Anna, what do you do?
   Anna: I'm an ______________.
   Bernie: Oh, splendid.
   Anna: What do you do?
   Bernie: I'm actually in the ______________ myself, so uh, not really

______.

3. **Bella:** What do you think of the guinea-fowl?
Anna: I'm a ______.
Bella: Oh, God.
Max: So, how's the guinea-fowl?
Anna: Best guinea-fowl I've ever ______.

Exercise 3 Put the following sentences in the right order according to the movie clip you have just watched.

1. Every one of them relates their sufferings in their respective lives.

2. Bernie arrives and has a nice talk with Anna.

3. Anna and William arrive to take part in Honey' birthday and exchanges greetings with Max and Bella.

4. Max suggests that they should give the last brownie as a prize to the person who could tell the saddest story about his or her own life.

5. They say goodbye to each other.

6. Honey arrives and has a very pleasant meeting with Anna.

Exercise 4 Divide the class into two groups and have a class debate. One group should argue that different social status is the obstacle of true love and marriage, while the other group should argue that it isn't.

Section B Reading

It is easy to assume that someone who has a fairly good mastery of a foreign language should be able to communicate successfully with people who speak that language as their mother tongue. However, even skilled speakers of a foreign language can still have a difficult time and end up in confusion and frustration. What might get in the way? Is it so difficult to use the language effectively and make themselves fully understood? The hint here lies, perhaps in the way in which they speak and the way they interact with the native speakers. To be more specific, who should take the initiative to speak, how much should they speak, what should they say in particular circumstances, and what should they also do in these circumstances? Here, we use the word "norm" to cover the examples that we've mentioned. In other words, we need to discuss the different rules and customs that apply when people communicate with each other in the context of different social activities.

As we have learned from the previous chapters, what is "above the water" is deeply rooted in what is "below the water." To make it clear, the norms of social interaction that a particular society adheres to are closely related to the values and beliefs that the members of that society generally hold. When we consider different social norms, we must certainly not ignore the values that underlie them.

In this chapter, we confine our comparison between China and some English-speaking countries, especially, the UK and the US.

Addressing

In many English-speaking countries, people address each other by just using their first names, e.g. Tom, Michael, Ellen, or Sophie. This is particularly true in the US, where equality is greatly valued on different levels of social life. Therefore, it is not strange for a student to call his or her teachers by their first name or a mother-in-law to be called in the same way by her daughter-in-law. Although some seniors may prefer to be called by their surname.

In China, and many Asian countries like Japan and Korea, it is embarrassing for elder people or people with higher position to be addressed by their first names. The hidden rule is that given names are limited to husband and wife, very close friends, and subordinates by superiors. The reason might be the strict hierarchy which has influenced China for more than one thousand years and the tradition of respecting the old.

The common practice in China is that position- or occupation-linked titles are often used to address people, like teacher (*laoshi*), manager (*jingli*), and director (*zhuren*). People use these titles to show their respect, while people who hear it will also feel honored and valued. A great diversity of titles are also used in the U.S., such as Doctor, Professor, Judge, President, Senator, Governor, Mayor, General, Colonel, or Captain.

Another interesting phenomenon is that when Chinese people address a stranger, they would use words such as Grandpa (*daye*), Grandma (*dama*), Uncle (*shushu*), Aunt (*ayi*), Brother (*dage*), or Sister (*dajie*). This would always confuse people from an outside culture, who might discern no relationship between them by blood. The extensive use of kinship terms is related to the tradition of treating strangers with kindness like family members and the belief that all people should live in harmony. In contrast, Americans would simply use "Sir" or "Ma'am" to address a stranger. And even among relatives, the kinship terms are not often used, as given names are preferred. "Brother" or "Sister" does exist in America as terms of address, however, they are normally found in a religious context.

Greetings

People in English-speaking countries generally greet each other by using some more formal acknowledgements like "Good morning", "Good afternoon", "Good evening", "How do you do?" "How are you?" and some less formal ones like "Hi!" and "Hello!" In the UK, people might typically use "Are you all right?" as the routine way of greeting.

On the other hand, the Chinese way of greeting seems to vary a lot. Up till about ten years ago, people usually greeted each other by saying "Have you eaten?", "Where are you going?", "What are you going to do?" These questions don't really function as greetings requiring a specific reply. Rather, they serve to focus attention on the other person. Thus, a simple reply of "*Nihao*", which equals to "Hello", would do.

Nowadays, the more common way to greet people in China is either to use "*Nihao/Ninhao*", which is more acceptable to foreign people, or to use the other person's name, which may sound strange to foreigners. On hearing his or her name being called on the street by a Chinese friend, a person from English-speaking countries would most probably respond with "Yes?" He or she is preparing for a question or a comment. But, actually, instead of either, only a simple greeting is being conveyed.

Saying Goodbye

When visiting a friend's home, Chinese and Americans have similar rules for saying farewells. That is, both groups would first express the intention to depart, usually with an excuse, and then actually leave. However, the length of each phase of this process and what people generally say and do during these two phases are not the same in each culture.

The length of the first phase is much longer for Americans. The time from the indication of leaving to the actual departure can last from a few minutes to as long as an hour. The guest offers an excuse for leaving and then continues the conversation or activity saying farewell and leaving. Otherwise, the guest might miss something important, a train, for example, or an exam. So, the guest leaves abruptly. While Chinese usually take only three to five minutes to wrap up the conversation after they show the intention to leave, with preparation for departure closely following.

However, the second phase seems to play a more important role in China and takes much longer. Generally, when visitors depart, a Chinese host will accompany them to the door and walk together with them for some distance. The conversation will continue while they are walking. And the longer the host walks to see the guests off, the more respect and hospitality are accorded to the guests. On the point of departing, the host might use words like "*man zou*", "*zou hao*", or "*you kong zai lai*", to ask the guests to take care and come back to visit again when they are free. In contrast, the second phase in the U.S. closely follows the first phase. People use expressions like "Take care", "See you", "So long", "Bye-bye", "Have a nice day" to end the visit. This kind of abrupt way of saying goodbye may cause their Chinese friends to feel that they are not valued and are not looked to for further development in the friendship.

But it should be noted that both in China and the U.S. it is so often the custom-to invite people back, even as a formality.

Expressing Gratitude and Thanks

If you visit a city in most English-speaking countries, "Thank you" might be the phrase you hear most during a day. You constantly hear it on the tube, on the bus, in the supermarket, on the street, in the office and in the classroom. Gratitude is expressed between strangers, friends, and husband and wife. At the same time, gratitude is expressed on matters of different scope – small favors and big ones. For example, a customer says thanks to the shop assistant who brings him or her the item the customer requests; a husband thanks his wife when she pours the wine for him at the dinner table; a manager says thanks to his employees who have won an important bid.

In contrast, "Thank you" is used with much lower frequency in China. Chinese people don't show gratitude for actions that they regard as a duty. And it is rarely expressed among very close friends and family members. This does not mean that they are impolite. Actually, they value the friendship and family affection so much that they firmly believe that they should be responsible for helping each other out in face of difficulties. And when "Thank you" does appear in conversation, they might feel "*jian wai*" (which signifies that they are not being treated as a trusted friend or family member) instead of happy or appreciated. Furthermore, "Thank you" is used for more important big favors. Nowadays, however, with more frequent cultural exchanges with the outside world, "Thank you" is also used for small matters, especially in urban areas.

Above are some especially common social activities people may encounter. Different norms exist in other social interactions as well, for example, how to give and respond to compliments, how to make phone calls, how to extend an invitation, how to make an appointment, and how to show hospitality, as will be discussed in the following audio section, etc. All these interactions require our constant attention and study, if smooth cross-cultural communication is to occur.

Understanding and Speaking Interculturally

1 Pair discussion: Recall your experience of interacting with your foreign teachers or foreign friends. Tell your partner what you say and behave in each of the social activities mentioned above. Have you suffered from the different norms?

2 Class discussion: Do you think social norm is something that will never change? If not, have you noticed any change in Chinese norm of social interaction? What might have led to those changes? Does western civilization play a role in it? What do you think?

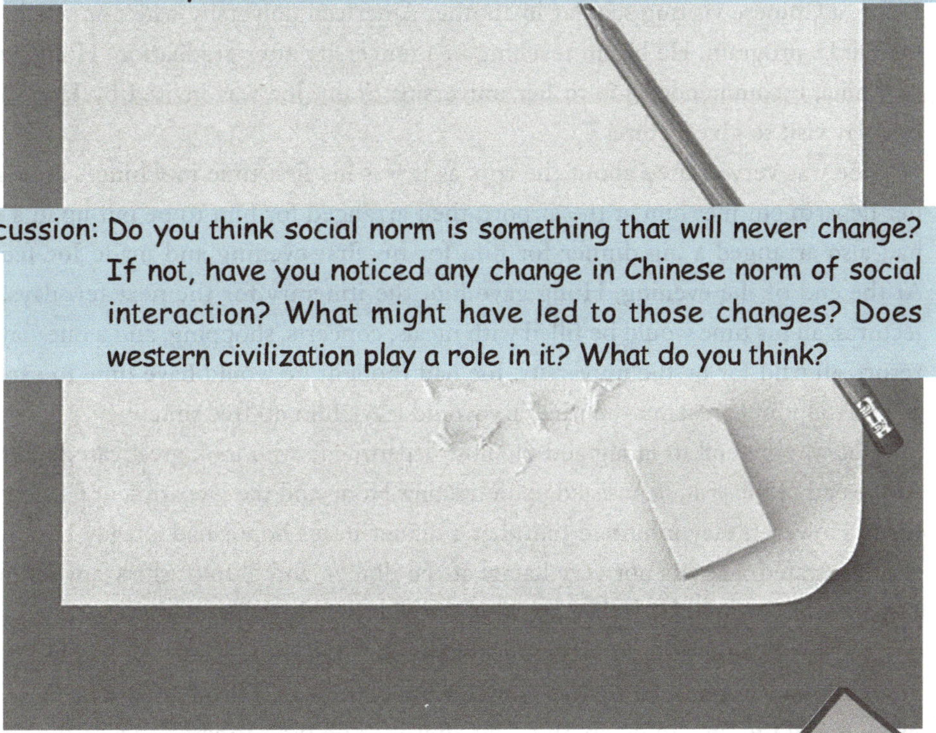

Section C Case

Introduction to the Case

Social norms are the rules that a group uses to determine what constitute appropriate and inappropriate values, beliefs, attitudes and behaviors. Failure to stick to the rules can result in some misunderstanding and even severe punishments.

The Scenario

Chinese Hospitality—Overdone

Joe is an assistant Professor in an American university. Two years ago, he made friends with Hong, a Chinese visiting scholar in another American university when he was in the final year of his Ph. D. program. He began teaching in a university after graduation. Hong, who had returned to China, recommended Joe to her university. Soon, Joe was invited by Hong's university for a five-day visit to give lectures.

Joe was very excited about the trip, as it was his first time in China. Hong and the Chair of her department met him at the airport, then arranged for him to be put up in a nice hotel. They had also arranged a big dinner for him for his first evening and made Joe feel very welcome. At the end of the evening, Hong gave him the itinerary for the next few days. Apart from the lectures, all his time would be filled with meals, concerts, shopping, and a one-day trip to a nearby resort, all paid for by the university. Joe had thought he would have time to explore the city and the surrounding area, but the itinerary would leave him no free time.

Joe was grateful to Hong and the host department, who took great care of him during his visit. At the end of the visit, he insisted upon treating Hong and the Department Chair to dinner to thank them. However, they informed him that a dinner in his honor had already been arranged. Joe was very frustrated. He was not very happy at the dinner, and did not show any enthusiasm when the Department Chair said that they hoped Joe would come back for another visit.

When it came time for Joe to leave, he did not know what to say. He knew he should be grateful for everything Hong had done for him, but he had also felt deprived and trapped since he never found the time to do anything by himself. The tight itinerary never allowed him to explore on his own; he felt especially annoyed that all the plans had been made without consulting him. Ironically, as soon as Joe left, Hong was very relieved. She felt Joe's visit had been successful but it had required most of her time to make sure that the visit would go smoothly. She never knew that Joe, still upset about the tight control placed on his schedule, complained to the person sitting next to him on the plane. "While in China, I sometimes felt like a prisoner!"

Understanding and Speaking Interculturally

Exercise 1 Listen for the first time and answer the following questions.

1. What did Hong and the Chair of her department do to welcome Joe?

2. What did Hong feel when Joe left and why?

3. Can you find how Joe's feelings changed about everything Hong had done for him during his trip in China?

Exercise 2 Listen for the second time and fill in the blanks.

1. Joe is an 1) ________ in an American university. Two years ago, he made friends with Hong, a Chinese 2) ________ in another American university when he was in the final year of his 3) ________.

2. At the end of the evening, Hong gave him the itinerary for the next few days. Apart from 4) ________, all his time would be filled with meals, 5) ________, shopping, and a one-day trip to a 6) ________, all paid for 7) ________.

3. Joe was 8) ________ Hong and the 9) ________, who took great care of him during his visit. At the end of the visit, he insisted 10) ________ Hong and the Department Chair to dinner to thank them. However, they informed him that a dinner in his honor had already been arranged. Joe was 11) ________.

4. The tight itinerary never allowed him to explore on his own; he felt 12) ________ that all the plans had been made without 13) ________. Ironically, as soon as Joe left, Hong was 14) ________. She felt Joe's visit had been successful but it had required most of her time to make sure that the visit would 15) ________.

Exercise 3 Exploring interculturally.

1. Can you explain why Joe said, "While in China, I sometimes felt like a prisoner!"?

2. Can you tell the differences between Chinese hospitality and American hospitality? Discuss the question with your partner by using some examples.

Part IV

Nonverbal Communication

Chapter 9

Body Language

Section A Movie clip

Introduction to the Movie *Mulan*

This movie is Walt Disney's retelling of the old Chinese folktale of Mulan, a young Chinese maiden who learns that her weakened and lame father is to be called up into the army in order to fight the invading Huns. Knowing that he would never survive the rigors of war, Mulan decides to disguise herself and join in his place. Unknown to her, her ancestors are aware of this and try to prevent it by sending a tiny disgraced dragon, Mushu, to force her to abandon her plan. The dragon agrees, but when he meets Mulan, he learns that she cannot be dissuaded. And so the dragon decides to travel with her, in an attempt to regain his dignity among the family ancestors by making her a war hero.

Introduction to the Selected Scenes

In Scene I, Mulan proceeds into camp and meets fellow soldiers, but under advice from Mushu on how to act like a real man, unwittingly starts a camp-wide brawl. In Scene II, Li Shang, the Captain in charge of the new troop training, begins a strict training schedule and is visibly disappointed at the low level of his new troop's abilities. Eventually he orders Mulan to return home, but she succeeds in impressing him by retrieving an arrow from a tall pole while weighed down with brass amulets. The troops, inspired by this, all improve and become good soldiers. In Scene III, Mulan leads her old comrades to rescue the Emperor, and finally wins the respect of the Emperor and others in the Imperial City.

Script of the Scenes

Scene I

Mushu: Okay, this is it. Time to show 'em your man walk. Shoulders back, chest high, feet apart, head up and strut. Two, three. Break it down. Hup, two, three. And work it!

Mushu: Beautiful, isn't it?

Mulan: They're disgusting.

Mushu: No, they're men. You have to act like them, so pay attention.

Soldier 1: Look. This tattoo will protect me from harm.

Yao: Hmm.

Soldier 2: I hope you can get your money back!

Mulan: I don't think I can do this.

Mushu: It's all attitude. Be tough, like this guy here.

Yao: What are you looking at?

Mushu: Punch him. It's how men say hello.

Monk Soldier: Oh, Yao, you've made a friend.

Mushu: Good. Slap him on the behind. They like that.
Yao: Whoa-ho-ho! I'm gonna hit you so hard, it'll make your ancestors dizzy.
Monk Soldier: Yao, relax and chant with me… Feel better?
Yao: Yeah. Ahh, you ain't worth my time. Chicken boy.
Mushu: Chicken boy? Say that to my face, ya limp noodle!
Yao: Oh. Sorry, Ling.

Hey! Whoa! You're dead! Oh, there he goes!

Scene II

(Lyres of the song)
We've got a long way to go.
Let's get down to business
To defeat the Huns
Did they send me the daughters
When I asked for sons
You're the saddest bunch I ever met
But you can bet before we're through
Mister, I'll make a man
Out of you
Tranquil as a forest
But on fire within
Once you find your center
You are sure to win
You're a spineless, pale, pathetic lot
And you haven't got a clue
Somehow I'll make a man
Out of you
I'm never gonna catch my breath
Say good-bye to those who knew me
Boy, was I a fool in school for cutting gym
This guy's got 'em scared to death
Hope he doesn't see right through me
Now I really wish
That I knew how to swim
Be a man
We must be swift as a coursing river

Be a man
With all the force of a great typhoon
Be a man
With all the strength of a raging fire
Mysterious as the dark side
Of the moon
Time is racing toward us
Till the Huns arrive
Heed my every order
And you might survive
You're unsuited for the rage of war
So pack up, go home you're through
How could I make a man
Out of you
Be a man
We must be swift as a coursing river
Be a man
With all the force of a great typhoon
Be a man
With all the strength of a raging fire
Mysterious as the dark side
Of the moon
Be a man
We must be swift as a coursing river
Be a man
With all the force of a great typhoon
Be a man
With all the strength of a raging fire
Mysterious as the dark side
Of the moon

Scene III

Chi Fu: That was a deliberate attempt on my life! Where is she? Now she's done it. What a mess! Stand aside! That creature's not worth protecting.

Li Shang: She's a hero.

Chi Fu: 'Tis a woman. She'll never be worth anything.

Li Shang: Listen, you pompous...

Emperor: That is enough.

Li Shang: Your Majesty, I can explain.

Emperor: I've heard a great deal about you, Fa Mulan. You stole your father's armor, ran away from home, impersonated a soldier, deceived your commanding officer, dishonored the Chinese army, destroyed my palace...and...you have saved us all.

Mushu: My little baby is all grown up and...and savin' China. You have a tissue?

Emperor: Chi Fu?

Chi Fu: Your Excellency?

Emperor: See to it that this woman is made a member of my council.

Chi Fu: Member...what? There are no council positions open, Your Majesty.

Emperor: Very well. You can have his job.

Chi Fu: What? My... Oh.

Mulan: With all due respect, Your Excellency, I think I've been away from home long enough.

Emperor: Then...take this, so your family will know what you have done for me. And this, so the world will know what you have done for China.

Yao: Is she allowed to do that?

Li Shang: Um... You... You fight good.

Mulan: Oh. Thank you. Khan, let's go home.

New Words

armor *n.* a defensive covering worn to protect the body against weapons 盔甲

dizzy *adj.* having a whirling sensation and a tendency to fall 眩晕的；眼花的

impersonate *v.* assume the character or appearance of, especially fraudulently 假扮；假装

pompous *adj.* characterized by excessive self-esteem or exaggerated dignity; pretentious 爱炫耀的；自负的

punch *v.* hit with a sharp blow of the fist 拳击；用拳头猛击

Tattoo *n.* a permanent mark or design made on the skin by a process of pricking and ingraining an indelible pigment or by raising scars 纹身

strut *v.* walk with pompous bearing; swagger 神气活现地走路；昂首阔步

Phrases and Expressions

chicken boy (slang) a coward
胆小鬼

limp noodles (slang) a coward
胆小鬼

see to something to deal with a task that needs to be dealt with
负责；注意

Notes

'Tis

It is used in spoken English, meaning "It is."

Understanding and Speaking Interculturally

Exercise 1 Answer the following questions according to the movie clips you have just watched.

1. In Scene I, how does Mushu advise Mulan to act like a real man? Does it work?

2. If you were Mulan, what kinds of body language would you employ to assert your "manhood"?

3. In Scene II, two kinds of sports games are involved. Please identify them.

4. In Scene III, how does the Emperor act to express his thanks to Mulan? How does Mulan behave to express her joy when receiving the Emperor's rewards? Do you think this would happen in real China?

Exercise 2 Match the roles in the movie clips with their personalities.

Roles	**Personalities**
1) Mulan	a) kind, affectionate and considerate
2) Mushu	b) courageous, strong-willed and optimistic
3) the Emperor	c) kind, decent and open-minded
4) Mulan's father	d) talktive, humorous and smart

Exercise 3 In Scene III, the body language of "hugging" is empolyed to express personal feelings. Brainstorm in groups about "hugs" in China, and fill in the chart below. After the discussion, each group should present their ideas to the class.

	Relationship gender age	why hug or not hug
Who you hug	1	
	2	
	3	
Who you don't hug	1	
	2	
	3	

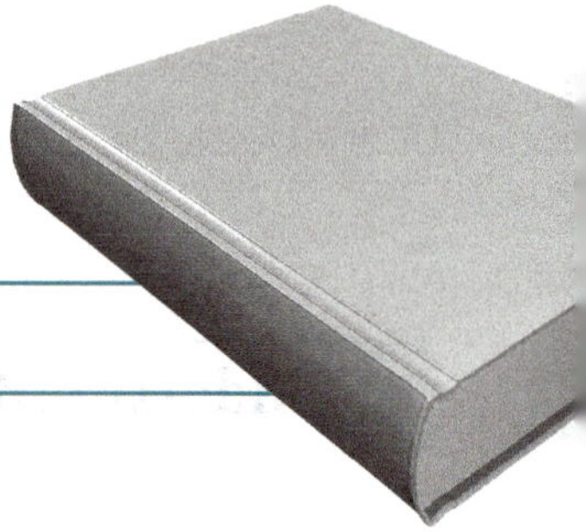

Section B Reading

The study of body language is known as kinesics. Kinesic behaviors include gestures, head movements, facial expressions, eye behaviors, and other physical movements that can be used to communicate. Of course, like all other forms of communication, no single type of behavior exists in isolation. Specific body movements can be understood only by taking the person's total behavior into account. As a matter of fact, many aspects of your body language may contain information that others use to form an impression of you. Consider, for example, the way you walk, which communicates your emotional state and your sense of confidence. Grayson and Stein (1981), in fact, after filming people walking in the streets of New York, then showed the films to prisoners, who indicated which walkers appeared vulnerable to attack. People who walked confidently with swinging foot movements were less likely to be selected as victims.

Paul Ekman and Wallace Friesen (1969) have suggested that there are five categories of kinesic behaviors: emblems, illustrators, affect displays, regulators, and adaptors. We will consider each type of kinesic behavior in turn.

Emblems

Emblems are nonverbal behaviors that have a direct verbal translation. Emblems that are familiar to most Chinese include the gesture of arm-waving to indicate hello or goodbye. The meanings of emblems are learned along the way in a culture, and are often used consciously by the members of that culture when they wish to present specific ideas to others.

Emblems can be a great source of misunderstanding in intercultural communication because the shared meanings for an emblem in one culture may be quite different in another. In Turkey, for example, to say "no" nonverbally, one would nod his head up and back, raising his eyebrows at the same time. By contrast, wagging one's head from side to side doesn't mean "no" in Turkish, it means "I don't understand." So if a Turk asks you, "Are you looking for the bus to Ankara?" and you shake your head "No", he will assume you do not

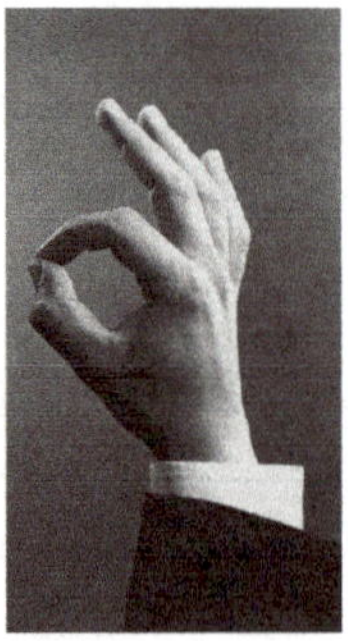

understand English, and will probably ask you the same question again, this time in, perhaps, German. (Brosnahan, 1988)

Illustrators

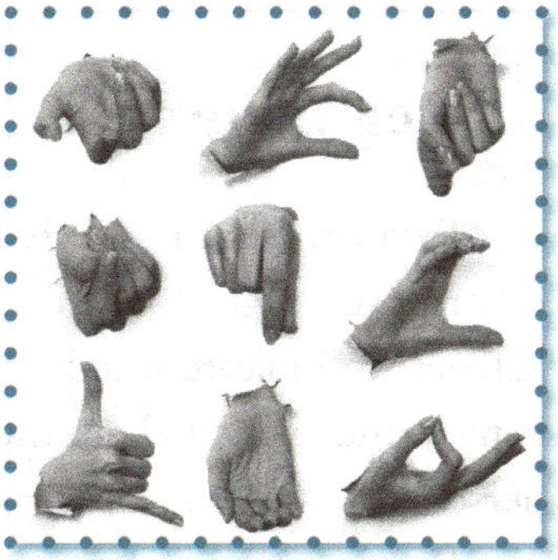

Illustrators are nonverbal behaviors that are directly tied to, or accompany, the verbal message. They help to emphasize a point that the speaker is making. For example, in saying "the huge mountain," you may simultaneously lift your arms and move them in a large half-circle. Similarly, you may use your hand to indicate directions to a particular place. Unlike emblems, however, none of these body movements has meaning in itself. Rather, the meaning depends on the verbal message it is tied to.

Illustrators are less culture-specific than emblems, which makes them more likely to be universally understood. Illustrators also show that we are highly involved and interested in the conversation.

Affect Displays

Affect displays are facial and body movements that show feelings and emotions. Expressions of happiness or surprise, for example, are displayed by the face and convey a person's inner feelings. Though affect displays are shown primarily through the face, postures and other body movements can also display an emotion.

Affect displays may be unconscious and unintentional, such as a look of shock, and a blush of embarrassment. Or affect displays may be conscious and intentional, as when we purposely smile and look at another person to show warmth and welcome. Cultural norms often govern both the kind and degree of affect displays shown. We Chinese, for example, present in public much less negative affect displays than most Europeans.

Regulators

Regulators are nonverbal behaviors that maintain or regulate turn-taking in conversations. In other words, regulators are used by speakers to indicate whether others should take a turn and by listeners to indicate whether they wish to speak or would prefer to continue listening. They also convey information about the preferred speed of conversations and the degree to which the other person is understood and believed.

Regulators are learned early in life and used automatically with little thought. In this sense, regulators are culture-specific. For instance, people from high-context cultures such as China and Korea are especially concerned with meanings conveyed by the eyes.

Adaptors

Adaptors are personal body movements that occur as a reaction to an individual's physical and psychological state. Scratching an itch, twisting the corner of clothes, tapping a pencil, and smoothing one's hair are all behaviors that fulfill some individual need.

Adaptors are usually performed unintentionally, without conscious awareness. They seem to be more frequent when one feels pressured, impatient, nervous or enthusiastic, and they are often interpreted by others as a sign of discomfort, uneasiness, or other negative feelings.

Understanding and Speaking Interculturally

1. Watch the movie clip of *Tom and Jerry*, examine the body languages of the Mouse and the Bird, and then work in pairs to supply the verbal counterpart of their body languages.

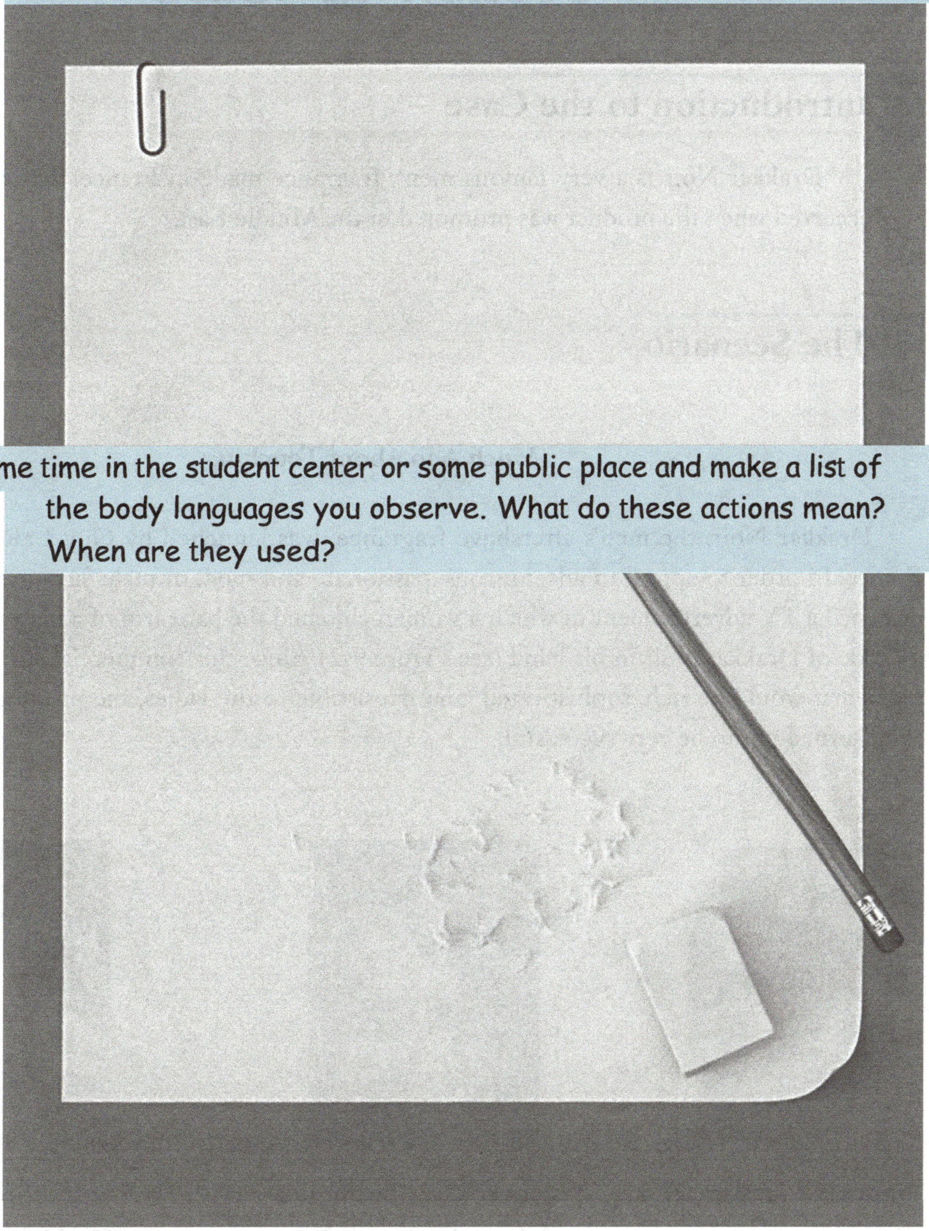

2. Spend some time in the student center or some public place and make a list of the body languages you observe. What do these actions mean? When are they used?

Section C Case

Introduction to the Case

Drakkar Noir is a very famous men's fragrance made in France. The facts in this case occurred when the product was promoted in the Middle East.

The Scenario

Much Ado About Touching

Drakkar Noir, the men's aftershave fragrance, was launched by Guy LaRoche in 1982 in France. In order to appeal to adventurous, passionate and modern male customers, the company designed a TV advertisement in which a woman clutched the bare arm of a man who was holding a bottle of Drakkar Noir in his hand (see Figure 9-2). Since this commercial almost guaranteed a scent that would be rich, sophisticated, and irresistible to the ladies, the promotion for Drakkar Noir turned out to be very successful.

Figure 9-1 Drakkar Noir

Figure 9-2 European Advertisement for Drakkar Noir

Figure 9-3 Saudi Arabian Advertisement for Drakkar Noir

Later on, the company decided to use the same advertisement to open its Middle Eastern market. Unfortunately, the promotion soon became a disaster. After a flurry of market research, the company realized the impropriety of the body language used in the advertisement to a Saudi Arabian audience, and soon replaced it with a woman using the tip of her finger to slightly touch a man's arm in a suit (see Figure 9-3). With this change in body language, the campaign finally helped lead to a good year for sales in this new market.

Understanding and Speaking Interculturally

Exercise 1 Listen for the first time and answer the following questions.

1. For whom was the perfume Drakkar Noir specially designed, men or women?
2. In which country was Drakkar Noir first launched?
3. Where did the sales campaign for Drakkar Noir suffer its setback?

Exercise 2 Listen for the second time and fill in the blanks.

1. Drakkar Noir, the 1) ________ aftershave fragrance, was launched by Guy LaRoche in 1982 in France. In order to appeal to the adventurous, passionate and 2) ________ male customers, the company designed a TV advertisement in which a woman 3) ________ the 4) ________ arm of a man who was holding a bottle of Drakkar Noir in his hand.
2. Since this commercial almost guaranteed a scent that would be rich, sophisticated, and 5) ________ to the ladies, the promotion for Drakkar Noir turned out to be very 6) ________. Later on, the company decided to use the 7) ________ advertisement to open its Middle Eastern market. Unfortunately, the promotion soon became a 8) ________.
3. After a flurry of market research, the company realized the 9) ________

______ of the body language used in the advertisement to a Saudi Arabian audience, and soon replaced it with a woman using the 10) ______ ______ of her finger to 11) ______ touch a man's arm in a 12) ______. With this change in body language, the campaign finally helped lead to a good year for sales in this new market.

Exercise 3 Exploring interculturally.

1. Why did the same advertisement succeed in France but fail in Saudi Arabia?
2. Why did the adapted version of the advertisement succeed?
3. What you can learn from Drakkar Noir's story?

Chapter 10

Time

Section A Movie clip

Introduction to the Movie *Outsourced*

Todd Anderson spends his days managing a customer call center for Western Novelty, an American novelty product company in Seattle, until the jobs in his entire department, including his own job, are outsourced to India. Adding insult to injury, he is sent to India to train his replacement. In India, Todd is assaulted by the sights and sounds of a completely different culture. However, through his team of Indian call center workers, he soon realizes that he too has a lot to learn—not only about India and America, but about himself. Before long, Todd discovers that being outsourced may be the best thing that ever happened to him.

Introduction to the Selected Scene

Over his first few weeks in India, Todd is initially concerned with improving his employees' minutes-per-call rating. He's bored by his job and yearns to return to the comforts of home. Between the accent and culture training and his explanation of Western Novelty items, Todd frantically tries to increase the effectiveness of the Indian office. During a trip to a McDonald's knockoff that doesn't serve cheeseburgers, he meets a fellow American who advises him, "I was resisting India. Once I gave in, I did much better." These words set Todd to thinking deeply about his future life in India.

Script of the Scene

Todd: When is this glass coming?

Puro: It is coming presently, sir.

Todd: Is the volume always this low?

Puro: This is low?

Todd: Well yes, you're obviously not riding on all the callers yet. Why is the MPI so bad? At 12 minutes per incidents, we're losing money on every call.

Puro: Bad?... When I started it was 15, I brought it down to 12.

Todd: This place is a disaster, if we don't get it down to 6, I'll be stuck in India for the rest of my life.

Puro: We'll get the MPI down, no problem.

Todd: Don't say no problem, when it is a problem. If we don't get it down to 6, you'll never get a promotion and you'll never get to marry what's-her-face.

Puro: Who's face, sir?

Todd: Your girlfriend, Bagy Swami, whatever her name is.

Puro: Everyone, please work harder, faster. OK?

Todd: OK, what else? Yes, Manmeet.

Manmeet: I do not understand item H403.

Todd: H403, ah...yea, a lot of Americans wear this to sporting events.

Manmeet: But why, sir?

Todd: It's hard to explain, they just do...

Female Employer: I do not understand the purpose of A221.

Todd: A221. That's a burger brand. Americans eat a lot of beef...and some people like to burn their initials into their food, with a red hot iron before they eat it.

Female Employer: Why?

Todd: That's a cow brand. You know, the thing you use to burn a symbol into a cow. In America, that's how you keep track of your cows, is branding.

Female Employer: With a red hot iron?

Todd: Yeah.

Manmeet: But, a...wouldn't the cow run away?

Todd: Oh, no, we only do it to baby cows, when they're small enough, to...hold them down. Yes, Asha?

Asha: A suggestion, Mr. Todd?

Todd: Go ahead.

Asha: You need to learn about India.

"Hey, its Todd... I'll be out of the country for a few days, so leave a message... You have no messages. Are you still there? You have no messages."

Recording

Female: "I told you, it's my grandson's first day at school... I want to get him some supplies, but I'm not sure what kids need these days."

Male: "Perhaps some rubbers, ma'am."

Female: "What did you say?"
Male: "I mean...if you have a pencil, you need some rubbers."

Todd: OK...who can tell me, what was wrong with this call? It's not a "rubber"...it's an "eraser."
Asha: No, sir, this is a rubber.
Todd: No, it's an eraser. "Rubber" means condom.
Manmeet: You mean like a "flat"?
Puro: They call it an "apartment."
Todd: No, a condom...birth control.
Manmeet: Does it work?

Dave: This is Dave.
Todd: Hi, Dave.
Dave: I just saw your numbers, you do realize you're not on vacation over there?
Todd: Yeah, I got to come here for vacation.
Dave: Unless you're planning on taking up residence, you'd better get the ball rolling.
Todd: Yeah, that's why I'm calling actually... An MPI in the 6's is not realistic.
Dave: I didn't say in the 6's, Todd, I said get it down to 6. 6.59 is not 6, its 7, you need to get it down to 6.0.
Todd: You're kidding me? We had a deal.
Dave: Seattle Agent calls, getting offline on Sunday. Expect a bump in calls on.
Todd: You know what a 6 is in the industry. Anything below 7. That's the definition.
Dave: Didn't you read your contract? We said get it down to 6, I'm holding it at 6.
Todd: Dave, you're a corporate slime ball.
Dave: Watch it, Todd, you lose your stock options, and you'll be living in a cardboard box.
Todd: Dave...
Dave: I gotta go.

Todd: Julie?... Hey, it's me. Yeah...how you doing? Just wanted to check in and say hi. Oh nothing...just wanted to hear your voice. I miss you. Oh, I know, I'm sorry, did I wake you? Yeah, I know... I know. Is somebody there?

Todd: How much to take me to Bombay? To Bhagat Singh Road, right now?
Taxi Driver: Oh no sir, Bombay is too far, it will use too much petrol, it will damage my car, it's impossible. OK, 6 000 rupees.
Todd: Don't sweat it, I'm gonna expense it.
Taxi Driver: OK sir, 5 000 rupees and not a rupee less.
Todd: Whatever.
Taxi Driver: OK, my deal is that, sir! I'll take you to Bombay for 4 000 rupees.

Waiter: Hello sir...how may I help you?
Todd: I'd like two cheeseburgers, a large fries...
Waiter: Sorry, but we don't have cheeseburgers here, sir.
Todd: What?... I thought this is McDonald's?
Waiter: Sorry, sir...this is MacDonnell's.
American: Get the Maharaja veggie burger. It's as close as you're gonna get.
Todd: I came all the way from Gharapuri for a cheeseburger.
American: You know they have a real McDonald's in Gharapuri, you still can't get a cheeseburger. You know what INDIA stands for, don't you? "I'll Never Do It Again." Did you hear about the guy who outsources his old job? He writes code in San Francisco...makes 70 grand a year...so he hires a guy in Bangalore to do his job for 12 grand. His boss thinks he's telecommunicating. He's got so much free time, he's thinking about getting another job just like it. We've got Indian doctors, reading American X-rays. Lawyers writing briefs, I'm in customer service.
Todd: Me too.
American: So, how long are you here for?
Todd: I have to get my MPI under a flat 6.
American: Not in India. Not unless you hire the accent neutral, that work for me, all you can hope for here is an 8.

Todd: I can't go home till I get a 6.
American: Well, you better find yourself a wife then.
Todd: She'll call me "Toad."
American: What?
Todd: My name is Todd, everyone says "Toad."
American: Listen here, Todd. Just a word of advice. I remember feeling, like you do. I was resisting India. Once I gave in, I did much better.

New Words

bump *n.* a rise or increase, as in prices or enrollment 上涨；增长

expense *v.* write off as an expense 把…作为开支勾销；报销

flat *adj.* free of qualification; absolute 无条件的；绝对的

initials *n.* the first letter of each word of a person's complete name considered as a unit 人名的首母缩写

resist *v.* remain firm against the actions, effects, or force of; withstand 抵制；抵抗

Phrases and Expressions

Don't sweat it. (American slang) Don't worry.（美国俚语）别担心。

get the ball rolling to begin something 开始做某事

slime ball (slang) a despicable or disgusting person 卑鄙的，令人厌恶的家伙

Notes

Outsource

The word is a term in management which means to farm out (work, for example) to an outside provider or manufacturer in order to cut costs (外界供应为缩减开支而把（如工作）包给外界的供应者或生产者). In this film, Todd's story is treated as a springboard for a smart look at the effect of cultural difference on work, friendship and love, and the global economy's impact on national and personal identity. The film shows that individuals in every nation are nearly powerless before the global economy, a force that shatters tradition and compels people to think of themselves as self-interested free agents.

MPI

an abbreviation of "Management Performance Indicators" 管理绩效指标

Understanding and Speaking Interculturally

Exercise 1 Fill in the blanks according to the movie clips you have just watched.

Dave: This is Dave.

Todd: Hi, Dave.

Dave: I just saw your __________, you do realize you're not on vacation over there?

Todd: Yeah, I got to come here for vacation.

Dave: Unless you're planning on taking up residence, you'd better get the ball __________.

Todd: Yeah, that's why I'm calling actually... An MPI in the 6's is __________.

Dave: I didn't say in the __________, Todd, I said get it down to 6. 6.59 is not 6, its 7, you need to get it down to __________.

Todd: You're kidding me? We had a deal.

Dave: Seattle Agent calls, getting offline on Sunday. Expect a bump in calls on.

Todd: You know what a 6 is in the industry. Anything ______. That's the definition.

Dave: Didn't you read your contract? We said get it down to 6, I'm ______ ______ it at 6.

Exercise 2 Match the words on the left with their speakers on the right.

1. "All you can hope for here is an 8."
2. "You need to learn about India."
3. "I have to get my MPI under a flat 6."
4. "We said get it down to 6, I'm holding it at 6."
5. "Bad?... When I started it was 15, I brought it down to 12."

a. Puro
b. Fellow American
c. Dave
d. Asha
e. Todd

Exercise 3 Discuss in the groups the Indian and American concepts of "Time" reflected in this movie. Support your argument with details selected from the scene.

Section B Reading

The study of how people use, structure, interpret, and understand time is called chronemics. Time is a potent force, communicating as powerfully as verbal language. In North America, for example, lateness for a business appointment communicates lack of interest. Usually we consider chronemics from two aspects: time orientations and time systems.

Time Orientations

Time orientation refers to the importance the members of a culture assign to the passage of time. Specifically, some cultures are past-oriented, others are present-oriented, and still others prefer a future-oriented worldview. (Samovar & Porter, 1995)

Past-oriented cultures regard previous experiences and events as most important. These cultures place a primary emphasis on tradition and the wisdom passed down from older generations. Therefore, they show a great deal of respect for parents and other elders, who are the links to these past sources of knowledge. Chinese and Native American cultures are typical examples of this time orientation.

Present-oriented cultures regard current experiences as most important. These cultures place a major emphasis on immediacy and on experiencing each moment as fully as possible. Consequently, people do not participate in particular events or activities with an eye to future concerns. Rather, they participate because of the immediate pleasure they may enjoy from these activities. In this sense, they are always aware of ways to appreciate the simple pleasures arising in daily activities. People in such cultures typically believe that unseen and even unknown outside forces, such as luck or fate, control their lives. Cultures such as those in the Philippines and many Central and South American countries are usually present-oriented.

Future-oriented cultures believe that tomorrow—or some other moment in the future—is most important. Current activities are not accomplished and appreciated for their own sake but for the potential future benefits they might yield. For example, one goes to university, studies for examinations, and works hard primarily not because one enjoys doing so, but more importantly, because these activities might lead to a rewarding future career. People from future-oriented cultures, including many European Americans, believe that their fate is at least partially in their own hands and that they can control the results of their actions.

Time Systems

Time systems are the hidden cultural rules that are used to arrange experiences in some meaningful way. There are three types of time systems: technical or scientific, formal, and informal (Hall, 1959).

Technical time systems refer to the precise, scientific measurement of time in units such as light years or microseconds.

Formal time systems involve the cultural understanding of units of time. Time units can vary greatly from culture to culture. Time can be defined according to the revolution of the moon around the earth, the changing seasons, the rise and fall of the tides, or the movements of the sun. It can also be linked to significant events such as the birth of a royal son or an important victory in battle.

Informal time system refers to the implied cultural rules of how time should be used or experienced. How long should you wait for someone who will be ready soon, for example: a minute, a while, or some other period? When is the proper time to arrive for an 8:00 P. M. party or a 9:00 A. M. business appointment? As a dinner guest, how long after your arrival would you expect the meal to be served? Cultures form unstated expectations about the timing and duration of such events.

Perhaps the most important aspects of a culture's informal time system are the degree to which it is monochronic or polychronic. (Hall, 1959)

A monochronic time system means that things should be done one at a time, and time is measured in precise, small units. In such a system, time is regarded as a commodity, something to be used, bought, wasted, saved or spent. People in cultures that view time in this way attach much importance to appointments and schedules, and view them as ironclad. For example, many European Americans carry a calendar book divided into hours, which tells them when, where and with whom to engage in activities. These events also have limits or boundaries, so that there is an expected beginning and ending point that has been scheduled in advance.

A polychronic time system means that several things are under way at the same time. People in cultures that observe time in polychronic fashion regard relationships as far more important than schedules. Appointments may be quickly broken, schedules readily set aside, and deadlines go unmet without guilt or apology when friends or family members require attention. In this sense, European Americans are often upset when they are kept waiting for a scheduled appointment, particularly when they discover that they are the third of three appointments that have been scheduled at exactly the same hour.

Cultural Differences in Perceptions and Use of Time

Misunderstandings may occur between people who have different time orientations. For example, someone from a present-oriented culture may view people from past-oriented cultures as too tied to tradition and people from future-oriented cultures as passionless slaves to materialism. Alternatively, someone from a future-oriented culture might view those from present-oriented cultures as self-centered, inefficient, and short-sighted. (Gonzalez and Zimbardo, 1985)

Cultures also differ in terms of the formal and informal time systems they use to determine how long an event should last, and even how long "long" is. Misinterpretations often occur when individuals from monochronic and polychronic cultures attempt to interact. Each usually views the other's response to time-specific appointments as disrespectful and unfriendly.

Understanding and Speaking Interculturally

1 What are the three time orientations? Which of them do Chinese hold? List the features of it against your own actions.

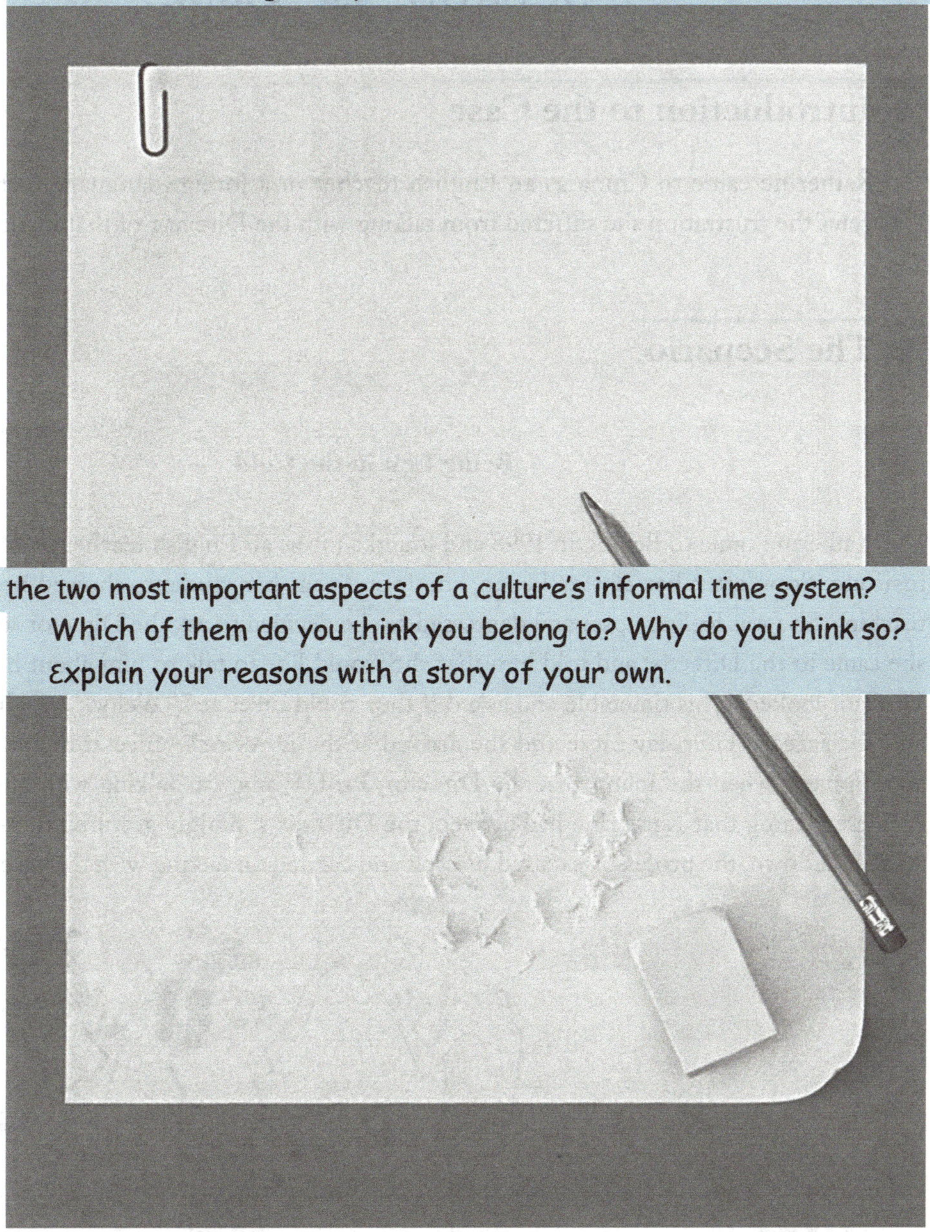

2 What are the two most important aspects of a culture's informal time system? Which of them do you think you belong to? Why do you think so? Explain your reasons with a story of your own.

Section C Case

Introduction to the Case

Katherine came to China as an English teacher in a foreign language institute. This case illustrates the frustration she suffered from talking with the Director of that institute.

The Scenario

Being Left in the Cold

Katherine came to Beijing in 1998 and found a job as an English teacher in a foreign language institute. Soon after her classes began, she found that her students showed no interest in her teaching. She was feeling upset and depressed so she decided to ask the Director for help. One day, she came to the Director and told him that she would like to talk to him about her problem. The Director looked at his timetable and asked if they could meet at 10 o'clock on Thursday morning and she agreed. Thursday came and she arrived at the Director's office at the exact time of their appointment when she found that the Director, Prof. Wang was talking with another teacher in Chinese. Seeing that Katherine had arrived, the Director smilingly gestured to her to take a seat. As she sat down, the professor excused himself and carried on talking with the teacher.

About five minutes later, the Director concluded his conversation and made a profound apology as he began to talk with Katherine. The Director showed great concern and asked her what the problem was. Just as she was describing her problem, another Chinese teacher came in, with a form that apparently needed the Director's signature. The Director smiled an apology to Katherine again and turned to talk with that teacher, also in Chinese. Katherine became impatient, wondering why their conversation should be interrupted since they had already made an appointment. She was so upset by their talking in Chinese in front of her that she became quite angry. Although their conversation continued, she was apparently unhappy about what had happened.

Understanding and Speaking Interculturally

Exercise 1 Listen for the first time and answer the following questions.

1. Why did Katherine go to the Director for help?

2. What happened when Katherine arrived at the Director's office?

3. What happened after Katherine began to talk with the Director?

Exercise 2 Listen for the second time and fill in the blanks.

1. One day, she came to the Director and told him that she would like to talk to him about her problem. The Director looked at his 1) ________ and asked if they could meet at 10 o'clock on Thursday morning and she 2) ________. Thursday came and she arrived at the Director's office at the 3) ________ time of their appointment when she found that Prof. Wang was talking with another teacher in 4) ________.
2. Seeing that Katherine had arrived, the Director 5) ________ gestured to her to take a seat. As she sat down, the professor excused himself and 6) ________ talking with the teacher. About 7) ________ later, the Director concluded his talk and made a profound 8) ________ as he began to talk with Katherine. The Director showed great concern and asked her what the problem was.

3. Just as she was describing her problem, another Chinese teacher came in, with a form that apparently needed the Director's signature. The Director smiled an 9) ________ to Katherine again and turned to talk with that teacher, also in Chinese. Katherine became 10) ________, wondering why their conversation should be 11) ________ since they had already made an 12) ________. She was so upset by their talking in Chinese in front of her that she became quite 13) ________. Although their conversation continued, she was apparently 14) ________ about what had happened.

Exercise 3 Exploring interculturally.

1. What is your opinion of the Director's behavior?

2. How would you explain Katherine's feeling to the Director?

Chapter 11

Space

Section A Movie clip

Introduction to the Movie *Pushing Hands*

The film tells the story about Master Chu, a retired Chinese Tai-Chi master, who moves to Westchester, New York, to live with his son Alex, his American daughter-in-law Martha, and their son Jeremy. The grandfather is increasingly distanced from the family as a "fish out of water" in Western culture. The film shows the contrast between traditional Chinese ideas of Confucian relationships within a family and the much more informal Western emphasis on the individual. The friction in the family caused by these differing expectations eventually leads to the grandfather moving out of the family home. In the process, he learns how he must adapt to his new surroundings before he comes to terms with his new life.

Introduction to the Selected Scenes

Martha does her writing at home, and Mr. Chu, the grandfather, also stays at home and practices his "pushing hands" everyday. Martha thinks he affects her writing severely in that she can not focus her attention on her new book. As a matter of fact, she feels heavy pressure. Her friend Linda suggests she buy a large house to insulate her from grandpa's interference. In the evening, Martha complains to Alex about her problem, trying to talk him into moving into a bigger place. Alex, however, rebuffs Martha's request, and the conversation ends unhappily.

Script of the Scenes

Linda: You're like a shit. Where is grandpa? He is so cute with the headphones on. Hi, grandpa!

Martha: No, Linda.

Linda: Hi! Do you think he remembers me? Come on, it is still what you've got to see. You'll get your own room to write in. Your grandpa can be out in the back chopping bricks. Whatever he does, you'd never know he existed.

Martha: I wish he didn't.

Linda: God, he's really getting you down.

Martha: Well, the way Alex acted for the past seven years, you'd have thought he didn't have a father. But, boom, one month ago they showed up on the doorstep. I haven't written a word since.

Linda: Now, Alex has to get the man out of here.

Martha: It's not that simple with Alex. Frankly, I don't think we could afford to get a bigger place, let alone buy a mansion!

Linda: Of course you can, especially if your mother's offer is still good.

Martha: Oh, Alex will never accept money from her, you know that.

Linda: Work on him. You've got to think more things if you want to learn more about man.

Martha: You've got a lot to learn about husbands. Sorry.

Linda: It's OK. I'm getting a dog.

…

Martha: Just one more sentence. OK. How is your computer virus?

Alex: Almost killed. And when can I start reading your new book?

Martha: There is no new book, can't you tell? Shit out as you're used out of as your father?

Alex: You don't know my father.

Martha: I've spent every single day in the same room with that man since he showed up here a month ago. Alex, it's impossible. He's taken over my work room. I just don't have the space to think.

Alex: Not enough space? In China, this house is big enough for four families.

Martha: Sure, but they speak the same language, so they can talk to each other. Alex, he's learned no word of English.

Alex: Then what about you? What have you done but make fun of him, treating him with distress bad?

Martha: Alex, I have tried.

Alex: I'm his only son. What do you want me to do?

Martha: You can at least consider moving into a bigger place. We can afford it.

Alex: No.

Martha: I don't see why we have to pay for his insurance and let him stay inside our home, but we can't accept a little loan from my mother.

Alex: That's not a little loan. It's a bribe, a big bribe, and you know it!

New Words

bribe *n.* something, such as money or a favor, offered or given to a person in a position of trust to influence that person's views or conduct 贿赂

chop *v.* cut by striking with a heavy, sharp tool, such as an ax 通过用斧子等沉重锋利的工具来砍劈

doorstep *n.* a step leading to a door 门阶

mansion *n.* a large, stately house 宽敞而庄重的房子

Phrases and Expressions

freak out
to become or cause to become greatly excited or upset 使变的极度兴奋或不安

get someone down
to make someone low in spirits or depressed 使情绪低落，沮丧

show up
to make an appearance 出现

Notes

Pushing hands

The title of the film refers to the pushing hands training that is part of the grandfather's tai chi routine. Pushing hands is a two person training which teaches tai chi students to yield in the face of brute force. Tai chi chuan teachers were persecuted in China during the Cultural Revolution, and the grandfather's family was broken up as a result. He sent his son to the West several years earlier and when he could he came to live with his family with the expectation of picking up where they had left off, but he was unprepared for the very different atmosphere of the West. "Pushing Hands" thereby alludes to the process of adaptation to culture shock felt by a traditional teacher in moving to the United States.

Understanding and Speaking Interculturally

Exercise 1 Fill in the blanks according to the movie clips you have just watched.

1. **Linda:** Hi! Do you think he remembers me? Come on, it is still what you've got to see. You'll get your own room to ______ in. Your grandpa can be out in the back ______ bricks. Whatever he does, you'd never know he ______.
   Martha: I wish he ______.
   Linda: God, he's really ______ you ______.

2. **Martha:** I've spent every ______ day in the same room with that man since he showed up here a month ago. Alex, it's ______. He's taken over my ______.

I just don't have the ______ to think.

Alex: Not enough ______? In China, this house is ______ enough for four families.

Martha: Sure but they speak the same language, so they can ______ ______ to each other.

Exercise 2 Decide whether the following statements are True or False according to the movie clip you have just watched. Write "T" for true and "F" for false.

_____ 1. Martha is not getting along well with her father-in-law.

_____ 2. The grandfather enjoys his life in New York very much.

_____ 3. Linda thinks Alex should ask his father to move out.

_____ 4. Martha demands a bigger place because she wants to live more comfortably.

_____ 5. Alex is on good terms with his mother-in-law.

Exercise 3 Discuss in the groups how would you solve Martha's problem if you were Alex. After the discussion, each group should present their ideas to the class.

Section B Reading

The study of spatial relations is known as proxemics. Intercultural communicators need to realize that cultures have different approaches to space and ways of using it. Usually we consider proxemics from two aspects: territory and personal space.

Territory

The need to protect and defend a particular spatial area is known as territoriality, a set of behaviors that people display to show that they "own" or have the right to control the use of a particular geographic area. In addition to private territories such as one's house, a corner in a dormitory, a car one owns or even a newspaper one buys to read, people may have public territories that are open to all, such as a table in a library, a seat in such public places as banks, post offices and parks, or a space in a parking lot.

Private territories are usually marked by using actual barriers such as fences, walls, flags and signs that say "Do Not Enter" or "Keep Off the Grass." In contrast, public territories are often marked informally by nonverbal markers such as clothes, books and other personal items that indicate a person's intent to temporarily control or occupy a given area. However, the marker used as a sign of temporary occupancy is valid as long as others respect it. Otherwise, invasion of the particular space may occur.

Cultural differences in territoriality can be exhibited in three ways. First, cultures can differ in the general degree of territoriality that its members tend to exhibit. For example, Hall and Hall (1990: 12) have suggested that "people like the Germans are highly territorial; they shield themselves behind heavy doors and soundproof walls to try to seal themselves from others in order to concentrate on their work. The French have a close personal distance and are not as territorial. They are tied to people and thrive on constant interaction and high-information flow to provide them the context they need."

Second, cultures can differ in the range of possible places or spaces about which they are territorial. For example, a study showed that a German's feeling of territoriality may be so strong that it extends to "all possessions, including the automobile. If a German's car is touched, it is as though the individual himself has been touched." (Hall and Hall, 1990: 10)

Finally, cultures can differ in terms of the typical reactions exhibited in response to invasions of territory. Members of some cultures prefer to react by withdrawing or avoiding conflicts whenever possible. Others respond by using barriers or other boundary markers to keep them from the possibility of intrusion. Still others react forcefully in an attempt to defend their "possessions" and their apparent sense of honor.

Personal Space

Personal space refers to the portable territory with invisible boundaries that expand or contract depending on the situation (Samovar & Porter, 1995). In other word, we carry body bubbles with us that are like invisible walls defining our personal space.

In one sense, personal space is culturally determined. For example, some cultures simply do not think of private, personal body space. Sometimes, fifty Africans can crowd into the same amount of space that holds only twenty North Americans. The reason is that the Africans' personal space suffers no sense of intrusion from crowding and touching.

Table11.1 Four Spatial Zones

In another sense, personal space results from varying relationships. In general, we establish shorter distances with people with whom we seek approval and maintain greater communication distances from those about whom we feel negatively. Also, longer distance may refer to figures of authority. Edward Hall (1966) has suggested that people interact within four spatial zones or distance ranges: intimate (0~50cm, reserved only for intimate lovers and family members), personal (>50~120cm, used only for friends), social (>120~270cm, kept with acquaintances), and public (>270cm, used for talking across a room and for public speaking).

Our difficulty in intercultural communication comes from conversing in unexpected and different zones, which happen to have cultural connotations . For example, in Middle Eastern countries, being close enough to breathe on another person is proper. In fact, to many people in such cultures, the breath is like their spirit or life, so sharing their breath in close conversation is like sharing their spirit. However, North Americans tend to prefer comparatively greater distances between themselves and others. As a result, many Middle Easterners converse in zones they perceive as personal, but which North Americans view as intimate. This is why some US government officials and visitors return from the Middle East, Southern Europe, or Latin America and say things like, “It’s all right if you don’t mind having people breathe in your face.” Meanwhile, North Americans themselves may be perceived as distant and cold because of how they define their personal space.

Understanding and Speaking Interculturally

1. What is personal space? According to Edward Hall, what are the four spatial zones within which people react?

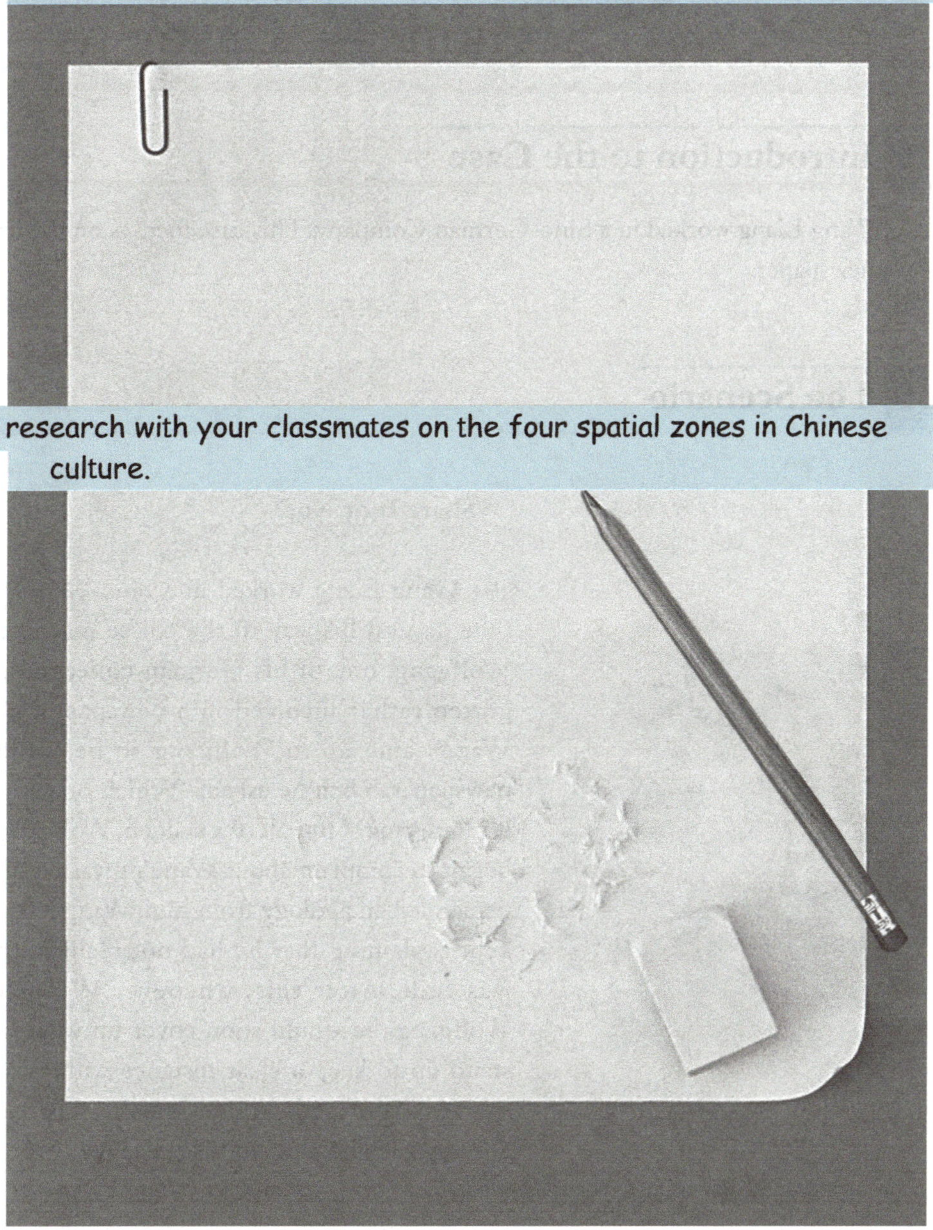

2. Conduct a research with your classmates on the four spatial zones in Chinese culture.

Section C Case

Introduction to the Case

Wang Liang worked in a Sino-German Company. This case focuses on the frustration caused by a newspaper.

The Scenario

Share It or Not?

Wang Liang worked in a Sino-German Joint Venture. One day, on his way to the coffee machine, he found that Wolfgang, one of his German colleagues, had seemingly gotten rather involved in a newspaper. Out of curiosity, Wang came up to Wolfgang so he could glance at the newspaper. Then he asked, "Which one are you reading? Is it interesting?" But all of a sudden, Wolfgang lost his temper, began to complain about Wang's invasion of his privacy, and demanded an apology from him. Wang felt rather upset, and kept explaining that he had not realized that his behavior was rude. After this, whenever Wang stepped toward Wolfgang, he would soon cover up what he was doing, or stand up to keep a clear distance with Wang. Wang Liang got very confused, wondering why his friendly behaviors aroused such hostility in his colleague.

Understanding and Speaking Interculturally

Exercise 1 Listen for the first time and answer the following questions.

1. What is Wolfgang's nationality?
2. What did Wang Liang do when he found Wolfgang was reading a newspaper?
3. How does Wolfgang react to Wang's behavior?

Exercise 2 Listen for the second time and fill in the blanks.

1. Wang Liang worked in a 1) ________ Joint Venture. One day, on his way to the coffee machine, he found that Wolfgang, one of his German colleagues, had seemingly gotten rather involved in a 2) ________. ut of curiosity, Wang 3) ________ Wolfgang so he could 4) ________ at the newspaper.
2. But all of a sudden, Wolfgang 5) ________ his temper, began to complain about Wang's invasion of his 6) ________, and demanded an apology for him. Wang felt rather 7) ________, and kept explaining that he had not realized that his behavior was 8) ________.
3. After this, whenever Wang stepped toward Wolfgang, he would soon 9) ________ what he was doing, or stand up to keep a clear 10) ________ with Wang.

Exercise 3 Exploring interculturally.

1. How would you react to Wang Liang's behavior?
2. Why did Wolfgang get angry?

Part V

Barriers and Bridges

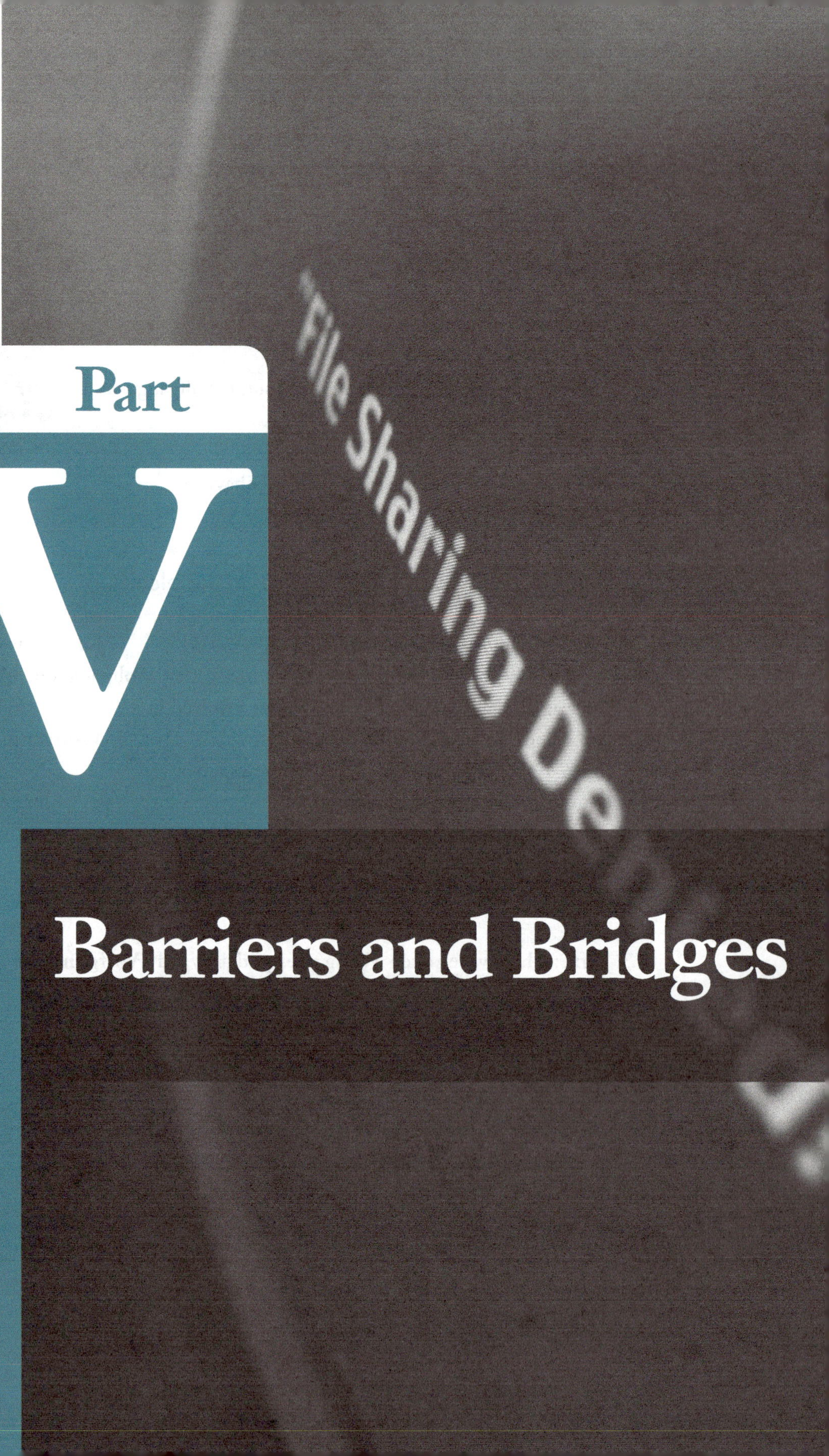

Chapter 12

Ethnocentrism and Stereotypes

Section A Movie clip

Introduction to the Movie *Crash*

People are born with good hearts, but as they grow up, they acquire prejudices. "Crash" is a movie that illustrates racial stereotypes that result in racial discrimination. The movie is set in Los Angeles, a city with a cultural mix of virtually every nationality. The story begins when several people are involved in a multi-car accident. From that point, we are taken back to the day before the crash, seeing the lives of several characters, and the problems each encounters during that day. Many of the characters switch from being bad-person-to-hero in ways that may surprise you.

Introduction to the Selected Scene

In the selected scene, the black guy Peter has been hitchhiking on the roadside and Tom Hanson, an officer in the local police department, is driving his car along the road. As a white officer, Tom has fewer stereotypes about black people and he has even tried to help them in earlier scenes of the movie. From the selected scene, we can see how even a kind person like Tom can make a mistake so big that he brings about a tragedy.

Script of the Scene

(Peter gets in the car.)

Peter: Really appreciate this.

Tom: No problem. So how long you've been out there tonight? It's cold.

Peter: Hour maybe.

Tom: Big surprise, huh?

Peter: Yeah, this ain't exactly "pick up a brother" territory.

Tom: True. So where you headed?

Peter: Anywhere the other side of the hill.

Tom: I'm goin' to El Segundo.

Peter: EL Segundo's cool.

Tom: You've been there?

Peter: Fuck no. (Laughing) That's some good music.

Tom: (Nodding) Uh-huh.

Peter: No, really. I'm startin' to understand it. Wrote me a country song myself just yesterday.

Tom: I'll bet you did.

Peter: (Sigh) Whatever.

Tom: (Noticing Peter's muddy shoes and torn jacket) So what's goin' on in the Valley tonight?

Peter: Ice-skatin'.

Tom: Ice-skatin'.

Peter: Love the Ice-skatin'. When I was a kid, I always wanted to be a goalie.

Tom: Come on!

Peter: What, you…you think that's funny or something?

Tom: I think you're having fun.

Peter: Yeah, whatever. (Seeing the patron saint on the dashboard and can't help laughing)

Tom: Something else funny?

Peter: Oh yeah.

Tom: Yeah? What's that?

Peter: People, man. People.

Tom: People like me?

Peter: No, no, no. I'm not laughin' at you, man. (Continue laughing)

Tom: Yeah, I can see that. Why don't you laugh outside?

Peter: Why are you getting all bent outta shape?

Tom: I'm not gettin' bent, man. Just pulling over.

Peter: Come on, man, keep drivin'. I said I'm not laughin' at you.

Tom: And I'm not telling you to get the fuck out of my car.

Peter: Why you bein' a fucking jerk? Just drive the car.

Tom: I've got a better idea. Get out now.

Peter: Fine. you want me to show you? I'll show you.

Tom: Get your hands out of your pocket. Put your hands where I can see 'em.

Peter: Who the fuck you think you're talkin' to?

Tom: Put your hands where I can see!

Peter: You wanna see what's in my hands? I'll show you what's in my fuckin' hands!

(Before Peter was able to show him what's in his hands, Tom had already pulled out his gunand squeezed the trigger.)

Tom: Oh, God.

New Words

dashboard *n.* the panel at the front of a car that displays the controls （汽车的）仪表板

goalie *n.* (infml) a goalkeeper（非正式）守门员

jerk *n.* (infml) a stupid person who does not care about the effects of his actions（非正式）（不顾行为后果的）蠢人；莽撞之人

territory *n.* area or land（某种特定的）地区；地方

Phrases and Expressions

get bent out of shape
to become very angry or upset 感到非常生气或沮丧

pull over
to stop the vehicle you are driving at the side of the road 将车辆停靠在路边

Notes

ain't
a short form of "am not", "is not", or "are not", that many people think is incorrect

El Segundo
a city in Los Angeles County, California

'em
a short form of "them"

outta
a short form of "out of"

patron saint
a holy figure looked to for protection and care

wanna
a short form of "want to"

Understanding and Speaking Interculturally

Exercise 1 Answer the following questions according to the movie clip you have just watched.

a) Why does Peter feel he needs to offer explanations even when Tom agrees to his liking the music playing in the car?

b) Why does Tom change his mind after noticing Peter's muddy shoes and torn jacket?

c) What does Tom mean by "Come on" when Peter tells him that he wanted to be a goalkeeper as a child?

d) Why do you think Peter begins to laugh when he sees the patron saint on the dashboard?

e) How does Tom react to Peter's laugh?

Exercise 2 Fill in the blanks according to the movie clip you have just watched.

1. **Tom:** True. So where you ______?
   Peter: ______ the other side of the hill.

2. **Peter:** Why are you getting all bent outta shape?
   Tom: I'm not gettin' bent, man. Just ______.
   Peter: Come on, man, ______. I said I'm not laughin' at you.

Exercise 3 Decide whether the following statements are True or False according to the movie clip you have just watched. Write "T" for true and "F" for false.

_____ 1. Tom is glad to pick up Peter in such a cold night.

_____ 2. Peter pretends that he has been to El Segundo.

_____ 3. Peter keeps laughing because he takes Tom for a stupid man.

_____ 4. Tom shots Peter because he hates black people.

Exercise 4 Discuss in groups what you would do if you were Tom. After the discussion, each group should present their solutions and ideas to the class.

Exercise 5 Find a partner and perform the scene with the help of the script.

Section B Reading

Ethnocentrism

What is ethnocentrism?

The concept of ethnocentrism was first introduced by the American academic and professor William G. Sumner, who defined it as "the view of things in which one's own group is the center of everything, and all others are scaled and rated with reference to it" (Lustig & Koester, 1996). Ethnocentrism is the belief that one's own culture is the best and all other cultures are inferior. So ethnocentrism actually refers to the attitudes of cultural superiority, one of the major barriers to intercultural communication.

How does ethnocentrism impede intercultural communication?

It is normal and natural for each of us to be proud of our own culture's achievements, values and characteristics, However, sometimes we go so far that we allow our pride to turn into an attitude that implies others are not as good as we are. In fact, many scholars believe that because we learn ethnocentrism so early in life, and primarily unconsciously, it might well be the major barrier to intercultural communication.

Steward and Bennett (Steward and Bennett, 1991) describe the negative impact of ethnocentrism on intercultural communication. First, ethnocentric beliefs about one's own culture may lead to a narrow and defensive identity. Chinese parents take care of their children so carefully that they interfere with every decision that their children are supposed to make. While Americans generally disapprove of this method of child-rearing , Chinese people regard it as the best way to demonstrate love for their children. This example illustrates that people tend to think their culture is "the only true culture", which is in fact not true. Second, when people form ethnocentric beliefs, they normally perceive members of other cultures in terms of stereotypes. Americans usually look upon the custom of arranged marriage prevailing in the East as something strange or offensive to human rights. This contributes, in part, to the view that Americans have of countries such as India or China. Third, since ethnocentric beliefs assume that one's own culture is normal and natural, ethnocentric judgments usually involve unfair comparisons that ennoble one's culture while degrading those of others.

Of course in today's globalized society, few people openly claim that their own culture is superior to other cultures. But people unconsciously tend to judge other cultures according to their own value systems. If their ethnocentric tendency is extremely strong, either verbally or nonverbally, people will discriminate against those people with different cultural norms and values. Very often, ethnocentrism serves as the starting point for most prejudicial beliefs, the source of many social problems. The most serious crime in human history arising from ethnocentrism is the massacre of Jews by the Nazis in Germany during WWII.

How can ethnocentrism be overcome?

Since ethnocentric attitudes are very harmful to intercultural communication, several steps can help overcome ethnocentrism. First of all, we should be fully aware that, while one culture is different from another, that is not evidence it is better than any other culture. Consider, for example, the cultures of China and the United States. Chinese people use chopsticks while Americans use a knife and fork when eating. Is one more correct than the other? Chinese people never open gifts in the presence of guests while Americans usually open the gift and share their pleasure together with their guests. Can we say Chinese people are more civilized than Americans? Or that American rules of politeness are better than those of the Chinese? Obviously neither of the two statements is true. Thus, we need to remember there exists differences between two cultures rather than superiority or inferiority between them.

Second, we should try to know more about ourselves in order to overcome the difficulties caused by deeply-rooted ethnocentrism. Identifying the attitudes, prejudices, and opinions that we all carry around can prevent many conflicts caused by ethnocentrism. Understanding our own communication styles may contribute much to successful intercultural communication. However, it is not easy to view ourselves objectively. If we perceive ourselves in one way, while those with whom we interact perceive us in another way, serious problems can arise. This requires us to be sensitive to feedback we receive, be more aware of our own communication style, and make appropriate adjustments in time.

Finally, developing empathy is a very effective way to overcome ethnocentrism. Empathy refers to the ability to be able to see things from the point of view of others in order to better understand other cultures. Empathy can be cultivated only if we become sensitive to the values and customs of the culture with which we are interacting. To resist ethnocentric attitudes, we should learn to suspend, or at least keep in check, the cultural perspective that is unique to our own experiences. In a word, developing and increasing empathy may help to reduce the difficulties we encounter in intercultural communication.

Stereotypes

What are stereotypes?

Only in Texas!

Only in China!

Stereotype, a perception process, is a form of generalization about some group of people. When people have little information about a group of people, they are likely to think of them in a very general way. If they interact with other people who also lack information about the same group, they tend to share the same oversimplified view of that group. So stereotyping is the process of overgeneralizing based on limited or inaccurate information. Take the above pictures as an example. If somebody visiting Texas sees the humorous situation displayed in the picture shown to the left and infers that this may happen only in Texas, he is making stereotypes about Texas. The same can be said about the picture on the right.

Why are stereotypes pervasive?

The reason for the pervasive nature of stereotypes is that human beings have cognitive and psychological needs to categorize and classify. In our daily life, there are numerous occasions when we need to generalize simply in order to make sense of our experiences. Since the world is so large and no one can respond to every situation as if it were entirely new and unique, we depend a lot on our generalizations to deal with the many kinds of people and situations we encounter. In spite of their conveniences, the generalizations we adopt are sometimes too broad or are based on inadequate or outdated information. Such inappropriate generalizations are dangerous and may cause difficulties in our intercultural encounters.

Although stereotypes may result in misleading communication , they are not innate to human beings. Rather, stereotypes are learned in a variety of ways. First, children acquire stereotypes from their parents, relatives and friends. Second, stereotypes develop through limited personal contact. Many may have resulted from direct experience with only one or two people from a particular cultural group. Finally, many stereotypes are provided by the mass media. Television has been guilty of providing distorted images of many ethnic groups.

What are positive and negative stereotypes?

As most stereotypes are based on relatively minimal experiences with particular individuals, they often tend to be inaccurate. This inaccuracy of stereotypes is indicated in two ways determined by how much emphasis is placed on positive or negative attributes of a particular culture. For instance, imagine that you have stereotyped a culture as being very efficient (a positive attribute) but also very rigid and inflexible in their business relationships (a negative attribute). If we tend to overestimate the importance of the culture's positive characteristics, such as its degree of efficiency, while simultaneously ignoring or underestimating its rigidity and other negative characteristics, we are forming a positive stereotype. Conversely, a negative stereotype occurs if we exaggerated the negative attributes while ignoring or devaluing its positive ones.

Stereotypes, especially negative ones, will make us blind to the actual characteristics of a particular cultural group. Take the author as an example. She had an unpleasant experience with her landlady in London and the stereotype formed as a result about cruel British people lasted many years. Yet this is a stereotype that does not apply to every individual in that society.

One more point to observe is that negative stereotypes often lead to prejudice, which is generally defined as negative attitudes toward other people based on assumptions about them. More severely, prejudice may develop into discrimination, which is the behavioral manifestations of that prejudice. Thus discrimination can be thought of as prejudice "in action." The segregation of different races in public places is a typical form of discrimination.

How do stereotypes hamper intercultural communication?

Due to their inaccuracy, stereotypes inevitably become one of the greatest obstacles in intercultural communication. First, stereotypes fail to specify individual characteristics. As we have suggested, stereotypes often are assumed to apply to all or most of the members of a particular group or category, resulting in a tendency to ignore differences among the individual members of the group. Therefore, stereotypes overlook individual characteristics. The result is that a specific person is not treated as a unique individual but as a typical member of a group or a category. Second, stereotypes also keep us from communicating successfully because they are oversimplified, overgeneralized, or exaggerated. Based on half-truths, distortions, and often untrue premises, this type of stereotyping error will provide us with incomplete and inaccurate images about people with whom we are interacting. Third, stereotypes tend to impede intercultural communication in that they repeat and reinforce beliefs until they are often assumed as "true beliefs." For years, women have been pictured as "weak ones" in society, an attitude that may prevent women from advancing in their career. Finally, stereotypes can lead to errors in interpretations and expectations about the behaviors of others. These incorrect interpretations and expectations may make our intercultural communication more difficult because people use their stereotypes to make incorrect judgments about specific individuals and events.

How can we go beyond stereotypes?

How can we learn about another culture without falling into stereotyping? It will help recognize that no two groups are either totally different or exactly the same. When we make generalizations or try to form stereotypes, we need to be very careful, always reminding ourselves that people are different even within one culture in spite of the many things they share. Thus, these generalizations may apply to some people to a certain extent at certain times, but certainly not universally true all the time.

Although stereotyping is an essential tool to enable human beings to communicate with each other, successful intercultural communication requires us to possess the ability to move beyond stereotypes and to respond to the individuals with whom we communicate. Stereotypes based on previous experiences should be used only as guidelines or suggested interpretations rather than as hard and fast categories or evaluations of a certain cultural group.

Understanding and Speaking Interculturally

1 Question: Look at the picture below, there is a man on the bus who killed a passenger. Who, do you think, is the killer?

2 Group work: Read the following poem and share your interpretations with group members.

We and They

Father, Mother, and Me
Sister and Auntie say
All the people like us are We,
And everyone else is They.
And They live over the sea,
While We live over the way,
But—would you believe it?—
They look upon We
As only a sort of They!

We eat pork and beef
With cow-horn-handled knives.
They who gobble their rice off a leaf,
Are horrified out of Their lives;
And They who live up a tree,
And feast on grubs and clay,
(Isn't it scandalous?) look upon We
As a simply disgusting They!

We shoot birds with a gun.
They stick lions with spears.
Their full-dress is un-.
We dress up to Our ears.
They like Their friends for tea.
We like Our friends to stay;
And, after all that,
They look upon We
As an utterly ignorant They!

We eat kitcheny food.
We have doors that latch.
They drink milk or blood,
Under an open thatch.
We have Doctors to fee.
They have Wizards to pay.

And (impudent heathen!) They look upon We
　As a quite impossible They!

All good people agree,
And all good people say,
All nice people, like Us, are We
And everyone else is They:
But if you cross over the sea,
Instead of over the way,
You may end by (think of it!)
looking on We
As only a sort of They

Notes

1. cow-horn-handled: 牛角做柄的
2. gobble: 狼吞虎咽地吃
3. grubs: 蛆
4. thatch: 茅草屋顶
5. Wizards: 术士
6. impudent heathen: 放肆的异教徒

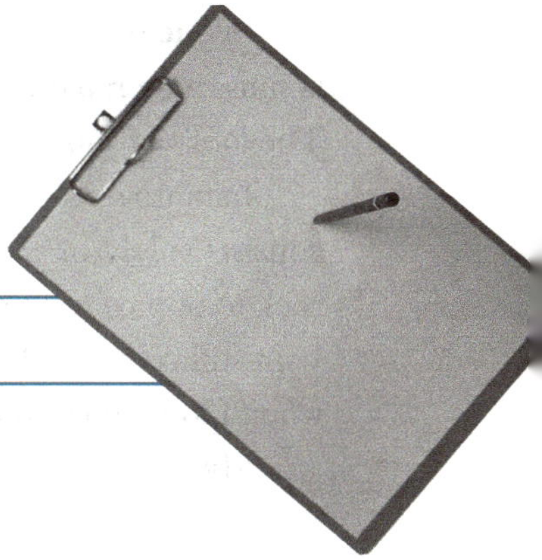

Section C Case

Introduction to the Case

"I know we're on planet earth but what planet are you on?"

Massachusetts teenager Kamaal Majeed believes that being content with himself and defining his own life are more important than going along with any racial stereotypes that his peers may try to force upon him. The following essay of his describes how he deals with the ethnocentric and stereotyping ideas of his peers.

The Scenario

Ethnocentrism and Stereotypes: Being Content with Myself

By *Kamaal Majeed*

Why don't you act black? Since my middle school years, I've been asked this question more than any other. It seems to me that too many people have what society programs into their brains, what should be expected of me, a black person, before ever interacting with me. But I believe in being who I am, not who others want me to be.

On my first day of high school, going into math class, two of my classmates pointed and laughed at me. I initially thought my fly was open, or that something was stuck in my teeth. But as I took my seat, I heard one of the students whisper, why is a black person taking honors? So my fly wasn't open. An honors-level class had simply been joined by a student whose skin was an unsettling shade of brown.

Many people think that my clothes should be big enough for me to live in, or expect me to listen exclusively to black music. In seventh grade, a group of my peers fixed their cold stares on my outfit. Cargo shorts and a plain, fitting T-shirt. They called out to me, go get some gangsta clothes, white boy.

In one of my Spanish classes, as part of a review exercise, the teacher asked me, Te gusta mas, la musica de rap o rock? Do you like rap music or rock music more? I replied, La musica de rock. The looks of shock on my classmates' faces made me feel profoundly alienated.

I am now in my junior year of high school. I still take all honors courses. My wardrobe still consists solely of clothes that are appropriate to my proportions. My music library spans from rock to pop to techno, and almost everything in between. When it comes to choosing my friends, I am still colorblind. I continue to do my best work in school in order to reach my goals. And yet, when I look in the mirror, I still see skin of that same shade of brown.

My skin color has done nothing to change my personality, and my personality has done nothing to change my skin color.

I believe in being myself. I believe that I—not any stereotype—should define who I am and what actions I take in life. In high school, popularity often depends on your willingness to follow trends. And I've been told that it doesn't get much easier going into adulthood. But the only other option is to sacrifice my individuality for the satisfaction and approval of others. Sure, this can be appealing, since choosing to keep my self-respect intact has made me unpopular and disliked at times, with no end to that in sight. But others' being content with me is not nearly as important as my being content with myself.

Notes

take honors

Take an honors course. Honors courses refer to programs in which students can get access to new material or new ways of thinking about material, as well as making them more skilled in analysis and communication.

unsettling

disturbing

techno

Any of various styles of dance music characterized by electronic sounds and a high-energy, rhythmic beat.

Understanding and Speaking Interculturally

Exercise 1 Listen for the first time and fill in the blanks with the information you hear.

What my peers expect of me	I'm being who I am
take ordinary courses	take 1)_______________ courses
wear something 2)_______________	wear clothes of appropriate size
like only 3)_______________ music	like 4)_______________ music as well

Exercise 2 Listen for the second time and fill in the blanks.

1. It seems to me that too many people have what society 1)_______________ their brains, what should 2)_______________ of me, a black person, before ever 3)_______________ me.

2. On my first day of high school, going into math class, two of my classmates pointed and laughed at me. I 4) ______ thought my fly was open, or that something was stuck in my teeth. But as I took my seat, I heard one of the students 5) ______, why is a black person 6) ______? So my fly wasn't open. An honors-level class had simply been joined by a student whose skin was 7) ______.

3. I am now in my junior year of high school. I still take all honors courses. My wardrobe still 8) ______ clothes that are 9) ______ to my proportions. My music library 10) ______ rock to pop to techno, and almost everything in between. 11) ______ choosing my friends, I am still colorblind. I continue to do my best work in school in order to reach my goals. And yet, when I look in the mirror, I still see skin of that same shade of brown.

4. I believe in being myself. I believe that I—not any stereotype—should 12) ______ who I am and what actions I take in life. In high school, 13) ______ often depends on your willingness to 14) ______. And I've been told that it doesn't get much easier going into adulthood. But the only other option is to 15) ______ the satisfaction and approval of others. Sure, this can be appealing, since choosing to keep my self-respect intact has made me unpopular and disliked at times, with no end to that in sight. But others' being content with me is not nearly as important as my being content with myself.

Exercise 3 Explore interculturally.

1. What are some of the ethnocentric ideas Kamaal Majeed's peers have about themselves?

2. How do you interpret the sentence "My skin color has done nothing to change my personality, and my personality has done nothing to change my skin color."?

3. Explore the origin of the name of our country "Zhongguo" and analyze the ethnocentric attitudes the name implies.

4. Have you formed any stereotypes towards certain groups of people around you? What are they? How do they affect your communication with them? Have you found any ways to overcome those stereotypes?

5. In your real life, have you ever met somebody like Kamaal Majeed who acts very differently from other members of his social group? How have you reacted to his behavior?

Culture Shock and Adaptation

Section A Movie clip

Introduction to the Movie *The Terminal*

Viktor Navorski has planned to visit New York to fulfil his father's wish of getting the autograph of a jazz player. When he arrives at New York City's John F. Kennedy International Airport, officials inform him that his visa has been canceled. During the time he was flying to the US, his country Krakozhia has experienced a political coup. The President and other leaders have been murdered by rebel forces. There is a new government in place and all travelling have been suspended by this new government. As a matter of fact, neither his passport nor visa had been valid. Over the next nine months, Viktor is forced to live in the terminal building, unable either to enter the United States or to return home. During his stay in the terminal, he experiences a lot of culture shock. However, he tries to adapt himself to the small "foreign" world he inhabits and eventually survives.

Introduction to the Selected Scene

In the selected scene, Viktor has just been told that a rebellion has taken place in his country. Although he can not quite understand English, he sees the news broadcast on TV. He is very anxious and tries to call home, but nobody at the airport is willing to help him understand how to use the telephone card. He is so depressed that he sits down to organize the food vouchers that the airport has provided him for meals. While he is trying to help a young girl with her suitcase, the cleaning person throws his food vouchers into the garbage can. As a result, he is not able to get food to eat, and has nowhere to sleep. Life in the terminal becomes really hard for him.

Script of the Scene

[The officer of Customs and Border Protection (CBP) and Viktor walk into the terminal Building]

CBP officer: Now, Mr. Novorski. Mr. Novorski. Mr. Novorski. This is the International Transit Lounge. You are free to wait here. These are food vouchers. You can use them in the food court. Your Krakozhia money is no good here. This is a 15-minute, prepaid calling card. You may call home, if you like. This, in case we need to contact you, is a pager. You must keep this with you at all times. Here is an ID badge for you to get into CBP. Beyond those doors, Mr. Novorski, I'm going to need you to look at me. Beyond those doors is American soil. Mr. Dixon wants me to make it clear that you are not

	to enter through those doors. You are not to leave this building. America is closed.
Viktor:	America closed. What I do?
CBP officer:	There is only one thing you can do here, Mr. Novorski. Shop.

(With these words, the officer leaves, leaving Viktor alone in the terminal, not knowing what to do. The TV is broadcasting the bad news about his country's rebellion. Watching this, Viktor becomes very anxious and shocked, he wishes somebody could help him.)

TV broadcaster:	...the international community tries to secure a peaceful resolution. Meanwhile, the populace has to wonder if they will ever find political stability or find the leadership to secure their place on the world stage. And next hour, looking to buy a 90-foot yacht?

(Viktor is anxious and begins to run in the terminal. The TV broadcast continues)

TV broadcaster:	...taken hostage. We're hearing that the Vice President has been killed, along with 4 cabinet members, 13 injured soldiers and 20 civilians. By dawn, rebel leaders had surrounded the state houses. In a symbolic gesture, the national flag of Krakozhia was torn down from the Presidential Palace and the Parliament building.

(Viktor tries to stop the TV program)

Viktor:	(pointing at the TV) Please, please, television.

(Viktor begins to speak his own language and no one understands him. In the end, he gets to the second floor.)

TV broadcaster:	This is just in from our overseas stereo. Last night a military coup overthrew the government of Krakozhia. Bombing and gunfire were heard through the night. Although the details are unclear, we are told that President Vogabagin and his aides have been taken hostage.
CBP officer:	Bonjour, monsieur. You are a Red Carpet Club member? (Viktor speaks his own language) I need to see your boarding pass and club card, sir? (Viktor continues speaking his own language) I'm sorry, sir. This is a private lounge. The public lounge is downstairs.

(Viktor returns downstairs, trying to make a phone call back home, but he can't understand the instructions on the card. So he tries to ask somebody for help.)

Passerby: Watch it!

Viktor: Please. Please. Telephone? Telephone?

Viktor: (to people walking by) Please. Please.

(Hopelessly, Viktor sits down to organize his food vouchers. A girl beside him is trying to close her suitcase and Viktor puts down the food tickets, intending to help her. Unfortunately, he tries so hard that the suitcase breaks. At the same time, his food vouchers are blown away on the floor and the cleaning person picks them up and throws them into the garbage can.)

Girl: Oh my God. Oh, my God, you broke my bag! I got this in Paris. This is my favorite bag. I can't believe you just broke my bag! Mom, Dad! He broke my bag!

(Finding his food vouchers gone, Viktor runs to the cleaning person, trying to get his vouchers back)

Viktor: Food document.

Cleaning person: Excuse me. Stop it. Stop it. Do you have an appointment? I don't let anyone to look at my trash without an appointment.

Viktor: er…

Cleaning person: I have an opening next Tuesday.

Viktor: Tuesday?

Cleaning person: Tuesday.

Viktor: Monday, Tuesday, Wednesday. Tuesday?

Cleaning person: Tuesday. It will be good time for you to come back and get lost. OK, goodbye. Sorry.

Viktor: Tuesday.

(Without food, Viktor has to find a place to sleep. He comes to Gate 67 and puts some chairs together, making himself a bed. Right when he was about to go to sleep, an airplane flashes exactly over Viktor. He is very scared and puts up his hands.)

Viktor: Don't shoot!

New Words

badge *n.* a small piece of metal, cloth, or plastic with a picture or words on it, worn to show authority, rank, membership of a group, support for a political idea or belief, etc 徽章；标记；象征

lounge *n.* a waiting room（机场的）等候室

pager *n.* a small device, carried in a pocket, that makes short high noises to tell the person carrying it that someone is trying to reach him 寻呼机

populace *n.* (fml) the people who live in a country（正式用语）平民；百姓；民众

voucher *n.* a kind of ticket that can be used instead of money for a particular purpose 代金券；凭证

Phrases and Expressions

take hostage
seize someone and use him as a prisoner 抓走某人扣作人质

boarding pass
a boarding card 登机证

Notes

Bonjour, monsieur
French words meaning "Good morning, sir."

Krakozhia
the fictional country of Viktor in the movie

the International Transit Lounge
a waiting room at an international airport

Understanding and Speaking Interculturally

Exercise 1 Answer the following questions according to the movie clip you have just watched.

1. Why does Viktor fail to get his food vouchers back?

2. From the movie clip, can you infer what kind of person Viktor is?

3. What kind of culture shock does Viktor encounter in the movie clip?

4. What do you think has caused his culture shock at the airport?

Exercise 2 Fill in the blanks according to the movie clip you have just watched.

1. **Viktor:** America closed. ________?
   CBP officer: There is only one thing you can do here, Mr. Novorski. ________.

2. **Viktor:** Food ________.
   Cleaner: Excuse me. Stop it. Stop it. Do you have an appointment? I don't let anyone ________ without an appointment.

Exercise 3 Put the following sentences in the right order according to the movie clip you have just watched.

1. Viktor helps the girl to close her suitcase.

2. Viktor is anxious to know what the TV is broadcasting about his country.

3. The CBP officer gives Viktor some instructions about staying in the terminal.

4. Viktor tries to retrieve his food vouchers.

5. Viktor is afraid of being shot while he sleeps.

6. No one will help Viktor with his telephone calling card, leaving him feeling isolated and alone in the terminal.

Exercise 4 Discuss in the groups what you would do if you were Viktor at such a difficult time. After the discussion, each group should present their ideas to the class.

Exercise 5 Divide the class into several groups and perform the scene with the help of the script.

Section B Reading

Culture Shock

What is culture shock?

Culture shock is defined as the following by Professor Linell Davis, an expert in both Western and Chinese culture with a rich educational background and research experience in both America and China.

Culture shock: Troublesome feelings such as depression, loneliness, confusion, inadequacy, hostility, frustration, and tension, caused by the loss of familiar cues from the home culture (Davis, 2007).

As this definition implies, the "shock" in culture shock emphasizes the pain and doubt that a person experiences when faced with a significantly new experience. This is perfectly normal when you are first confronted with a new culture and may occasionally occur in other situations as well. That is to say, people from the same culture may also experience culture shock. Take our trip to another city within our country as an example. On our first arrival, despite understanding the local language, we may not be accustomed to the local food, the weather or even the way people behave. At one time or another, we may experience all the feelings described in the previous definition. As a result, the unpleasant feeling of discomfort will settle over us, even though it is not a foreign culture that has triggered it.

Many factors bring about culture shock. Some factors involve the characteristics of the communicating participants and others are related to the situation to which the participants are trying to adapt. The traditional explanation for the onset of culture shock is somewhat linked with the sorrow people feel after losing their beloved ones. Modern theories concerning the factors causing culture shock include the following three: the theory of negative events, the theory of decrease in social support and the theory of different values.

Symptoms of culture shock

People experiencing culture shock may undergo a series of uncomfortable changes both physically and mentally. Generally speaking, the symptoms of culture shock are first experienced psychologically. When someone arrives in a new culture, he may feel very lonely as the result of being in an unfamiliar environment. The loneliness and helplessness cause anxiety and unease, resulting in withdrawal. As time goes by, the mental discomfort may cause many physical discomforts as well, such as insomnia, inattentiveness, loss of appetite and even headaches.

Over time the increasing mental and physical discomfort may lead to disruptions and fragility in the person's social life. For example, he may constantly make phone calls back home or write letters to relieve stress, indulge in smoking or drinking, or become increasingly engaged in religious activities. Consequently, the person may lose self-confidence and become over-dependent on others. In a word, someone suffering from culture shock may lead a life of great difficulty in a foreign culture.

Intercultural Adaptation

The adaptation process

Intercultural adaptation refers to the process of acclimatizing to the demands of a new cultural environment. It addresses the needs of travelers or new immigrants to cope with the distress caused by incongruity between the host culture and one's native culture. Adaptation is a process with identifiable stages. Learning about the process will not prevent culture shock, but it will help people understand what is happening to them.

Although scholars have not reached a consensus view as to the exact number of stages or their names, there is general agreement that the process of intercultural adaptation follows the "U-curve" pattern shown in Figure 13-1. Taking into consideration the reverse culture shock when returning to one's home culture, the "W-curve" pattern results, as in Figure 13-2.

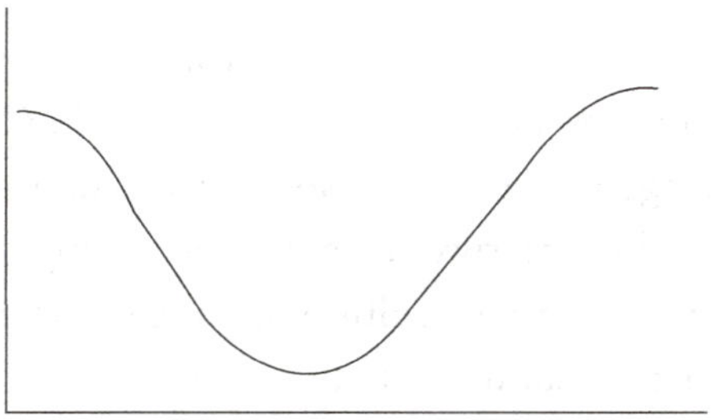

Figure 13-1 U-curve Pattern

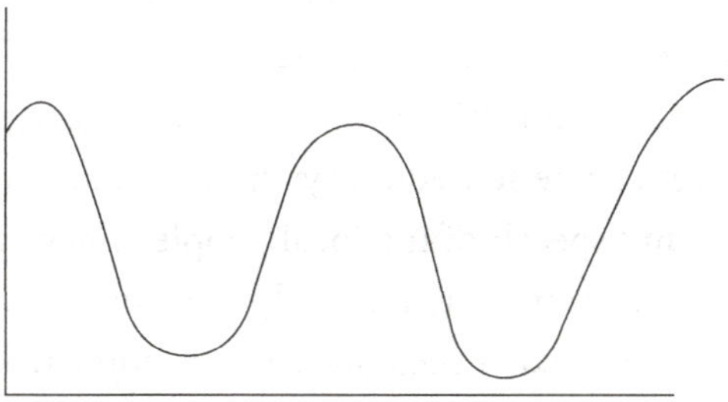

Figure 13-2 W-curve Pattern

Stages of intercultural adaptation

According to Davis (2007), typically people experience the following stages as they adapt to a new cultural situation. As illustrated by Figure 13-3, the diagram illustrating the stages of the adaptation process depicts a line that rises and falls over time, representing an individual's sense of well-being and comfort.

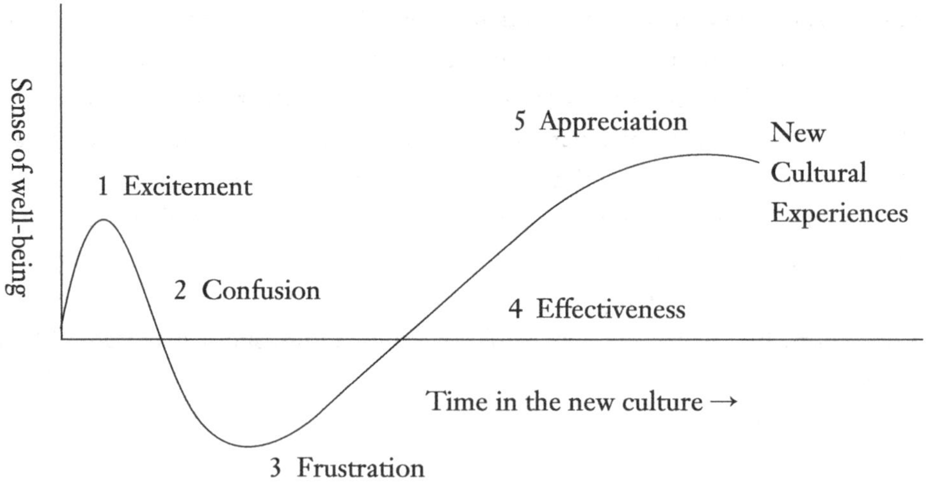

Figure 13-3 Stages of Adaptation to A New Culture

Stage One: Excitement about the new situation

The excitement that characterizes this stage typically continues through the early period after arriving in a new culture. Most people who go abroad to live temporarily or permanently in a new culture choose to do so willingly, usually with some specific purpose in mind such as furthering their education, pursuing economic or professional opportunities, or simply experiencing something new. Thus, they usually anticipate the experience with a great deal of excitement, stirring up more energy than usual. On the chart this is shown as an increase in feelings of well-being above the baseline.

Stage Two: Confusion when faced with the hidden aspects of culture

As the diagram shows, with the onset of confusion, the line falls sharply, meaning that someone in an unfamiliar culture often experiences a sudden decline in mood or spirit. Cultural differences can be sensed everywhere. Often at this stage newcomers misread or misinterpret the behavior and speech of the local people. They also tend to interpret meanings according to their own cultural grammar. This helps explain why a person in a new culture often feels disoriented and unable to predict accurately what people from the new culture will do or say.

At this time, the newcomer can avoid or postpone many of these problems by living in an enclave, a special community of people from the home culture. Here the newcomer feels understood and can get realistic help in coping with the new culture. Yet living in an enclave is not a final solution to intercultural adaptation problems, although it eases the strain of the early period of life in the new culture. However, the newcomer eventually has to move out from the enclave emotionally as well as physically in order to adapt to the new culture successfully.

Stage Three: Frustration when old ways of dealing with situations fail to work

At this point, the person's mood and sense of well-being are at their lowest point as represented by the bottom of the curve shown in the diagram of the adaptation process. The confusion, self-doubt and depression of the second stage are replaced by more negative attitudes toward the new culture. Instead of blaming or doubting himself, the newcomer starts to put the blame for his difficulties on the new culture and its people.

To some degree, this is an improvement, because it shows that the newcomer is paying more attention to what local people around him are actually doing. Encountering unpleasant experiences with people from the host culture, the newcomer may first feel very angry and frustrated, without knowing how to deal with them. But as time goes by, his anger and frustration will spur greater attentiveness, which will equip him with some helpful experiences at communicating interculturally.

Stage Four: Effectiveness as new skills are acquired

During the third stage the newcomer has negative feelings but acts more assertively to deal with the new culture. In time these efforts pay off, and the newcomer becomes more effective at coping with his surroundings. He is gaining intercultural skills that lead to more positive experiences. As a result, once he starts to feel more positively about the new culture, his outlook becomes more optimistic.

At this stage, the person (no longer a newcomer) is now a sensitive observer of life in the new culture and uses that ability to observe and to learn new behaviors. By this time, he knows what facial expressions and body movements are called for in most situations. He knows what he can say or should say, and knows what to avoid saying. He is able to make more accurate judgments about the behaviors of the host country's people, and he can choose his responses deliberately rather than being overwhelmed by feelings of doubt or anger. These new behaviors bring him some success and this in turn helps him to become more relaxed. In a word, the person is able to accept both the similarities and the differences between his home culture and the new culture. He is becoming more sensitive to local people and, as a result, his relationships with them are becoming warmer and more personal. Life is definitely becoming more comfortable.

Stage Five: Appreciation as new skills and attitudes enable the person to live more fully in the new situation

In this stage the person moves beyond effectiveness in the new culture to an attitude of appreciation. He is developing a more personal understanding of the new culture and values it. The person is able to live a full life, experiencing the full range of human feelings in the new culture. The person can love, trust, laugh and solve problems, participating in a range of activities possible at home. He is becoming more creative and expressive and acquiring the ability to take initiative and responsibility.

From the diagram of the adaptation process, we see that in the appreciation stage the person may be functioning at a higher level and is likely to feel even better than during the excitement stage. The person has grown not just in terms of valuable skills, but also as a human being. The intercultural experience can be a profound learning experience.

Stage six: More challenging intercultural experiences

When a person has successfully adapted to a new culture, he has learned how to "learn" culture. That is a valuable attribute for anyone living in the global village. He is now ready for new intercultural experiences. He will repeat the same adaptation process when he returns to the home culture. He will experience culture shock again as he has already grown used to the foreign culture and perhaps lost touch with his own home culture. This is known as "reentry shock", sometimes a more complicated process because people at home do not expect him to have changed and experience difficulty in understanding him. To overcome this shock, he must undergo the adaptation process one more time. Through the repeated experiences, he will continue to undergo the stress of adaptation, but with acceptance of the vicissitudes of adaptation as a part of life. The person is wiser now and is able to cope with it. If he moves to other new cultures as part of his life, he may become an expert in adaptation.

How can better adaptation be achieved?

In order to adapt to a new culture successfully, we need to develop competence in intercultural communication. It is commonly agreed that competence of this sort can be evaluated from the cognitive, affective and behavioral perspectives. Related to these three dimensions, knowledge, a willing motivation and a mastery of skills are required to better understand a new culture and effectively adapt to it.

Accelerating our adaptation process first requires a commitment to learning about both the culture of others and understanding our own. A standard method can be adopted to help reach this goal, that is, to understand the general rules for interpreting a certain culture. Second, a willingness to explore various cultural experiences without prejudgment is necessary. With strong motivation, we tend to behave more actively and be more tolerant, important qualities in intercultural communication. Finally, an ability to behave appropriately and effectively with culturally different people is required. Appropriate behavior effectively excludes any prejudiced or stereotyped assumptions about other people. Although it is hard to predict what kind of people are more adaptive to a new culture, the requisite knowledge, motivation and skill can certainly help promote the adaptation process.

In terms of appropriate communication skills, the tools of description, interpretation and evaluation are highly recommended in order to enhance successful intercultural communication. A competent communicator should be able to distinguish among statements that are descriptive, interpretative and evaluative. A statement of description details the specific perceptual cues and information a person has received, without judgments or interpretations, resulting in undistorted opinion that helps to reduce intercultural conflicts. Unfortunately, in our everyday interactions, most common speech consists essentially of interpretations and evaluations of what we receive from other interacting participants. Without doubt, these interpretive or evaluative statements will often mislead us into making erroneous judgments or decisions in our intercultural contacts.

The purpose of descriptive statements is that they allow us to identify the sensory information that forms the basis of our interpretations and evaluations. Focusing on descriptive statements, we are less likely to make biased judgments. Through repetitious practice of this tool in interactions with people from diverse cultures, we will experience a greater potential to achieve better adaptation.

Understanding and Speaking Interculturally

1 Pair work: Work with your partner, discuss the stereotypes about the following groups of people and how stereotypes affect our communication.

College professors
Bankers
Northern Chinese
Fat people
Millionaire
Mother
American old people

2 Role play: Divide the class into groups of 4 or 5. Suppose each group is a Chinese group living overseas. The students are supposed to act in a short play, which will reveal the possible difficulties and problems caused by culture shock. Possible solutions need to be detected in the play as well.

3 Suppose a particular student is late for school. Different statements concerning this fact are made as the following:

1) Sam is five minutes late.
2) Sam does not care very much about this particular class.
3) I am really offended by that attitude.
4) Sam also arrived late each of the previous times the class has met.
5) Sam is always late for everything.
6) I like a student who chooses to be enthusiastic about only classes she really likes.

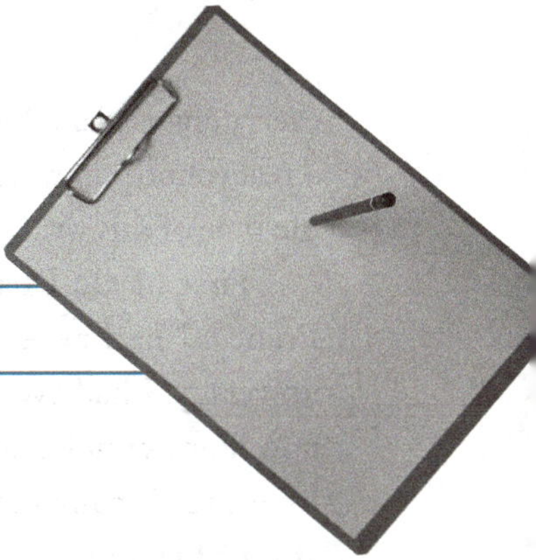

Section C Case

Introduction to the Case

In order to improve her English, Francine Nnyina went to the College of New Jersey to study for one year as an exchange student from France. With the help of teachers and friends in the new school, Francine Nnyina successfully overcame her culture shock as part of her American educational journey.

The Scenario

Culture Shock: The Story of a French Exchange Student

By *Francine Nnyina*

During the current semester, spring 1998, I have been studying at the College of New Jersey on exchange from France, where I live as an international student. Though I am a citizen of the western African country of Cameroon, I spent the majority of my life in the Central African Republic where I completed my elementary through high school education.

Eight years ago, I moved to France to study English at the Universite de Saint-Denis (Paris VIII). I decided to come to the United States a year ago when I realized that in order to further my English studies, I needed to live in an English-speaking country.

Classes in France are organized the same way they are here in the U.S., in a semester system. The only difference is that students can graduate after three years instead of four. I was about to graduate when I resolved to spend some time in America. I decided to learn more about English-speaking culture before I move ahead for my master's degree in Translation from English to French.

When I first came here everything looked so big: the streets, the buildings and the cars. I was not too surprised because America has always been presented to me as the country of dreams where everything is giant. I was excited by the idea that America was no longer just an imaginary country, but a real country in which I had to live for a while. I have already been here for a month-and-a-half (at the time of this writing), and I have noticed some major differences between the countries.

First of all, I have found that in terms of studies, there is much more work here than in France. I had never faced such an amount of work during the three years I had spent at my university. I had even studied American literature, but did not have as many books to read as I do now. For example, my Women Writers class requires at least six books, not counting the excerpts. I have read many novels, and written many essays on them, but I think what I have to do here is at least five times as much as what I did in France.

I guess the difference between the French educational system and the American system is that in France, the courses cover a particular subject in depth, whereas here the classes embrace a large range of topics, but more superficially. However, the interesting point is how the classes are more alive here than in France because the American students are more apt to speak and to express their opinions clearly on a subject.

The classes here are also smaller, which could make them more interactive. But they aren't because most students do not try to study together. This would allow those who understand quickly to help those who do not, but instead each student works alone.

The other thing that astonishes me is the difference in terms of technology. The students here have easier access to computers, allowing them to go to websites for research. In France, some people have computers at home, but the majority do not have access to computers at all. At my university, there are two or three computer laboratories, but they do not meet the needs of around 6,000 students. I have never even heard a professor mention an address for a website. The fact is that they know how hard it is for students to access the Internet.

What I find fantastic is how the professors are more approachable here than in France. The students can easily communicate with them during their office hours without an appointment and through e-mail. The professors really care a lot for their students, especially for me since they know that it sometimes can be difficult for me to understand everything. I really appreciate their attitude because it has helped me a lot.

Understanding and Speaking Interculturally

Exercise 1 Listen for the first time and answer the following questions.

1. What is the nationality of the student?

2. Which course is she studying in the United States?

3. What difficulties has she experienced in the U.S.?

Exercise 2 Listen for the second time and fill in the blanks.

1. During the current semester, spring 1998, I have been studying at the College of New Jersey 1) ______ from France, where I live as an international student. Though I am a citizen of 2) ______ of Cameroon, I spent the majority of my life in the Central African Republic where I completed my 3) ______ education.
2. Classes in France are organized the same way they are here in the U.S., in a 4) ______. The only difference is that students can graduate after three years 5) ______ four. I was about to graduate when I 6) ______ spend some time in America. I decided to learn more about 7) ______ before I move ahead for my master's degree in Translation from English to French.
3. I guess the difference between the French educational system and the American system is that in France, the courses cover a particular subject 8) ______, whereas here the classes embrace a large range of topics, but 9) ______. However, the interesting point is how the classes are 10) ______ here than in France because the American students are more 11) ______ and to express their opinions clearly on a subject.
4. What I find fantastic is how the professors are 12) ______ here than in France. The students can easily communicate with them during their office hours 13) ______ and through e-mail. The professors really 14) ______ their students, especially for me since they know that it sometimes can be difficult for me to understand everything. I really 15) ______ because it has helped me a lot.

Exercise 3 Explore interculturally.

1. Can you explain what is behind the culture shock the girl experienced?

2. Have you ever encountered any culture shock in your communication with your foreign teachers or foreign friends? Tell your partner about your story.

Acculturation and Identity

Section A Movie clip

Introduction to the Movie *My Big Fat Greek Wedding*

Toula Portokalos is a 30-year-old Greek woman who lives in Chicago and works in her family's restaurant called Dancing Zorba's. Living in America, the Portokalos family has never forgotten that their roots are Greek. The children all attend Greek school and the father Gus talks about traditional Greek culture. As for Toula, all her father wants is for her to marry a nice Greek boy. But Toula is looking for more in life. Her mother convinces Gus to let her take some computer classes at college. With those classes under her belt, she then takes over her aunt's travel agency. She meets Ian Miller, a high school English teacher and dates secretly for a while before her family finds out. Her father is depressed at her dating a non-Greek man. He has to learn to accept Ian, just as Ian must learn to accept Toula's huge family and their Greek culture.

Introduction to the Selected Scene

In the selected scene, Toula describes the kind of life her family leads in Chicago, with its Greek heritage. Their house is built in the Greek style with statues of gods guarding it. In order to show where they are from, a Greek flag hangs on the house. Toula attended Greek school to learn Greek, and when she grew older, her father has insisted she marry a Greek man. Even in everyday life, her father has never forgotten to search for the source of every word in the Greek language.

Script of the Scene

(Toula and her father are in their car.)

Toula's father: You better get married soon. You're starting to look old.

Toula: My Dad has been saying that to me since I was 15 because nice Greek girls are supposed to do three things in life: marry Greek boys, make Greek babies and feed everyone until the day we die.

(They get out of the car and enter their restaurant "Dancing Zorba's.")

Toula: When I was growing up, I knew I was different. The other girls were blonde and delicate. I was a swarthy 6-year-old with side-burns. I so badly wanted to be like the popular girls, all sitting together, talking, eating their Wonder Bread sandwiches.

(Toula and her peers are eating)

Girl: What's that?

Toula: It's Moussaka.

Girl: Moose ka-ka.

Toula: And while the pretty girls got to go to Brownies, I had to go to Greek school. At Greek school, I learned valuable lessons like "If Nike has one goat and Maria has nine, how soon will they marry?"

(Toula repeats Greek after the teacher)

Toula: My Mom was always cooking foods filled with warmth and wisdom and never forgetting that side dish of steaming-hot guilt.

Toula's mother: Niko, don't play with the food. When I was your age, we didn't have food.

Toula: Ma?

Toula's mother: What?

Toula: Why do I have to go to Greek school?

Toula's mother: When you get married, don't you want to be able to write your mother-in-law a letter? Niko, come on, eat!

Toula: We lived in a normal, middle-class Chicago neighborhood of tasteful, modest homes. Our house, however, was modeled after the Parthenon, complete with Corinthian columns, and guarded by statues of the gods. In case the neighbors had any doubts about our heritage, they could just check out our subtle tribute to the Greek flag. My Dad believed in only two things that Greeks should educate non-Greeks about being Greek and that any ailment, from psoriasis to poison ivy, could be cured with Windex. Six years later, I was 12. Athena, my older, perfect sister, was 15. And my brother, Nike, was 11. Every morning my Dad would lecture us on "the history of our people, the great civilization, the Greeks."

Toula's father: Ok, now, name three things the Greeks did first.

Athena: Astronomy, philosophy and democracy.

Toula's father: Bravo! Very good! (driving Toula and her friends to school) Now give me a word, any word and I show you, how the root of that word is Greek.

Toula: Sweet Lord, again.

Toula's father: How about "arachnophobia"? "Arachno" that comes from the Greek word for spider and "phobia" is a phobia, it means "fear."

So, "fear of spiders." There you go.

Girls: Ok, Mr. Portokolas, how about the word "kimono"?

Toula's father: Kimono? Good one. Kimono, Kimono. Of course, kimono comes from the Greek word "cheimonas", which means "winter." So what do you wear in wintertime to stay warm? A robe. You see, "robe", "kimono." There you go.

(The girls get out of the car)

Toula's father: Bye-bye.

Girls: Good bye, Mr. Portokolas.

Toula's father: Toula, You should be proud to be Greek.

New Words

ailment *n.* an illness that is usually not very serious 小病

arachnophobia *n.* fear of spiders 蜘蛛恐惧症

kimono *n.* a traditional piece of Japanese clothing like a long coat, that is worn at special ceremonies（日本的）和服

moose *n.* a large brown animal like a deer that lives in North America and northern Europe 麋；驼鹿

poison ivy *n.* a bush or vine that causes the skin to blister and itch 野葛

psoriasis *n.* an illness which makes your skin dry, red, and flaky 牛皮癣；银屑病

swarthy *adj.* having dark skin 肤色黝黑的；黑不溜秋的

Phrases and Expressions

side dish

a small amount of food such as a salad that you eat with a main meal 小菜；配菜

steaming-hot

very hot 十分炎热的；滚烫的

tribute to

be a clear sign of the good qualities that someone or something has（某些优良品质的）标示；证明

Notes

Brownies

a young girls' service organization, usually for members between 7 and 10

ka-ka

indirect expression for "shit", usually by grade school children

Moussaka

a cooked salad made up primarily of tomatoes and eggplant that is popular in Greece and Turkey

Parthenon

A temple in honor of the Greek goddess Athena, built in the 5th century BC. It is the most important surviving building of Classical Greece, and is one of the world's greatest cultural monuments.

Wonder Bread

a favorite brand of white bread in America

Windex

A cleaning product for glass and hard surfaces, manufactured since 1933 and popular in the United States and Canada since the mid-20th century.

Understanding and Speaking Interculturally

Exercise 1 Fill in the blanks with the information from the movie clip to make clear what kind of life Toula was living in America.

Item	Description
house	
food	
school	
daily life	

Exercise 2 Fill in the blanks according to the movie clip you have just watched.

1. **Toula's father:** You better get married soon. You're starting to ______ ______.

   Toula: My Dad has been saying that to me since I was 15 because nice Greek girls are supposed to do three things in life: ______ ______ until the day we die.

2. **Toula:** We lived in a normal, middle-class Chicago neighborhood of tasteful, modest homes. Our house, however, was modeled after the Parthenon, complete with Corinthian columns, and guarded by statues of the gods. In case the neighbors had any doubts about our heritage, they could just check out our subtle tribute to the Greek flag. My Dad believed in only two things that ______ ______ and that any ailment, from psoriasis to poison ivy, could be cured with Windex. Six years later, I was

12. Athena, my older, perfect sister, was 15. And my brother, Nike, was 11. Every morning my Dad would lecture us on __________________.

Exercise 3 Explore interculturally.

1. Why does Toula's father hang a Greek flag together with an American flag on their house?

2. Why does Toula's father insist on her marrying a Greek boy?

3. If you were Toula's father, would you hold on to your original culture and stick to your native identity, or would you manage to assimilate into the new culture? Why?

Section B Reading

In the preceding chapter, the adaptation process has been described in terms of a curve. However, this graphic depiction excludes other aspects of the adaptation process. For instance, it does not account for those whose experiences remain consistently favorable, for those who fail to adapt at all and return home prematurely, or for those whose level of discomfort changes little throughout the entire process. In fact, the pattern for every individual may be somewhat different. So a more general term, "acculturation," is used to subsume various forms of cultural or individual adaptation.

What Is Acculturation?

Acculturation is a type of cultural change that results from continuous firsthand contact between two distinct cultural groups. It refers to the process by which individuals change their psychological characteristics, change the surrounding context, or change the amount of contact in order to achieve a better fit (outcome) with other features of the system in which they carry out their life (Lusting & Koester, 1996).

In light of this definition, when individuals acculturate, they learn how to adapt to a given situation. There is no doubt that each individual will adapt in different ways due to different cultural backgrounds and their psychological make-up as well. Acculturation not only refers to the changes that the acculturating individual or group will make; the host group will also undergo changes in response to the influences introduced by people from other cultures.

What Are Typical Acculturation Strategies?

As mentioned in the previous section, when encountering a new culture, different people may react differently to their new environment. Many scholars have made great efforts to define those differences. The best-known model was developed by John W. Berry (1987), and comprises four acculturation strategies.

Berry based his strategy model on the answers to two prevailing questions that individuals must confront in their daily life. The first question concerns whether to maintain or reject their own cultural values. The second question concerns whether to accept or reject the host culture's cultural values. By recognizing both the extent to which immigrants wish to maintain their traditional culture and the degree to which they desire contact with the host society, a conceptual framework results containing four types of acculturation strategies. These are: assimilation, separation, integration and marginalization.

Integration occurs, when individuals accept both their native cultural values and those of the host culture. Individuals who adopt the strategy of assimilation discard their own cultural values and identity, and accept those of the host culture. Separation ensues when individuals accept their own cultural values and identity, and reject those of the host culture. Marginalization refers to individuals' rejection of the values and identities of both cultures. The following table summarizes the four strategies.

		Is it considered valuable to maintain one's original cultural identity and characteristics?	
		Yes	No
Is it considered valuable to maintain relationships with host groups?	Yes	Integration	Separation
	No	Assimilation	Marginalization

Table 14.1 Strategies of Acculturation

Berry's research with various immigrant groups shows that integration is the preferred mode of acculturation, followed either by assimilation or separation, while marginalization is the least preferred mode. However, it is obvious that individuals and groups do not have complete freedom to choose their particular strategy for acculturation, since the "choice" of strategy largely depends on how the dominant society responds to the acculturating group. For example, integration can only be freely chosen and successfully pursued by acculturating individuals or groups when the dominant society is open and inclusive in its orientation towards cultural diversity. Thus, a mutual accommodation is required for integration to be attained. This is why acculturation, unlike adaptation, results in changes in the host culture, as well.

What Is Identity?

Identity is an umbrella term used throughout the social sciences to describe an individual's comprehension of him or herself as a discrete, separate entity. In the discipline of intercultural communication, identity actually refers to the mental image of oneself and other individuals (Samovar, Porter & Stefani, 2005).

What Has Acculturation Brought to Identity?

As previously stated, acculturation represents a kind of cultural shift. This kind of change inevitably leads to changes in identity. These are particularly remarkable in groups known as intercultural transients, such as international business travelers, different groups of laborers and sailors, who frequently move between their initial host country and home, maintaining more than one place of residence. A primary challenge for transients is how to negotiate their cultural identity. Who are they? To which culture do they belong? Which cultural values do they embrace?

By experiencing Berry's four acculturation strategies, people achieve different cultural identities. Some adopt an identity as a member of the host culture, foregoing their original birth culture. Others try to maintain their original identity in the process of acculturating. In the case of marginalization, those associated with this strategy actually deny both their original identity and the identity their new culture has to offer. This group of people is often viewed as lost in terms of their cultural identity. Perhaps, if they move across different cultures freely, they may never feel a complete sense of self-identity wherever they go. No matter where they happen to live, they never quite feel at home anywhere.

Moving to a new culture, no one can avoid the identity conflict. Generally, identity conflict occurs when a new component of identity is incompatible with an existing one. Many factors determine the level of identity conflict. Factors such as tolerance of ambiguity, length of residence and the degree and quality of contact with host nationals affect the outcome of identity conflict, in addition to cultural distance and perceived discrimination.

What Can Be Done?

In order to reduce identity conflict, it is helpful to try to negotiate some compromises among different cultural identities. It is often recognized that travelers and immigrants may not only be influenced by the host culture, but also largely retain their cultural values or, alternatively, develop an entirely new, expanded identity that transcends either the original cultural identity or the identity of the host culture.

Kim proposed the term "intercultural identity" to refer to the perfect negotiation of cultural identities. Intercultural identity assumes an open-ended, adaptive, and transformative "self-other" orientation. The term involves two key elements—individuation and universalization in self-other orientation. Individuation involves both a clear self-definition and the definition of "other" as a singular individual rather than a member of a conventional social category. In this capacity, one is better able to see oneself and others in terms of unique individual qualities rather than group stereotypes. This element of individuation is significant, given the fact that the greatest error potential in intercultural communication lies in the overgeneralization about cultural individuals or groups.

The other element, universalization, focuses on the universal aspect of human nature, which will enable people to see the common humanity that exists across different cultures and to observe their common features, even among the points of difference. As people advance in the process of identity transformation, they are able to adopt vital outlook that rises above the provincial interests of one's own group membership. Instead, the individual sees himself or herself to be a part of a larger whole that includes other groups, as well. In fact, this element of intercultural identity helps us be more tolerant of all kinds of cultures and ethnicities.

In conclusion, intercultural identity assumes a more open, flexible and inclusive mindset towards both ourselves and others. Changing cultural identities is not an act of "surrendering" one's personal and cultural integrity, but an act of cultural respect for differences. This process will lead us to function more appropriately and effectively as we engage in intercultural communication in our rapidly globalizing world.

Understanding and Speaking Interculturally

1 Brainstorm: Write the phrase "I am..." on a piece of paper and quickly finish the sentence in various ways. Notice what are some of the most important images of yourself. For example, you may write down "I am a Chinese."

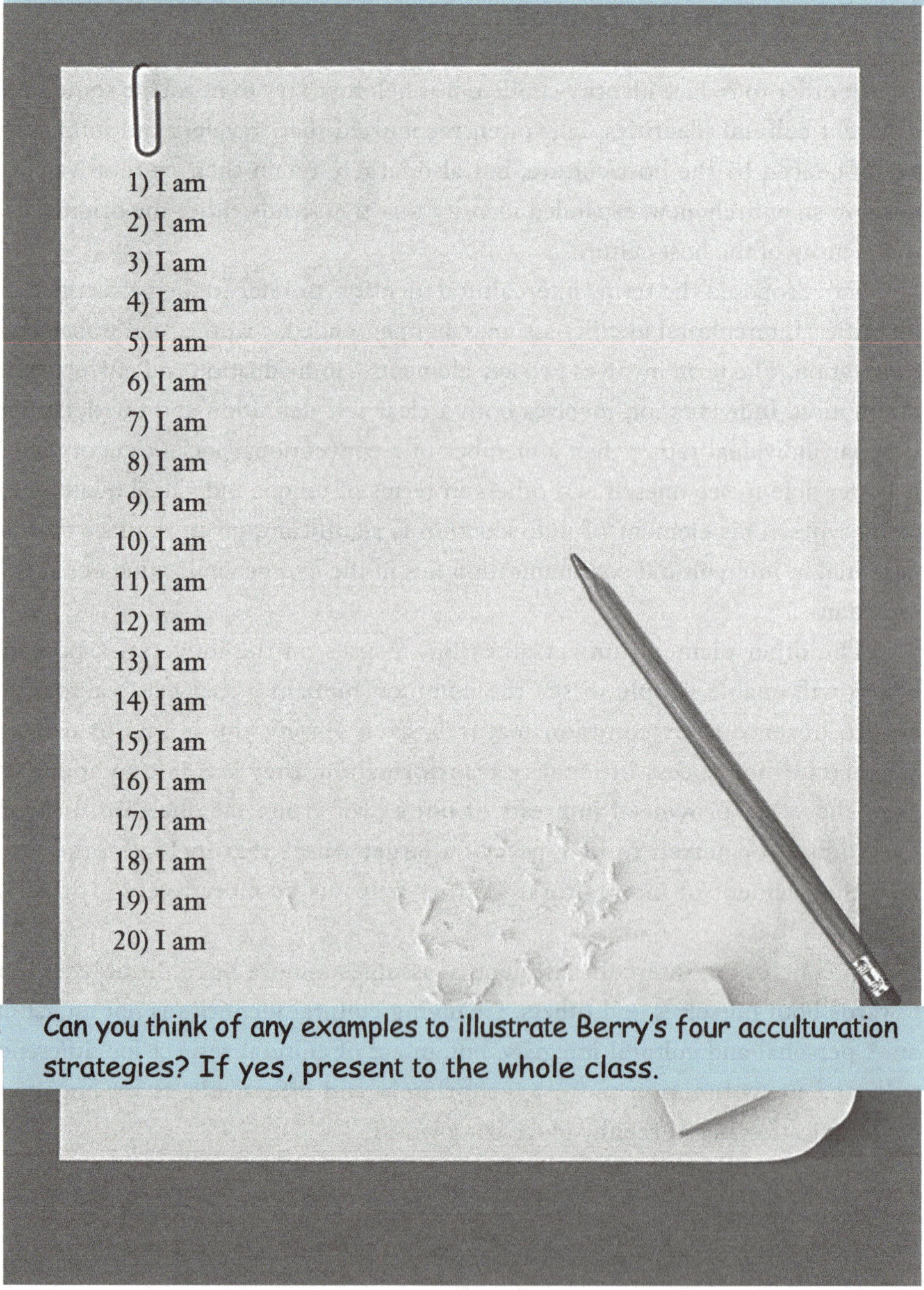

1) I am
2) I am
3) I am
4) I am
5) I am
6) I am
7) I am
8) I am
9) I am
10) I am
11) I am
12) I am
13) I am
14) I am
15) I am
16) I am
17) I am
18) I am
19) I am
20) I am

2 Question: Can you think of any examples to illustrate Berry's four acculturation strategies? If yes, present to the whole class.

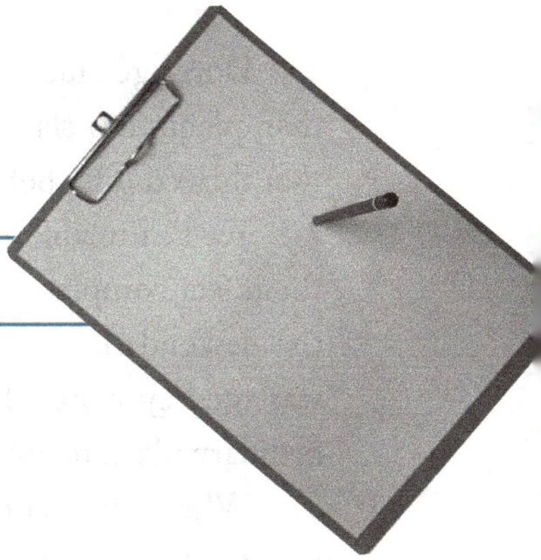

Section C Case

Introduction to the Case

"I don't know who I am anymore."

Commentator John McWhorter says he doesn't need a DNA analysis to know where he comes from. He says he's content with his family history the way it is: He's a black American, he admires his ancestors, but says that's all he needs to know.

The Scenario

African-American Identity: More Than DNA Tests

By *John McWhorter*

When I was a little kid, I was reminded that I would never know exactly where in Africa my ancestors lived. Even though some people thought they have found where their roots are, they actually just go back to a particular plantation, that's all.

But now with the wonders of modern science, all I have to do is hand over a scraping from my cheek and my DNA will be able to tell me whether I trace back to Senegal, Angola or somewhere in between. I suppose I'll sooner or later have it tested. But I can't say that I've ever felt like I didn't know where my roots were in the meantime because my roots are right here in the USA.

Don't get me wrong. There is certainly nothing bad about tracing ourselves back further than plantation slavery. I respect those who find comfort in connecting themselves to kingdoms that thrived long before Europeans encountered them.

Yet I'm unable to join those who say that finding out their ancestors lived in Ghana makes them feel complete or that they found home. As a matter of fact, I've always thought of myself as the descendant of Africans who made the best out of the worst. Although in Africa degradation was the key word, this leaves out the strength, the human spirit that's always burned bright in ordinary black people living lives of dignity.

Where do I come from? I come from a people who the very year I was born, 1965, had turned America upside down and gained the right to vote in the south. I come from my grandmother who was a child in Atlanta, was a playmate of the very Martin Luther King who went on to gain us that Voting Rights Act.

Africa was a very, very long time ago. Ghanaians today are given to calling black American visitors obruni, foreigners. And to me, this is natural and gives no insult.

What I come from is black American people. They produce no shame in me. They are my heroes. They are my home. They are enough.

Understanding and Speaking Interculturally

Exercise 1 Listen for the first time and answer the following questi

1. Can you infer which country the commentator John McWhorter comes from?

2. As an American, what did he think of his African background?

Exercise 2 Listen for the second time and fill in the blanks.

1. But now with the 1) ____________ of modern science, all I have to do is 2) ____________ a scraping from my cheek and my DNA will be able to tell me whether I 3) ____________ to Senegal, Angola or somewhere in between.

2. Yet I'm unable to join those who say that finding out their 4) ________ lived in Ghana makes them feel complete or that they found home. 5) ________, I've always thought of myself as the 6) ________ of Africans who made the best out of the worst.

3. Where do I come from? I come from a people who the very year I was born, 1965, had turned America 7) ________ and gained the right to vote in the south. I come from my grandmother who was a child in Atlanta, was a playmate of the very Martin Luther King who went on to gain us that 8) ________.

4. Africa was a very, very long time ago. Ghanaians today are given to calling black American visitors obruni, 9) ________. And to me, this is natural and 10) ________.

5. 11) ________ is black American people. They produce 12) ________ in me. They are my heroes. They are my home. They are enough.

Exercise 3 Explore interculturally.

1. How did the commentator define his identity as an African-American?

2. Have you ever encountered anybody who suffer from an identity crisis in the process of acculturation? If yes, share your story with your partner.

3. In the global village, what can be done to avoid identity crisis?

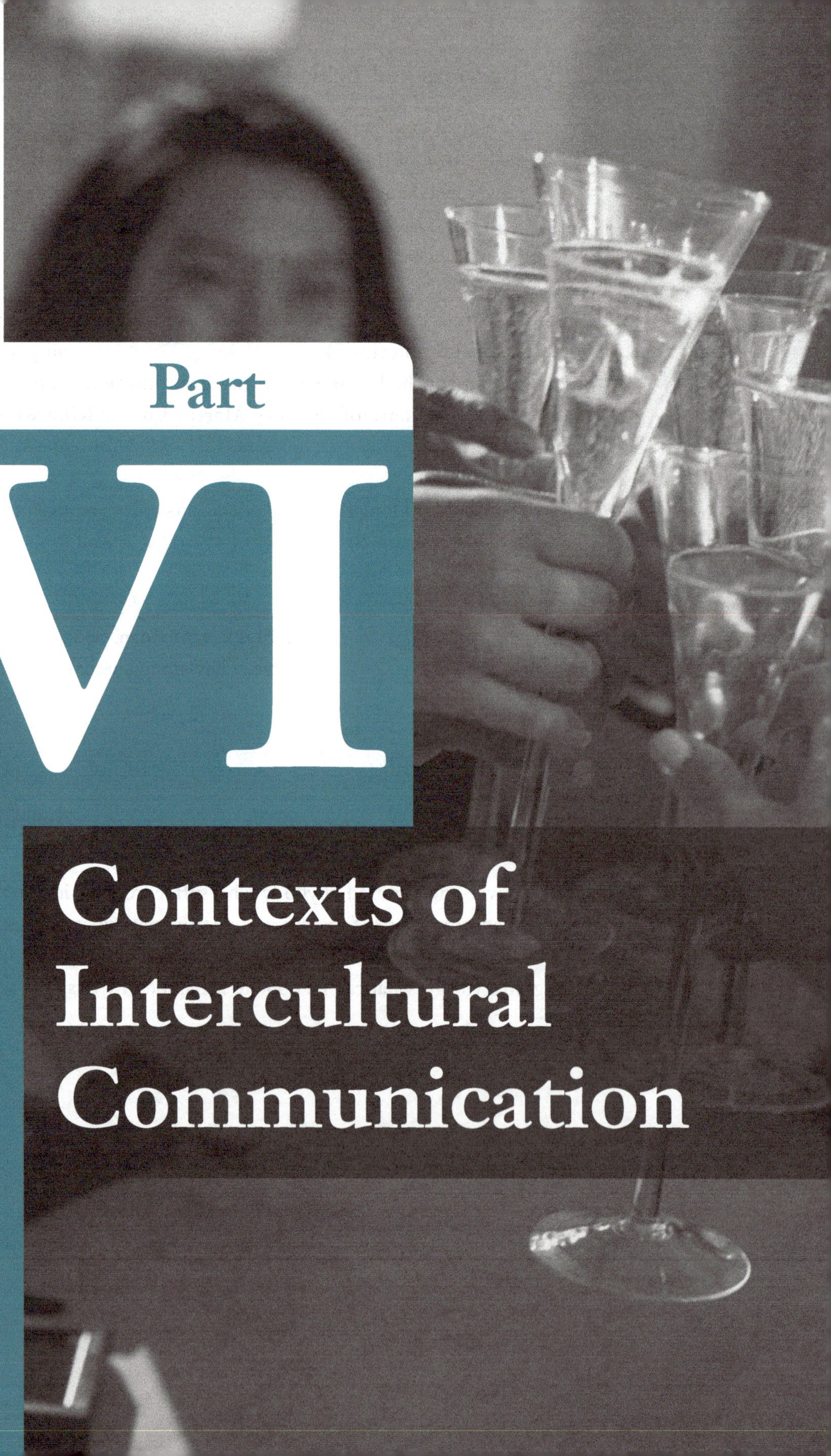

Part VI

Contexts of Intercultural Communication

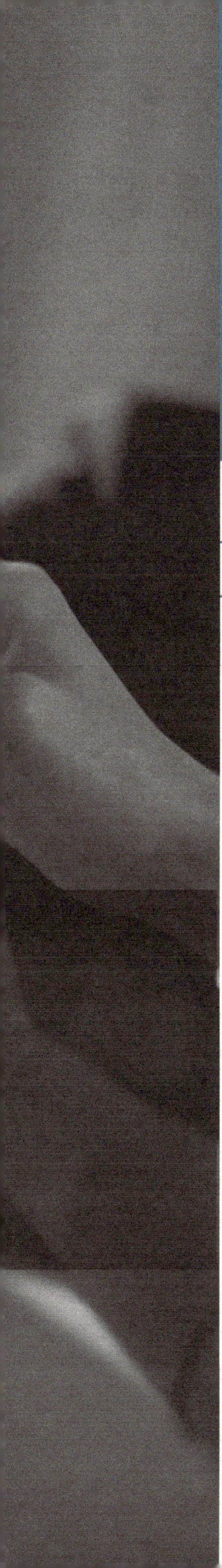

Chapter 15

Education Context

Section A Movie Clip

Introduction to the Movie *Mona Lisa Smile*

Katherine Watson (Julia Roberts) travels from California to the New England campus of Wellesley College in the fall of 1953 to teach art history. In the post-war era, Katherine expects that her students, the best and the brightest in the country, will take advantage of the opportunities presented to them. Soon after her arrival, however, Katherine discovers that the environment at the prestigious institution is steeped in conformity.

When Katherine encourages her students to think independently, she comes into conflict with the more conservative faculty and alumni.

In a world that has told the students how to live their lives, Katherine teaches them how to think for themselves. Through her students' efforts to find their own way, Katherine learns to chart a different course for herself, as well.

Introduction to the Selected Scene

Katherine is conducting her art class on Van Gogh and encouraging her students to reflect on the non-conformist views of the artist, when Betty rushes into the classroom fresh from her honeymoon. According to the unwritten tradition of the college, teachers would not pay particular attention to the attendance of married women, but Betty's behavior upsets Katherine and leads to a confrontation between the two.

Script of the Scene

Katherine: They can paint their own. Van Gogh in a box, ladies. The newest form of mass-distributed art: paint by numbers. Now everyone can be Van Gogh. It's so easy. Just follow the simple instructions...and in minutes, you're on your way to being an artist.

Baker: Van Gogh by numbers?

Katherine: Ironic, isn't it? Look at what we have done to the man... who refused to conform his ideals to popular taste. Who refused to compromise his integrity. We have put him in a tiny box and asked you to copy him. So the choice is yours, ladies. You can conform to what other people expect or you can…

Betty: I know. Be ourselves.

Baker: You're a sight for sore eyes.

Betty: I would've been on time but, silly me, I thought class was in the classroom.

Katherine: Glad you could join us, Mrs. Jones. We thought we'd lost you.

Baker: There's an unwritten rule for married girls—

Katherine: Don't bother.

Katherine: Since your wedding, you've missed six classes, a paper and your midterm.

Betty: Well, thank God I didn't miss the paint-by-numbers lecture. I was on my honeymoon and then I had to set up house. (To Baker) What does she expect?

Katherine: Attendance.

Baker: Most of the faculty turn their heads...when the married students miss a class or two.

Katherine: Then why not get married as freshmen? That way you could graduate without actually ever stepping foot on campus.

Betty: Don't disregard our traditions just because you're subversive.

Katherine: Don't disrespect this class just because you're married.

Betty: Don't disrespect me just because you're not.

Katherine: Come to class, do the work, or I'll fail you.

Betty: If you fail me, there will be consequences.

Katherine: Are you threatening me?

Betty: I'm educating you.

Katherine: That's my job.

New Words

conform *v.* keep to or comply with (generally accepted rules, standards, etc) 遵从，顺应

distribute *v.* separate into parts and give a share to each person or thing 分发，分配

faculty *n.* the collective body of teachers in an academic institution 大学的某系、科、院的全体教员

integrity *n.* quality of being honest and morally upright 诚实而正直

ironic *adj.* using or expressing irony; full of irony 讽刺的

sore *adj.* hurting when touched or used; tender and painful; aching （指身体局部）一触或一用就痛的，易痛的，疼痛的

subversive *adj.* trying or likely to weaken or destroy a political system, an accepted belief, etc 削弱或破坏某政治制度、公认的信仰等的；颠覆性的

Notes

You're a sight for sore eyes

It's such a relief to see you after we have had such a long class.

Van Gogh

Dutch painter. His favorite subjects were still-lifes, landscapes, and peasant figures working in the countryside. Among his most famous paintings are The Potato Eaters (1885), Starry Night (1889), and Self-Portrait with Pipe and Bandaged Ear (1888; he had sliced off his ear after a quarrel with the painter Paul Gauguin). His work had a powerful influence on the development of modern painting. He is considered the greatest Dutch painter since Rembrandt.

Understanding and Speaking Interculturally

Exercise 1 Answer the following questions according to the movie clip you have just watched.

1. What does "Van Gogh by numbers" mean?

2. What has Van Gogh refused to do?

3. Why is Katherine not pleased when Betty comes in?

Exercise 2 Fill in the blanks according to the movie clip you have just watched.

1. **Betty:** Don't disregard our traditions just because you're ______ ______.

   Katherine: Don't disrespect this class just because you're ______ ______.

2. **Betty:** Don't ______ me just because you're not.

   Katherine: Come to class, do the work, or I'll fail you.

   Betty: If you fail me, there will be ______.

Exercise 3 Discuss in groups the two different cultures that have caused the confrontation between Katherine and Betty. After the discussion, each group should present their ideas to the class.

Exercise 4 Divide the class into several groups and perform the scene with the help of the script.

Section B Reading

Intercultural communication usually takes place in three general settings: education, business and health care. Since education is an important social context in which cultural influences are much in evidence, schools are a primary vehicle for teaching and learning cultural values.

Learning Styles and Culture

Students from different cultures have different cognitive styles. To learn is not simply to acquire information. It involves various complex cognitive strategies, in which culture plays an important role in establishing a general framework for learning. Some cultures stress competition, while others emphasize cooperation. That helps to explain why Americans and Euro-Americans are more individualistic and competitive in classrooms than Asian students, who pay more attention to cooperation and group harmony. Moreover, individualistic students tend to find solutions on their own by adopting a trial-and-error method, or by undergoing a form of self-learning. Some students from Japan, however, prefer to receive instructions from, and imitate, the teacher. (Samovar, Porter & Stefani, 2000).

Cultures also influence and determine motivation in learning. Some students are more intrinsically motivated: they perceive that their studies will be helpful for them in pursuing a career. In other words, they are studying for themselves. They know the importance of study for their future life, and tend to be better motivated in their education. Other students brought up in cultures such as those of Singapore and China, observe that good scores and performance in school are rewarded by parents and teachers. These students are extrinsically motivated. As they grow up and the impact of rewards from teachers and parents diminishes, they may sometimes feel lost and lack proper motivation in their study. In this case, teachers should consider different approaches to motivating students more strongly.

Students seldom study alone; they typically study in groups in the classroom, where they must manage their relationships with other students and the teacher. In this respect, the differences in verbal communication and non-verbal communication mentioned in the previous chapters also apply.

The US, once called "a melting pot," is now frequently described as a "mosaic." However described, one meaning remains: its cultural diversity. Traditionally, education in the US was centered on Euro-American culture, while other cultures were simply ignored. With the increasing attention paid to cultural diversity among students and their learning styles, educators now are trying to accommodate different cultures they represent into the classroom. For example, many textbooks used to anthologize male white writers only, but now the works of many female, African-American, or Asian writers are also incorporated in order to give a much fuller picture.

Culture's impact on learning styles is also observed in Chinese classrooms. With the increasingly important role that China is playing in the world, more and more foreign students have become interested in learning the Chinese language, as well as enrolling in Chinese universities. This raises great challenges for Chinese educators, who are used to the homogeneous population of Chinese students.

Teaching Styles and Culture

Not only does students' cultural diversity pose a significant challenge for teachers, but the different cultural backgrounds of teachers themselves may also affect the learning style in classrooms dramatically, making the learning atmosphere more difficult, puzzling, or interesting. This requires both that students develop competence to adapt to the teacher's culture, and that teachers develop cultural awareness to accommodate their students.

Nowadays, foreign teachers are quite common in Chinese universities. To attend their class is a totally different experience. Some students enjoy the class, while others feel uncomfortable. The ability to adapt to the cultural difference in class is crucial in such classrooms.

A Chinese teacher shares the same cultural framework with his students in a Chinese university, and students tend to take that framework for granted. The Chinese always stress moral education, demand cooperation and interdependence, and pursue harmony. It is fairly common for a Chinese teacher to have perfect control over the educational process in the classroom,. Students, for example, are expected to take notes, and to raise their hands to ask for permission to ask questions in class. The teacher is seeking a correct answer to questions, which facilitates his teaching. For students and teachers alike, smooth cooperation and harmony are valued on both sides in class. However, these shared cultural norms are usually only only perceived when some strong cultural contrast occurs, or even conflict between the students and teacher.

In a foreign teacher's class, students are more often encouraged to ask questions, as well as to answer questions. Some students may even feel that they are being forced to answer too many questions, while whether the correctness of their answers may seem not to matter to the teacher. In this case, students may lose their confidence or interest. The foreign teacher is attempting to foster students' critical thinking, the ability to ask questions and to challenge authority. Yet the students may prefer to learn what is considered correct by the authorities. They wish to have their ability confirmed. Apart from the stress on originality and critical thinking, ideological conflicts may also occur. Ideological prejudice is not something we can easily become aware of or totally discard. It is something that has been instilled into our very way of thinking from our formative years. Everyone has an ideological stance, no matter what it is. Some foreign teachers, for example, may feel it difficult to accept the policy of family planning in China. They may think this represents a kind of violation of human rights. Chinese students, however, have already taken it for granted; they are familiar with the particular circumstances in China that have given rise to this policy.

It is also worth noting that Chinese and foreign teachers may give quite different grades to the same student, especially in writing or in a debate. So students should ask them to explain the reason for doing so. This would often reveal fundamental orientations toward particular criteria and values. It is a good opportunity to know how to do one's best in another culture's context. Those who go to work in a foreign company after graduation often find this knowledge quite helpful in their work.

Learning the Language, Learning the Culture

In the educational context, there are several possibilities for encountering foreign cultures. The most ordinary one is when we study a foreign language. This is particularly the case in China, as the English language is taught at various educational levels.

In TESL (Teaching English as a Second Language), it is traditionally held that the main purpose and criterion for studying a foreign language is to communicate. Most English textbooks are written according to this principle. Apart from the need to learn vocabulary and grammar, they stress that students should understand what an English speaker says, as if words and sentences were all that we have to know in order to understand. In other words, "Current communicative methods of second language teaching generally view language as a means of bridging an 'information gap'." (Corbett, 2003) Unfortunately, this is not so. Even if students knew the meaning of every word and observed all the proper grammatical rules, they may still fail to understand what a passage of speech implies. Language is not the only arch in the bridge that connects to other countries. A solid and comprehensive knowledge of cultural differences is also indispensable. It is quite necessary for us to incorporate the study of culture into the core curriculum in TESL, because the goal of second language teaching is "not so much 'native speaker competence' but rather an 'intercultural communicative competence.' "

In an educational context, there are several ways to adapt oneself to another culture. The first step is, of course, to acquire knowledge of that culture. Students should read widely about religion, political systems, and history. Christianity has a long history in the West, and its influence on Western culture can never be overestimated. Apart from religion, knowledge about political systems, such as how a leader is elected, can also be rewarding. Public attitudes and the domestic atmosphere are totally different in the U.S., compared with that in China, during an election period.

Reading foreign literature is also a good way to learn culture. As J. H. Miller says, reading literature is the quickest way to be absorbed in one's own culture. His words also apply when we want to know another culture. Besides, many characters in classic or even popular literature have already become a staple part of the culture. For example, Hamlet's "To be, or not to be" may at first sound puzzling to a Chinese student, but later they are glad and proud to quote this line when talking to foreigners.

The arts industry also has no national boundaries. Hollywood movies cross borders everywhere. We should support our own national arts industry, but that does not mean we should shut our door to foreign products, including cultural products. Watching movies can quickly introduce you to a foreign culture.

Understanding and Speaking Interculturally

1. Recall you foreign teacher's class. Have you ever felt any differences in values? What are they and what are the possible causes?

2. What are the effective ways to learn another culture? Have you adopted any of them to learn the American culture? Do they help to improve your English?

3. Do you think there are value differences among your Chinese teachers? Have you ever perceived them? What are the possible causes?

Section C Case

Introduction to the Case

"I don't know" is a common answer to a teacher's question in a Chinese classroom, but it is not the case in a foreign teacher's class. Listen to the following case and find out what would be expected in a foreign teacher's class.

The Scenario

The Wrong Answer

When I was a freshman I had an American teacher. One day when we were on the subject of poetry, he wrote a sonnet by Shakespeare on the blackboard and asked the students what it meant. To tell the truth, I would have had difficulty in understanding it even if it had been translated into Chinese. There was a long silence during which everyone, afraid of answering, lowered their heads. Unfortunately the teacher chose me to answer the question. I mustered up all my courage and said, "Sorry, I don't know."

That was always my reply to difficult questions in my Chinese classes. I expected him to go on and ask one of my classmates as my Chinese teachers would do.

To my surprise he spent the rest of the class (a nightmare for me) explaining how childish my answer was. "As an adult, you should at least have some idea about a question, no matter how difficult it is. Even though your answer is totally wrong, it is much better than 'I don't know.' "

I did not know why I could not say "I don't know." It was always safe for me to say that in my Chinese classes. After I had several more American teachers I began to realize that Chinese teachers concentrate on the results of learning and teaching, while American teachers generally emphasize the process. Chinese teachers expect students' answers to be correct, while American teachers welcome any answer because all answers are the fruit of the student's thinking. That is why a Chinese teacher prefers the decent "I don't know" to a wrong answer, while an American teacher feels annoyed by it.

Understanding and Speaking Interculturally

Exercise 1 Listen for the first time and answer the following questions.

1. What class did the student have?
2. What was his reply to the American teacher's question?
3. What was the response of the American teacher?

Exercise 2 Listen for the second time and fill in the blanks.

1. That was always my 1) ________ to difficult questions in my 2) ________ classes. I expected him to 3) ________ and ask one of my classmates as my Chinese teachers 4) ________.

2. To my surprise he spent the rest of the class 5) (________) explaining how 6) ________ my answer was. "As an 7) ________, you should at least have some idea about a question, no matter how 8) ________ it is. Even though your answer is totally

9) ____________, it is much 10) ____________ than 'I don't know.' "

3. I did not know why I could not say " 11) ____________." It was always 12) ____________ for me to say that in my Chinese classes. After I had several more American teachers I began to 13) ____________ that Chinese teachers concentrate on the 14) ____________ of learning and teaching, while American teachers generally 15) ____________ the 16) ____________. Chinese teachers expect students' answers to be 17) ____________, while American teachers welcome any answer because all answers are the 18) ____________ of the student's thinking. That is why a Chinese teacher prefers the 19) ____________ "I don't know" to a wrong answer, while an American teacher feels 20) ____________ by it.

Exercise 3 Explore interculturally.

1. Can you explain why the student chose to say "I don't know" in the class?
2. Can you explain why the teacher got annoyed by the student's answer?
3. What do you think is the cultural difference that has caused this problem?

Chapter 16

Business Context

Section A Video clip

Introduction to the Video *How To Make a Cake?*

Perhaps we have never seen a Western kitchen before. This movie introduces kitchen vocabulary to us, and teaches us how to make a cake. From it, we can become familiar with some of the differences between the Chinese way of cooking and the Western way of cooking.

Script of the Scene

Hi. Do you remember I said we were going to make a cake? I'm getting ready. When we make cakes we always look in a cookbook. This cookbook is very thick. It has a lot of different recipes in it. Now that we know exactly how much flour, sugar and butter that we have to put in the cake. We can begin to put these things in. I already have flour. Now I have to add some sugar because our cakes are always very sweet. You have to put in exactly the right amount. You don't want to put in too much more or less. It's not like Chinese cooking. Chinese cooking everyone has a different recipe. A little this a little bit of that. You don't say how much. But for our cooking everything is very clear exactly how much. This is three quarters of a cup of sugar. We also have special spoons that are all the same size. It's standard size. This is tablespoon. This is a teaspoon. We also have a half-teaspoon and a quarter teaspoon. So we have our standard cup and standard spoons and using these every time, so the cake will be the same. It will never be higher or lower or too salty or too sweet. You have this in China too. It's called baking powder. We also add eggs to our cake. These are fresh eggs. We don't need the yellow part. So we have to take it out first. Here the egg white. We can put them in, add some water. Then we add two tablespoons of oil. Do you know vanilla? In Chinese it's 香草. We add vanilla for some flavor in the cake to make it taste good. Now we beat the cake. "Beat" doesn't mean "打." "Beat" means to use a mixer, a mixing machine. Have a look. It doesn't look like cake. It looks like milk. But after you bake it, I promise you it looks like cake. This is the pan we need to use. Today I'm going to make many small cakes. In English, the small cake made in this kind of pan is called a "cupcake." It's like made in a small cup. First you have to put some butter in it. After mixing the cake then you have to pour it in the pan. If you want to, you can add some other things to the cake. You can put in some nuts or some raisins or some prunes. When you are ready you have to put them in the oven.

They'll cook now. They cook for about half an hour. When they're done. I wish I could give you one.

New Words

Butter *n.* 黄油

Cupcake *n.* 小圆蛋糕

Flour *n.* 面粉

Mixer *n.* 搅拌器

Raisin *n.* 葡萄干

Tablespoon *n.* 大汤匙

Teaspoon *n.* 茶匙

Understanding and Speaking Interculturally

Exercise 1 Answer the following questions according to the movie clip you have just watched.

1. The woman said: "You have to put in exactly the right amount. You don't want to put in too much more or less. It's not like Chinese cooking. Chinese cooking everyone has a different recipe. A little this a little bit of that. You don't say how much. But for our cooking everything is very clear exactly how much." Do you agree with her? Why or Why not?

2. Is it easier to cook Chinese dishes than to make a cake? Why or why not?

Exercise 2 Fill in the blanks according to the movie clip you have just watched.

1. We also have ________ that are all the same size. It's ________ size. This is tablespoon. This is a teaspoon. We also have a ________ and a ________ teaspoon.

2. "Beat" means to use a ________, a mixing machine. Have a look. It doesn't look like cake. It looks like milk. But after you bake it, I ________ you it looks like cake. This is the ________ we need to use. Today I'm going to make many small cakes. In English, the small cake made in this kind of pan is called a "________."

Exercise 3 Discuss in the groups why you could taste the same flavor in a Macdonald's hamburger everywhere in the world, while the same Chinese dishes may vary according to different chefs. After the discussion, each group should present their ideas to the class.

Section B Reading

Intercultural Business Contact

Perhaps no setting illustrates the challenges of intercultural communication so much as business. This is especially important given the shift toward globalized business models underway around the world. Increasingly, collaborative business ventures are taking place across international borders, as trade expands and companies seek new opportunities and new markets. As a result, intercultural skills are assuming greater importance.

Business is sometimes described as the art of getting things done, the typical goal being to turn a profit according to some pre-conceived definition or measurement. It requires planning, setting objectives, establishing specifications and reaching agreement on "deliverables." In cultural terms, it reveals much about a people, including their aspirations and social protocols. An important note here: We typically speak of business culture in national terms, differentiated by country. However, it is also useful to keep in mind that companies sharing a national origin may display radically different organizational cultures, a fact that can significantly affect what happens when one company acquires or merges with another.

As with any human activity, business offers rich opportunities to observe differences in customs and other cultural norms. Not surprisingly, the customs, habits of behavior and popular expectations that give a particular culture its most visible shape will have an impact on the business activities conducted among people who share the same cultural background. The trick is not necessarily to alter one mode of behavior in favor of another. Rather, it is a matter of using communication to bridge customs and highlight expectations.

Communication, of course, is the mainstay of business activities, providing the context for even the most fundamental processes, such as negotiations, meetings, reports and presentations. Achieving successful communication depends not simply on the effective exchange of information, but in particular on the degree of cultural understanding that the parties to a commercial transaction have about one another, understanding that affects how each side perceives intent and meaning. Thus, communication includes the spoken and the unspoken. A failure to perceive and interpret correctly the cultural signals passing back and forth in the course of doing business can negate even the best of intentions.

As a general rule for interpreting and "reading" culture, beliefs, assumptions and values offer useful windows into how people might be expected to behave and react. What does a particular culture believe about its society, the motivators that drive it and the goals it pursues? What matters most? What do people assume about one another's behavior? In the context of business activities that span cultural boundaries, these questions provide a basis for communication. They can serve as important tools for surfacing information needed to predict the degree of understanding that will enable business partners to work together or at cross purposes.

Examples of Intercultural Business Communication

Let's look at a few examples. As with any cultural topic, while examples are easily subject to stereotyping, they are used here to emphasize, perhaps through some exaggeration, a few basic principles.

First, consider the issue of time, a common point of reference in business. A sometimes effective way to distinguish one culture from another is to observe the role that time plays in it. Is time a decisive indicator of when an event will occur, or an approximation that helps people to form a relationship with the event in their own minds? Some cultures view the expression of time as an absolute. If a meeting (or social event, such as a dinner engagement) is scheduled to begin at 9 in the morning, that is when it will start. Lateness is considered improper, a cause for explanation. (This has been my experience of Scandinavian culture.) Other cultures, conversely, tend to treat time as an aspect of the natural world that lends rhythm to life. It is valuable not as a measure of productivity but as a larger symbol of structure and meaning. Its reduction to a precise moment in the day is of strictly advisory value. In the culture first described, failure to be prompt may be seen as rudeness or carelessness, both negative qualities for doing business. In the second culture, promptness might almost be considered unnatural, reflecting arrogance or un-sociability, a drawback where business is cast in a wider context of relationships. Given the practical and legal importance of schedules and agreements in much of the business world, it makes sense to develop a cultural awareness of the standards by which time is judged, and determine the relative value of precision. Communication is the means for doing so.

A more immediate question about time, of course, requires knowing the local time your business associate observes. A common mistake made in business agreements, formal or informal, is to fail to define whether specific times—for delivery or meetings, for example—refer to local time or some other time zone.

In another example, the exchange of business cards at the point of initial meeting represents an opportunity for two kinds of communication. Many Westerners view the gesture as a mechanical act, providing essential contact information necessary for doing business. Some Asian cultures, however, may see the business card as an extension of one's identity, a symbol of importance. Receiving a business card requires a moment of tacit acknowledgment before moving on with the conversation, holding the card in such a way to reflect its value and meaning.

Yet another example hinges on the proper moment for plunging into "doing business." The traveler from the US is sometimes described as being impatient to arrive at agreement, to get down to what he or she perceives as the real purpose of a business meeting. Seen from a different perspective, meetings offer opportunities to establish or continue building upon relationships. While social interplay—casual conversation about families or personal experiences—may seem ancillary to the business agenda, it is, in fact, an essential precursor to what follows. It may, for instance, provide insight into what someone values, how they organize their lives, even how they think. These are critical keys to judging intent, honesty and motivation.

No discussion of intercultural business communication should overlook the impact that choice of language and expression can have. For instance, while it is often difficult to speak without idioms—those culture-bound expressions that mean more than the actual words convey—idioms without a common cultural context can obscure our meaning and cause confusion. Imagine trying to negotiate a business deal with an American who peppers his comments with phrases such as "getting to first base," "hitting a home run" or "getting stuck in left field." Without a basic knowledge of baseball, these idioms are likely to go unappreciated. Similarly, a speaker who tends to build his end of the conversation around repeated references to "I," "me" and "my" may create a different cultural impression than if he defaults to "we," "us" and "our." Thus, the language of business communication tends to reflect images of ourselves that we should consider carefully.

Product branding and advertising also represent important communication opportunities. Both depend for their success on the ability of the reader, viewer and consumer to "connect" (often unconsciously) with language and imagery used to arouse interest in a product or service. Thus, a brand name, logo or advertising campaign should create positive feelings, the reason why so much care goes into choosing the most appropriate promotional strategy. A brand name that makes a strong impression in one culture can cause difficulties in another. For example, many years ago, General Motors introduced a car known as the Nova., a name with connotations suggesting novelty, an astronomical phenomenon or something especially modern. However, in Spanish-speaking cultures, "Nova" is heard as "no va," a phrase that in Spanish means "does not go." This is not a quality a carmaker wishes to have associated with one of its products. (For this reason, many auto manufacturers market cars whose product names are made-up words that will be inoffensive in any culture.)

Besides the preceding examples of intercultural communication, many others can be found in the naming of product brands, product advertising, style of business negotiation, style of business decision making and problem solving, in short, in all the activities that comprise the world of business. In fact, it is difficult to imagine doing business today without encountering such examples.

Tips for Effective Intercultural Business Communication

Thus, effective intercultural business communication requires looking for and paying attention to the signals that help assess whether someone will be a capable, resourceful and honorable business partner. Here a few more to consider:

Does a business associate speak in terms of consensus or achieving objectives unilaterally?

Is a company's culture open to uncertainty or does it prefer predictability?

Does an organization seem to reward initiative or is power concentrated among senior executives?

What is a company's attitude toward creativity?

How are business relationships valued?

Are rules viewed as applicable to everyone in the company or relaxed depending on circumstances?

The preceding examples suggest criteria and standards to apply in approaching business across borders. They are lenses that can be useful for understanding both communication strategies and "in-the-moment" communication challenges. Important skills to foster, in order to succeed at intercultural communication in business are little different from the skills needed in other cultural contexts: listening carefully, observing open-mindedly, asking clear questions, and always looking for signals to beliefs, values and assumptions.

It is also important, in turn, to consider the ways in which one's own cultural data are perceived. This means presenting needs and objectives as clearly as possible and being ready to define everything, taking nothing for granted. In general, communication behaviors that view business opportunities in terms of relationship-building are most likely to overcome intercultural challenges.

Understanding and Speaking Interculturally

1 Group discussion: In groups discuss your understanding of the sentence: "Perhaps no setting illustrates the challenges of intercultural communication so much as business."

2 Match the following explanations with the idioms below.

( ) getting to first base
( ) hitting a home run
( ) stuck out in left field

a. Assigned to a position far from the center of the action
b. Taking the first big step toward accomplishing a goal (as in the beginning of a project)
c. Achieving something noteworthy in a dramatic way (as in a huge success when introducing a new product)

3 In some countries, if you ask children what their fathers do, they will say "My dad drives a truck" or "My dad is a stock broker". But in others, the child will tell you "My father works for Mitsubishi" or "My dad works for Hitachi." What are the underlying cultural values?

4 What might the style of negotiation suggest about the culture of the participants?

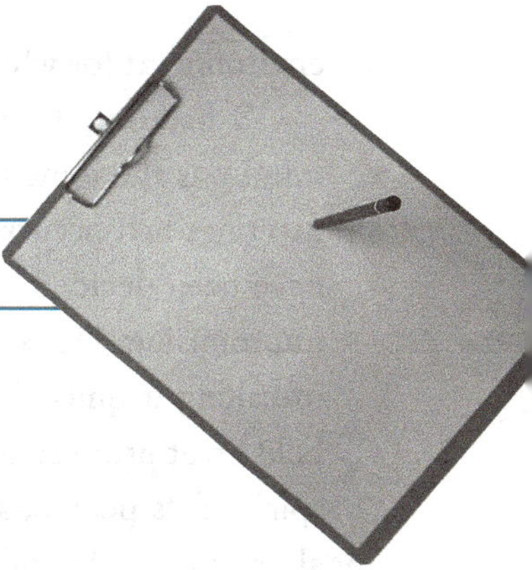

Section C Case

Introduction to the Case

The following cases illustrate the close relationship between culture and business. The first case shows us the importance of knowing the different business etiquettes in the countries of different cultural background. Through the American businessman's experience in India, the second case tells us the influences that different cultural patterns have on business.

The Scenario

Case 1 Correct Form of Address

An American businessman in a meeting in South Korea, addressed the wife of the CEO, Mr. Kim, as Mrs. Kim. That embarrassed both the interpreter and the Kims. He should have addressed her as Mrs. Lee. Because in South Korea it is the custom for women to maintain their maiden name after they marry.

Case 2 Doing Business in India: A Cultural Perspective

Joel stood by the windows of the Hilton and watched the lights twinkling in the harbor–tiny, glittering explosions of life. It was a quarter past nine in majestic Mumbai. Some local residents were unwinding by the beach dining al fresco. Many were scurrying back home from work, while the homeless were looking for a place to lay their heads for the night. The street below was bustling with activity and the loud, blaring sounds of rush hour traffic contributed to the environment for which the city is famous.

It had only been a few days before that Joel landed in the subcontinent. In the back of his mind was the joint-venture that he had planned with a mid-sized Indian firm. Negotiations and meetings had occurred one after another over the past few days, but nothing concrete seemed to have been decided upon, yet. His future in this new, chaotic and strange land seemed bleak and unpromising. He couldn't seem to get a grip on events. Frustrated, Joel was almost on the verge of calling it quits. The Indian economy had been booming for the past few years. The country held great promise for the future. Liberalized business policies had unleashed the entrepreneurial spirit of its people, and many multi-national firms, attracted by the dusty plains of Deccan, had already set up big offices throughout the nation.

Joel and his associates had been very excited at the prospect of entering into a joint venture with this particular Indian firm and were quite optimistic about the outcome. Negotiations had started off quite well initially, but slowly, problems and misunderstandings arose as deterrents to finalizing the deal. Joel had attended several meetings in the past week and had expected a completed deal by that morning, but it seemed as if the Indians didn't feel rushed to come up with a feasible deal and project plan. They had spent hours debating the objectives and long-term effects of the venture, but the discussions had rambled on and on without any concrete points being reached. Even after they had agreed on certain decisions during discussions, the process was further prolonged by the necessity of the Indians' going back to consult senior colleagues for approval.

An enraged Joel tried to speed up matters, as many more issues had to be addressed, but the Indians felt that he was only interested in finalizing and implementing the deal. He didn't seem to be concerned about debating the finer concepts behind the deal also, they began to question his intelligence, abilities and sincerity. His informal way of addressing them also made them feel uncomfortable and disrespected. All in all, they didn't really trust him and the deal that he had been nurturing all along and had been so eagerly looking forward to advancing.

Notes

beach dining al fresco 海滨露天茶座

bleak *adj.* gloomy and somber; dreary 寒冷的，阴冷的，荒凉的，凄凉的

Deccan 德干高原，印度中部偏南一高原

detriment *n.* damage, harm, or loss 损害，伤害，损失

enrage *v.* put into a rage; infuriate 激怒；使狂怒

grip *v.&n.* a tight hold; a firm grasp 紧握，掌握，控制

Mumbai 孟买（原称 Bombay）

scurry *v.* go with light running steps 急赶，急跑，急转，以轻快而交替的步子走动

unleash *v.* release or loose from or as if from a leash 释放

Understanding and Speaking Interculturally

Exercise 1 Listen for the first time and answer the following questions.

1. In case one, what mistake did the American businessman make?

2. What did Joel do in India? How did Joel think about the future of his situation in the first few days after arriving in India? How did Joel feel about it after several days of negotiations with his India partners?

Exercise 2 Listen for the second time and fill in the blanks.

Joel and his associates had been very excited at the 1) ______ of entering into a joint venture with this particular Indian firm and were quite 2) ______ about the outcome. Negotiations had started off quite well initially, but slowly, problems and misunderstandings arose as 3) ______ to finalizing the deal. Joel had attended several meetings in the past one-week and had expected a 4) ______ deal that morning, but it seemed like the Indians didn't feel 5) ______ to come up with a 6) ______ deal and project plan. They had spent hours debating the objectives and long-term effects of the 7) ______, but the discussions had rambled on and on without any 8) ______ points being reached. Even after they had agreed on certain decisions were reached during discussions, the 9) ______ was further prolonged by the necessity of going back to 10) ______ colleagues for approval.

Exercise 3 Explore interculturally.

1. Can you find the influences of culture upon different system for addressing names?

2. Describe the cultural values that underlie the Indian and American business rules from case two.

References

1. Berry, J. W., Kim, U., Minde, T. & Mok, D.(1987) "Comparative studies of acculturative stress" in *International Migration Review*, 21, 491-511.
2. Brosnaham, T. (1988). *Turkey: A Travel Survival Kit*.(2nd ed.) Victorial: Austuralia Lonely Planet.
3. Corbett, J. (2003) "An Intercultural Approach to English Language Teaching". In *Languages for Intercultural Communication and Education*. Buffalo, NY Multilingual Matters.
4. Davis, L. (2001) *Doing Culture: Cross-Cultural Communication in Action*. Beijing: Foreign Language Teaching and Research Press.
5. Dou, W. L. (2007). *Fundamentals of Intercultural Communication*. Beijing: University of International Business and Economics Press.
6. Ekman, P. and Friesen, W. V. (1969). "The repertoire of nonverbal behavior: Categories, origins, usage, and coding" in *Human Communication Research*,17: 232-265
7. Gonzalez, A. and Zimbardo, P. G. (1985). "Time in Perspective" in *Psychology Today*,19: 20-26
8. Grayson, B. and Stein, M. I. (1981). "Attracting assault: Victims' nonverbal cues" in *Journal of Communication*, 31(1): 68-75
9. Gu, Y. G. (2000). *Cross-Cultural Communication*. Foreign Language Teaching and Research Press.
10. Hall, E. T. (1959). *The Silent Language*. NY: Anchor Press / Doubleday.
11. Hall, E. T. (1966). *The Hidden Dimension*. Garden City, NY: Anchor Press / Doubleday.
12. Hall, E. T. (1976). *Beyond Culture*. Garden City, NY: Anchor Press / Doubleday.
13. Hall, E. T. and Hall, M. R. (1990). *Understanding Cultural Differences*. Yarmouth, ME: Intercultural Press
14. Hawkes, T. (2003). *Structuralism and Semiotics*. NY: Routledge.
15. Hofstede, Geert. (1980). *Culture's Consequences: International Differences in Work-related Value*, Beverly Hills, CA: Sage
16. Hofstede, G. (1991). *Cultures and Organizations: Software of the Mind*. McGraw-Hill.

17. Lustig, M. W. & Koester, J.(1996). *Intercultural Competence: Intercultural Communication Across Cultures (2nd ed.)*, NY: HarperCollins College Publisher.
18. Martin, J. N. & Nakayama, T. K. (2007). *Intercultural Communication in Contexts.* (4th ed.). Boston: McGraw-Hill
19. Rogers, E. M. & Steinfatt, T. M. (1999). *Intercultural Communication*. Prospect Heights: Waveland Press, Inc.
20. Samovar, L. A., Porter, R. E. & Stefani, L. A. (2000). *Communication Between Cultures.* (3rd ed.). Beijing: Foreign Languages Teaching and Research Press.
21. Stewart, E. C. & Bennett, M. J.(1991). *American cultural patterns: A cross-cultural perspective*, Yarmouth, ME: Intercultural Press.
22. Tylor, E. B. (1871). *Primitive Culture: Researches into the Development of Mythology, Philosophy, Religion, Language, Art, and Custom.* London: John Murray
23. 顾曰国. 跨文化交际. 外语教学与研究出版社，2000年.
24. 胡文仲. 跨文化交际学概论. 外语教学与研究出版社，1999年.
25. 汪福祥、马登阁. 文化撞击案例评析. 石油工业出版社，1999年.
26. 张爱琳. 跨文化交际. 重庆大学出版社，2003年.

Key for Reference

Chapter 1

Section A

Exercise 1

4.0, one seventy-nine, fashion, Extracurricular, sorority's charity project, commanding, philanthropist, recall, legal

Exercise 2

1. I remembered what happened in *Days of Our Lives* yesterday.
2. I'm able to use "I object."
3. I often chaired the discussion of very important issues like switching our toilet paper from Charmin to generic.
4. I was once in a Ricky Martin video.

Exercise 3

1. F 2. F 3. T 4. T

Exercise 5

1. Elle Woods is considered diverse by Harvard Law School because she's a fashion major and her extracurricula activities are so different from what the other candidates do, who are usually history, politics, or philosophy majors. Elle Woods is admitted by Harvard Law School mainly because they are looking for diverse type of students, which is determined by their education principles. From it we can learn that the education system developed in American culture encourages the development of individuality. From this movie clip we can also get to understand that culture shapes people's speech and behaviors, which in turn influences the communication between people.

Section C

Exercise 2

1. relieve, settled, librarian
2. dreamed, *mahjong*, dull
3. agricultural, vast, rent
4. casually, tenants, talents

Exercise 3

1. When his son went to work, Zhao was quite lonely and did not have any friends. This kind of life was quite different from his farming life in China, where there were always many friends and neighbors around, talking, drinking tea and playing *mahjong* together during the leisure time. Chinese culture is a group-oriented culture, in which people depend on each other heavily for a good life.
2. Chinese people are very practical and thrifty. For them, it is wasteful to use land only to raise flowers. Confucian teachings, which originated in the group-oriented cultures, are the guidelines that help shape this national temperament.
3. When Zhao was in America, he found that his loneliness was not relieved, and he missed his old friends a lot. That summer was the happiest time for him mainly because he was able to talk with other elderly Chinese again. From this example, we can learn that culture governs people's mind and helps determine whether they are happy or not. Another example in this case is the choice of Chinese families to grow vegetables on their rented land. Here we can

learn that culture governs people's behavior and provides guidelines for what to do and what not to do.

Chapter 2

Section A

Exercise 1

5, 2, 6, 4, 1, 3, 8, 7

Exercise 2

accident, sign, back, strange, chance, insane, faith

Exercise 3

1. When Sara hands her phone number to Jonathan, the paper is blown into a trash. Jonathan takes it as an accident, but Sara regards it as a sign of fate, which is telling her not to develop their relationship. Their different outlook to life causes the breakdown of the process of communication.

Section C

Exercise 3

1. Generally, Asian people are very courteous and indirect in their communication. Because they put great emphasis on group harmony, they are very tolerant, even when they are offended. These collectivistic values, shaped by Confucian teachings, were spread from China to many

Asian countries.

2. Westerners are generally very direct and frank in their mode of communication. And they have a strong sense of protecting their own rights. Individualistic values are the underlying principles governing their behavior.

Chapter 3

Section A

Exercise 1

1. d 2. f 3. a 4. c 5. b 6. e

Exercise 2

1. intellectual property right
2. determining, evidence, lawyer
3. duty, informing, abuse, medical
4. subject, deliberate, neglect
5. investigation, considerable, witnesses, violent, abuse
6. otherwise, unsafe, supervision, trial

Exercise 3

1. T 2. F 3. F 4. F 5. F

Exercise 4

1. Xu Datong invites John to be his lawyer because John is the best friend of his. In China, people usually try to seek help from all kinds of social relationship when they are in trouble. From it we can learn the heavy interdependence between Chinese people, which is a major

characteristic of collectivist culture.

2. From the photos of Dennis' injury, John agrees that Xu Datong has abused his own son. That's why John doesn't defend Xu Datong. From it we can learn that American people put more emphasis on the truth and facts rather than personal relationship, which is an important characteristic of individualist culture.
3. "Because he's Chinese." This is what is said by Jane Ning when asked by John Quinlan in the ending part of the movie. As a Chinese man, Xu Datong considers it as his responsibility to shoulder up all the troubles by himself, which is what is expected from a responsible and filial man in the Chinese culture.

Section C

Exercise 2

1. beating, warned, lunchtime, hated, Spanked, police
2. retirement, primary, detailed, expect, protect, refused, Things

Exercise 3

1. In China, the "beating" principle used to be a very popular way for parents to discipline their children. "Parents hit you for your own good". This is the general agreement among parents. In the traditional Si Shu (private school) in ancient societies, even teachers can give students corporal punishment. In the US, although parents are not forbidden to carry out mild physical punishment, parents are generally very careful about doing so. And American children are well aware of their rights. Calling the police is one way to help protect their rights, although it is rarely used.
2. Learning Chinese requires a lot of practice in reading and writing. In China, primary school students generally spend plenty of time doing this kind of practice in school. Many of them, whether willing or unwilling to do it, are required by their parents to continue this practice when they come back from the school. In the US, however, children are taught to protect their time from the day they are born, although we can also hear some complaints that children's schedules are filled with activities their parents plan for them. That is why Xue Suling couldn't carry out her original plan. From it we can know that individual rights are highly valued by Americans, something that is often observed in the individualistic American culture.

Chapter 4

Section A

Exercise 2

T, F, F, T

Section C

Exercise 2

1. at risk, philosophy, loyalty, interpersonal
2. technical experts, supervisors, managerial positions
3. rewards, promotions, and retention, individual performance, uncertainty and ambiguity, job security

Exercise 3

1. From this case, we learn that the Mexican culture is reserved and group-oriented. It pays high attention to group harmony and personal relationships.
2. The American culture is more individualistic, result-oriented, and analytic.
3. Because of the strong cultural differences between the American management and the Mexican staff, the change that the American management made was very difficult to accept for the Mexican staff: it was challenging, and it ignored the fundamental values in human relationship under Mexican circumstances.

Chapter 5

Section A

Exercise 2

unique, follow, appreciate, promised, respectfully

Section C

Exercise 2

1. F 2. T 3. T 4. F

Exercise 3

1. "Uncertainty avoidance" indicates how much a society feels threatened by ambiguous situations and tries to avoid them by providing rules, believing in absolute truths, and refusing to tolerate deviance. It refers to the extent to which a culture will avoid or tolerate uncertainty. Some cultures, such as Greece, Portugal, Belgium, Japan, Peru, France, Chile, Spain and Argentina, are averse to the unknown. Avoiding uncertainty can be difficult without adopting rules of behavior to compensate for uncertainty. Such cultures emphasize uniformity and dislike deviance. People from cultures that place a premium on avoiding uncertainty would try to get straight answers to questions. Such cultures may be rather emotional in the process of gathering information. Foreign teachers need detailed instructions. They hope to reduce the ambiguity in their expectations for the working in China. Thus they turn to Chinese officials to tell them exactly their responsibilities, rights, the regulations, the available facilities, the accommodation, the levels of the students, etc. Such information helps reduce their anxiety.
2. According to Hofstede's research, collectivist cultures tend to be Asian and Latin American, while the individualistic cultures tend to be North American and European. Collectivist cultures emphasize common interests, cooperation, conformity and inter-dependence. They also emphasize tight social frameworks, in which people tend to help their in-group and

expect their in-group to take care of their needs. The in-group includes one's extended family, relatives, acquaintances, friends, classmates, and colleagues. In individualistic cultures, people tend to see to their own needs and those of their immediate family. They emphasize more "I" than "we". Thus, if someone in America wishes to get a book from another library, he would directly consult the staff working at that library to see whether the library is available to him. If it is available, he then could inquire about the procedures for obtaining books from that library. He probably would not think of turning to his friends or any other connections to help him at first. In China, however, one would probably first try to find someone he knows to help him.

3. According to Hofstede's research, America ranked No.1 in individualism worldwide. In America, even friends still respect each other's privacy. And they still maintain certain distance to acknowledge one another's independence. Even friends should try not to be very demanding. If friends ask for help, they should make their requests rare and reasonable. While in China, friends belong to one's in-group, so friends connote a closer relationship. One could always expect his friend to help him, and vice versa. In China, friends are the people that one can depend upon and trust.

Chapter 6

Section A

Exercise 1

artist, paintings, package, fainted

Exercise 2

1. Offering a compliment.
2. Her Chinese friend gave the painting she complimented to her as a gift, which was not what she expected.

Exercise 4

1. In the West, the meaning of the sentence "I like your sweater" is very clear because of the low-context style of communication, in which most of the information in the communication is transmitted in the verbal speech.
2. In Asian societies, the meaning of the sentence "I like your sweater" is not clear because of the high-context style of communication, in which people may transmit a large amount of information in the context rather than in the verbal speech.

Section C

Exercise 2

1. Filipina, McDonald's
2. watering, grateful
3. hesitation, expect

Exercise 3

1. No, she didn't really mean it. She wanted to have one hamburger very much. She refused her classmate's offer just because she was Chinese. She knew the hamburger was quite expensive, so she didn't want to ask a favor of her classmate. If she had done so, she would have thought she had taken financial advantage of her classmate. Chinese culture is a typical high-context culture in which people's mode of communication is rather indirect and tentative. Sometimes they don't mean what they say simply for the sake of courtesy.
2. Generally, Westerners consider an invitation as genuine if it specifies a definite time, place and activity. In this case, all three criteria were very clear, so the Phillipine girl took the invitation as genuine, and was very happy to accept it. What she didn't know was that this invitation was not intended to be genuine by the girl who invited her, her Chinese classmate, who extended the offer just out of courtesy. For people raised in low-context cultures, who adopt the direct and frank mode of communication, they must take care to discern the real intentions of those raised in high-context cultures.

Chapter 7

Section A

Exercise 1

Well, it's only natural that you should be anxious, but it's all over now.	Mrs. Pearce
All alone you hurdled every obstacle in sight.	Maids/manservant
I'm nothing to you. Not as much as them slippers.	Higgins
Karpathy? That dreadful Hungarian?	Pickering
You'll be mentioned in history.	Eliza

Exercise 2

1. cage, achievement, backed, fantastic
2. glorious victory, history, dreading
3. subjective, imagination, prayers, comfortable

Exercise 3

1. T 2. F 3. T 4. F

Section C

Exercise 1

1. No. It was left off the list of the five Beijing Olympic mascots.
2. The Western association of the dragon as a fearsome, threatening animal contrasts with its symbolism for honesty, good fortune, and happiness in the minds of Chinese people.
3. The dragon is used as a totem because dragons actually existed, like other totem animals.

Exercise 2

1. 1) retire 2) harmonious 3) observation
2. 4) view 5) snake 6) unified 7) empire
3. 8) framework 9) artifact 10) vanished 11) spies
4. 12) promoted 13) plot 14) bestseller 15) soul

Chapter 8

Section A

Exercise 1

1. They are all celebrating Honey's birthday party.
2. Max suggests that they should give the last brownie as a prize to the saddest act there.
3. She is stuck in the house day and night, has to give up her favorite thing—smoking and can't have a baby.

Exercise 2

1. baby sister, key moments, adore you, Lucky me
2. actress, stock market, similar fields
3. vegetarian, tasted

Exercise 3

3, 6, 2, 4, 1, 5

Section C

Exercise 1

1. Hong and the Chair of her department met him at the airport, put him up in a nice hotel, arranged a big dinner for him for the evening and gave him the itinerary for the next few days.
2. Hong was very relieved when Joe left. She felt Joe's visit had been successful but it had required most of her time to make sure that his visit would go smoothly.
3. At the beginning, Joe felt very excited at his first trip to China and very grateful for everything Hong and her department. But later, he was very annoyed and felt deprived and trapped because of the tight itinerary.

Exercise 2

1. 1) assistant Professor　2) visiting scholar　3) Ph. D. program
2. 4) the lectures　5) concerts　6) nearby resort
   7) by the university
3. 8) grateful to　9) host department　10) upon treating
   11) very frustrated
4. 12) especially annoyed　13) consulting him　14) very relieved
   15) go smoothly

Exercise 3

1. Because the itinerary arranged by Hong and her department without consulting with Joe was so tight that he had no free time to explore the city and the surrounding area on his own.

Chapter 9

Section A

Exercise 1

1. Shoulders back, chest high, feet apart, head up and strut; punch and slap other soldier on the behind.
3. Boxing and Chinese Kongfu.
4. The Emperor bows to Mulan, and Mulan embraces the Emperor. These would not happen in real China because Chinese culture is high in power distance. Standing at the top of the Chinese social system, emperors would hold an attitude of entitlement, to express "I deserve this." In this sense, they would only offer rewards rather than exhibit body languages to express their thanks to the ministers and citizens.

Exercise 2

1) b 2) d 3) c 4) a

Section C

Exercise 1

1. Men. 2. France. 3. In the Middle East.

Exercise 2

1.	1) men's	2) modern	3) clutched	4) bare
2.	5) irresistible	6) successful	7) same	8) disaster
3.	9) impropriety	10) tip	11) slightly	12) suit

Exercise 3

Question 1& 2: Each culture has a well-defined system of meanings for different forms of touching. Some generalizations can be made with regards to high-touch versus low-touch cultures. Americans, the English, Germans and Northern Europeans are said to belong to low-touch cultures, exhibiting very limited tactile contact in public. Hispanics, people of Eastern European descents, Italians, the French, Arabs, and Jews are all said to belong to high-touch cultures. Care must be taken, however, not to over generalize in that each culture, whether considered to be high- or low-touch, defines for its members whom they can touch, as well as when and where they cannot touch. As above mentioned, although both the French and Arabs are generally considered high-touch, the French culture permits a mutual directional touching between different sexes while in Arabian cultures, the male follow a much higher touch pattern to the female, than the female do to the male. As regard to the Drakkar Noir ad in France, the touching involved is quite "high" and is from the female to the male. In French culture, it is proper, but in Saudi Arabia, it is too much, or let's say, it invites the conclusion that the female is behaving indecently, which can negatively affect the male's image. In the adapted version, the touching was reduced and neutralized. As a result, the picture in the ad implies that the man is so irresistible that the lady can't help getting close to him in spite of her awareness of the cultural rule.

Chapter 10

Section A

Exercise 1

numbers, rolling, not realistic, 6's, 6.0, below 7, holding

Exercise 2

1. b　　2. d　　3. e　　4. c　　5. a

Exercise 3

Americans regard time as a commodity, something to be used, bought, wasted, saved or spent. So they attach much importance to the efficiency of using time, and are much accustomed to a fast pace of life. In India, relationship is far more important than schedules and efficiency, and in this sense, people live in a much slower and more relaxed way. In this movie, Todd is sent to India to get its MPI down from 15 minutes per call to 6. Todd thinks it is not realistic, and the fellow American Todd meets in MacDonnell's says "No way in India." By contrast, Puro, the Indian charger, regards an MPI of 12 is already very satisfactory.

Another point is that Americans are very specific about time, which is quite different from how Indians treat it. In this movie, Todd argues sharply with Dave about the targeted MPI: should it be 6.0 or something between 6.0 and 6.59. However, when Todd asks Puro when the glass of his office will arrive, Puro says "It's coming soon." As a matter of fact, it finally comes three weeks later.

Section C

Exercise 1

1. She found that her students showed no interest in her teaching, and was feeling upset.
2. She found that the Director was talking with another teacher in Chinese.
3. Another Chinese teacher came in, and the Director turned to talk with that teacher, also in Chinese.

Exercise 2

1.	1) timetable	2) agreed	3) exact	4) Chinese
2.	5) smilingly	6) carried on	7) five minutes	8) apology
3.	9) apology	10) impatient	11) interrupted	12) appointment
	13) angry	14) unhappy		

Exercise 3

Questions 1&2: This case is about the cultural difference in two different time systems, namely Monochronic Time and Polychronic Time. The Director follows a Polychronic culture which schedules several activities at the same time, does not see appointments as ironclad commitments and often breaks them, and is more subject to interruptions. So, it is quite natural for him to keep talking with a Chinese teacher when it is already five minutes past his appointment time with Katherine, and later tolerate interruptions during his talk with her. By contrast, Katherine follows a Monochronic time system which schedules only one activity at one time, is very particular about appointments, and attaches great importance to efficiency. In this sense, she could not cope with the Director's conversation with other teachers, especially in Chinese, during her appointment time. Although the Director has realized that his behavior may not seem polite to Katherine, and even apologizes to her, his apology does not compensate for Katherine's frustration.

Chapter 11

Section A

Exercise 1

1. write, chopping, existed, didn't, getting, down
2. single, impossible, work room, space, space, big, talk

Exercise 2

1. T　　2. F　　3. T　　4. F　　5. F

Section C

Exercise 1

1. Germany.
2. He got close to Wolfgang to take a glance at the newspaper.
3. Actually, he got very angry.

Exercise 2

1. 1) Sino-German	2) newspaper	3) came up to	4) glance
2. 5) lost	6) privacy	7) upset	8) rude
3. 9) cover up	10) distance		

Exercise 3

Questions 1&2: This case is about the cultural differences in the understanding of personal space. Some cultures simply do not give private, personal space high consideration. Sometimes, fifty Africans can crowd into the same amount of space that holds only twenty North Americans. The reason is that the Africans' sense of personal space suffers no intrusion from crowding and touching. In this case, Wang Liang, coming from the Chinese culture, is not as sensitive about personal body space as is his German colleague. In other words, he tends to have respect primarily for the physical boundaries of personal territory, but pays little attention to certain less visible invasions, for example the invasion by eyesight. In this sense, he never realizes that his behavior may be regarded as rude. By contrast, Wolfgang's culture is more sensitive to privacy. To be specific, the boundary of his personal territory could extend to personal items, for example, the newspaper he was reading in this case. Therefore, when he found that Wang Liang was reading his newspaper without his permission, he felt an invasion of his private personal space, and thus became very angry.

Chapter 12

Section A

Exercise 1

1. Peter tries to give explanations because people usually have some negative stereotypes about black people. So even when Tom agrees to what he said, he is still worried that his words might not be trusted. That is how stereotypes hamper our communication in daily life.
2. Tom changes his attitude because the deeply rooted stereotypes about black people can never be completely removed from his heart, no matter how much he sympathizes them. From the dirty shoes and the torn jacket, Tom may assume that Peter has just been involved in some violence or some bad behavior.
3. When Tom said "Come on", he does not mean to encourage Peter. Instead, he means "Come on, don't try to fool me." His reaction to Peter's dream of becoming a goalie results from his ethnocentric ideas about himself. He may think it is impossible for black people to realize such a dream that only white people can hold. That's why he does not quite believe what Peter tells him about his dream.
4. Because Peter himself has exactly the same thing.
5. Tom gets into a rage because he thinks Peter was laughing at him for being so stupid as to pick up such a dangerous black person.

Exercise 2

1. headed; Anywhere
2. pulling over; keep driving

Exercise 3

1. T 2. F 3. F 4. F

Section C

Exercise 1

1) honor 2) very big 3) rap 4) rock

Exercise 2

1. 1) programs into 2) be expected 3) interacting with
2. 4) initially 5) whisper 6) taking honors 7) an unsettling shade of brown
3. 8) consists solely of 9) appropriate 10) spans from 11) When it comes to
4. 12) define 13) popularity 14) follow trends 15) sacrifice my individuality for

Chapter 13

Section A

Exercise 1

1. Viktor can't retrieve his food tickets because he knows very little English and can't explain to the cleaning person what exactly he has lost. If he were able to tell the cleaning person he had no food to eat without the tickets, the cleaner would have returned the tickets to him.
2. From the movie clip, we can infer that Viktor is a kind, patriotic person. He has a strong love towards his country. When he learns what has happened to his country, his eyes are full of tears. Although his situation is desperate, he does not forget to help others. During difficult times, he doesn't complain. Instead, he tries to solve problems by himself. Making a bed for himself is a good example.
3. First of all, his passport and visa have became invalid, forcing him to stay in the terminal. Secondly, he knows very little English and it is thus very hard for him to communicate with people. So he has a lot of difficulties finding out what's going on around him. Thirdly, he has lost his food tickets and has nothing to eat. Finally, he has no place to sleep.

4. The most fundamental reason for his culture shock lies in his poor English. He can understand very little, he can hardly make himself understood either. Another reason is his bad luck. If everything goes as planned, he will stay in New York for a few days and his poor English would not be the cause of so much trouble. So before we enter a new culture, we should be well prepared in order to reduce the chances of culture shock.

Exercise 2

1. What I do, Shop
2. document, to look at my trash

Exercise 3

3, 2, 6, 1, 4, 5

Section C

Exercise 1

1. Cameroon.
2. English.
3. Francine Nnyina has experienced many difficulties known as culture shock in her American education. The following are the details:
   1) a lot more work to do in America that in France;
   2) focus on the depth of a subject in France, but the width of a subject in America;
   3) students in American class are more active that those in France;
   4) smaller class in America, but students work alone;
   5) more advanced technology and better equipments in America;
   6) professors are more approachable in America than in France.

Exercise 2

1. 1) on exchange　　2) the western African country

3) elementary through high school

2. 4) semester system
5) instead of
6) resolved to
7) English-speaking culture

3. 8) in depth
9) more superficially
10) more alive
11) apt to speak

4. 12) more approachable
13) without an appointment
14) care a lot for
15) appreciate their attitude

Chapter 14

Section A

Exercise 1

House: built in a Greek style with columns and guarding statues of gods; featuring the Greek Flag

Food: usually Greek food

School: Greek school

Daily life: full of Greek atmosphere

Exercise 2

1. look old; marry Greek boys, make Greek babies and feed everyone
2. Greeks should educate non-Greeks about being Greek; "the history of our people, the great civilization, the Greeks"

Exercise 3

1. Toula's father hangs a Greek flag on their house in order to show the neighbors where they came from and how proud they are to have this heritage.
6. Toula's father insists on her marrying a Greek boy because her father believes only men with

Greek heritage are nice, reliable people. Although he has been living in Chicago his whole life, in his heart, he has such a strong Greek identity that it is really hard for him to accept a non-Greek as his son-in-law.

Section C

Exercise 1

1. Ghana.
2. The commentator is very proud of his African background. As he wrote, his ancestors are great people with great courage and never-ending spirits that make them live lives of dignity. Therefore, he respects them so much that he takes pride in talking about their stories.

Exercise 2

1.	1) wonders	2) hand over	3) trace back
2.	4) ancestors	5) As a matter of fact	6) descendant
3.	7) upside down	8) Voting Rights Act	
4.	9) foreigners	10) gives no insult	
5.	11) What I come from	12) no shame	

Exercise 3

1. The commentator describes himself as an American with African background without going to either extremes. After going across the long river of acculturation, he has identified himself as a pure American. In the meanwhile, he cherishes the spiritual treasure inherited from his African ancestors and manages to be inspired by this spirit in a positive way. So it is not surprising that he thinks there is no need to know exactly which specific country his ancestors used to live in. It is due to his wise interpretation of identity that he does not suffer from an identity crisis.

Chapter15

Section A

Exercise 2

1. subversive, married
2. disrespect, consequences

Section C

Exercise 2

1.	1) reply	2) Chinese	3) go on	4) would do
2.	5) a nightmare for me	6) childish	7) adult	
	8) difficult	9) wrong	10) better	
3.	11) I don't know	12) safe	13) realize	14) results
	15) emphasize	16) process	17) correct	18) fruit
	19) decent	20) annoyed		

Exercise 3

1. To say "I don't know" is the safest in classroom. It avoids embarrassment if your answer is not correct and saves labor.
2. Because the student's answer made the teacher suppose that he was not thinking critically, or lacked confidence in his own opinion.
3. The attitude towards results is the main difference in this case. The Chinese student is more concerned with whether he could get the right answer, while the American teacher emphasizes that students should have their own independent thinking and the confidence to tell.

Chapter 16

Section A

Exercise 2

1. special spoons, standard, half-teaspoon, quarter
2. mixer, promise, pan, cupcake

Section C

Exercise 2

1) prospect	2) optimistic	3) deterrents	4) completed	5) rushed
6) feasible	7) venture	8) concrete	9) process	10) consult senior

Exercise 3

1. The system for addressing names differ in different cultures. That makes it difficult to guess at a person's proper name and title. For example, the procedure of making introductions varies in different cultures. In the U.S. and Great Britain, first names are used. While in other cultures, the introductions are more formal. Titles are used in Germany, Italy, and China, for example. Titles indicate a person's profession or education. In Asian countries, such as China and Korea, the surname precedes the personal name. In some Hispanic cultures, people will have two surnames, one is from their father and the other is from their mother. In Latin American cultures, people will add their mother's maiden name to their surnames. When a woman gets married, she drops her mother's maiden name and add her husband's father's name. So if you go to a country with a different cultural backdrop, it is wise for you to learn the particular customs in the naming system and the use of titles.
2. Indians viewed time differently from the Americans. The Indians in this case viewed Joel as a pushy American who was only concerned about signing the deal. In the United States, efficiency, adhering to deadlines and a host of other similar habits are considered normal and are expected. In India, however, one needs to understand that one is dealing with people

from a different cultural background, that think and interact differently. Since Indians dislike being restricted by time, it is considered normal for them to delay and take longer in their negotiations. Unlike Americans who esteem efficiency and value time, the Indians prefer a slower pace of life and exhibit patience for waiting before making decisions. As a result, what is considered reasonable and feasible in America may not appear so in India and vice-versa.

As Indians are used to a system of hierarchy in the work place, senior colleagues are obeyed and respected. Supervisors are expected to monitor an individual's work and shoulder the responsibility for meeting deadlines. Therefore, it is important to double-check and keep track of time. Educated Indians have learned to adapt to Western methods of monitoring one's own work and completing it on schedule. In a group discussion, only the senior most person might speak, but that does not signify that the others agree with him. They may maintain silence, without contradicting him (or you) out of respect for seniority. Westernized Indians, on the other hand, can be quite assertive and direct, and it is acceptable to treat them in the same manner. Politeness and honesty go a long way in establishing the fact that your intentions are genuine.

图书在版编目 (CIP) 数据

跨文化交际视听说 /《大学英语选修课 / 学科课程系列教材》项目组编. 北京：高等教育出版社，2009. 3（2024. 11 重印）

（大学英语选修课 / 学科课程系列教材）

ISBN 978 — 7 — 04 — 026347 — 3

Ⅰ. 跨… Ⅱ. 大… Ⅲ. ①英语 – 听说教学 – 高等学校 – 教材②文化交流 – 高等学校 – 教材 – 英文 Ⅳ. H319. 9 G115

中国版本图书馆CIP数据核字（2009）第038552号

出版发行	高等教育出版社	咨询电话	400 – 810 – 0598
社　　址	北京市西城区德外大街 4 号	网　　址	http://www.hep.edu.cn
邮政编码	100120		http://www.hep.com.cn
印　　刷	涿州市京南印刷厂	网上订购	http://www.landraco.com.
开　　本	787 × 1092　1/16		http://www.landraco.com.cn
印　　张	16.75	版　　次	2009 年 3 月第 1 版
字　　数	376 000	印　　次	2024 年 11 月第 18 次印刷
购书热线	010–58581118	定　　价	35. 00 元

本书如有缺页、倒页、脱页等质量问题，请到所购图书销售部门联系调换。

物 料 号　26347 – 00